WITHDRAWN

A Possible India

A Possible India
Essays in Political Criticism

Partha Chatterjee

DELHI
OXFORD UNIVERSITY PRESS
CALCUTTA CHENNAI MUMBAI
1997

Oxford University Press, Great Clarendon Street, Oxford OX2 6DP

Oxford   New York
Athens   Auckland   Bangkok   Calcutta
Cape Town   Chennai   Dar es Salaam   Delhi
Florence   Hong Kong   Istanbul   Karachi
Kuala Lumpur   Madrid   Melbourne   Mexico City
Mumbai   Nairobi   Paris   Singapore
Taipei   Tokyo   Toronto
and associates in
Berlin   Ibadan

ISBN 0 19 564333 X

Typeset by Rastrixi, New Delhi 110070
Printed in India at Pauls Press, New Delhi 110020
and published by Manzar Khan, Oxford University Press
YMCA Library Building, Jai Singh Road, New Delhi 110001

To Samar Sen *(1916–1987),*
who might have enjoyed this book

Possible, *a.* ME . . . **1.** That may be (i.e. is capable of being); that may or can exist, be done, or happen; that is in one's power, that one can do, exert, use, etc. *b.* That can or may be or become; as *a possible object of knowledge* = something that can or may be known . . .

The Shorter Oxford English Dictionary

Preface

I have long resisted the temptation to do a single-volume study of Indian politics, despite the fact that, over the years, many people have reminded me that this was entirely expected of me as an Indian political scientist. The reason for my reluctance was not that I did not take seriously my professional responsibilities towards the discipline to which I belonged. On the contrary, it was precisely because I took those responsibilities seriously that I hesitated to undertake the task. To put it plainly, the reason was that I did not know how to write such a book.

The problem as I saw it was one of defining my location in relation to the object of study: namely, the institutional structures and political processes of the Indian state. Since the beginning of my professional life in the early 1970s, I have been acutely conscious of the fragility of this relationship. Having reached adolescence in the restless decade of the 1960s, when every young mind in West Bengal was touched by the dream of liberation, I brought into my first academic exercises on contemporary politics a conceptual and analytical language that was derived — unabashedly — from Marx, Lenin and Mao Zedong. To use this language with conviction, one needed not just to glance from time to time at the image of an alternative state of the social world, but to possess and display that image as an object of one's own creation, and hence of proprietorship. One needed, in other words, to occupy that high ground of criticism from which one could match, claim for claim, argument for argument, evidence for evidence, the whole panoply of ruling doctrines; in short, to advance, on behalf of a class, an alliance or the people as a whole, a rival claim to rule. I do not know if in brandishing this language of power, I managed to sound convincing. What I do know, however, is that I had a certain degree of freedom to find my own way through that dense and fiercely contested doctrinal terrain; after all, I was not bound by any party line and did not

need to have my writings screened for their ideological correctness. In any case, the years 1975–7 drastically realigned my relation to the study of Indian politics.

The declaration of Emergency in June 1975, its sudden lifting
after a year and a half, and the elections of March 1977 confirmed
for many of us what we thought were the characteristic properties
of the structure of political rule in post-colonial India. We
described these structural properties in terms of the balance
between the constituent elements of the ruling class coalition.
Electoral democracy, it was clear, was an important enabling
condition for the working of this balance; the limits of electoral
democracy too would be set by the requirements of maintaining
the balance. What was new, however, in our understanding of
Indian politics was the discovery, after 1977, that this particular
structure of class rule, more sophisticated and effective than in
many other post-colonial countries of the world, also afforded
significant strategic opportunities for popular struggles for democracy. In time, with the rapid decline through the 1980s of the
Congress as the principal political organization of India's ruling
classes, the incorporation of the substantial part of the Left into
the institutions of governance, and the new attempts in the 1990s
of the Hindu Right to occupy the ground lost by the Congress,
our description of the structure of class rule in India necessarily
took on a much less unified and much more contingent quality.

There was no position I could truthfully occupy from which
I might claim to provide a panoptic view of Indian politics.
Nevertheless, I did continue to write on the subject — nearly
once a week on an average — mainly at the behest of Samar Sen,
editor of the Calcutta weekly, *Frontier*. I now know how enormously rewarding an experience this was, for I was required to
write history as it happened; not as a journalist would, since I
had neither the opportunity nor the skills of reporting, but as a
critic trying to match structure to event, institution to process,
claim to fact.

I offer this volume in place of the book on Indian politics that
I will never write. It is constructed from my writings over the
last twenty years, and includes a variety of genres — essays,
reviews, polemics, editorial comments, and journal entries. I have
selected and arranged this material so as to produce an account
of structures in motion, described from shifting vantage points,

sometimes with the advantage of historical hindsight, but often alongside the events themselves. I believe this gives a more engaged, rich and truthful account of my understanding of post-colonial politics than a more smoothly constructed synthetic volume.

I do think there is an overall theoretical concern that has emerged out of these twenty years of my engagement with the study of Indian politics. It is a concern with democratic politics — where democracy is not, as the republican cliché still proclaims, government of the people, but *the politics of the governed*. The perspective is oppositional, negative, resolutely critical. It is sceptical of all utopian talk — liberal, populist or socialist. Contrary to liberal preaching, it is conscious of the fact that the critical issue of governance in many post-colonial countries is increasingly being posed as the opposition between capitalist growth and democracy. At the same time, this perspective makes one wary of using a populist language of power, since it cannot intelligibly conceive of a state of the social world in which the masses will be anything other than objects of government. It is a perspective that has taught one to rely on one's own strength, to fight strategically and to dream within the realms of the possible.

As in the case of *The Present History of West Bengal*, the companion volume to this book, I must thank Timir Basu, editor of *Frontier*, for giving me permission to use many of my writings published in that journal. I am also grateful to Arup Mallik for letting me use a translated version of an article we had jointly authored in our youth. This manuscript was put together during the winter of 1995, which I spent at the International Institute of the University of Michigan at Ann Arbor: my thanks to my colleagues and students there. As always, I remain grateful to the staff of the Centre for Studies in Social Sciences, Calcutta, for their unstinting help. And finally, I thank Nitasha Devasar of Oxford University Press, Delhi, for making the fiftieth year of India's independence (which also happens to be the fiftieth year of my life) the occasion for the publication of this book.

Calcutta   PC
March 1997

Acknowledgements

Chapter 1: 'The Indian Big Bourgeoisie: Comprador or National', *Frontier*, Annual Number 1985, pp. 32–8.

Chapter 2: 'Jawaharlal Nehru and the Decade After Freedom', *Indian Historical Review*, 6, 1–2 (1979–80), pp. 237–45; 'The Last Years of Jawaharlal Nehru', *Frontier*, 17, 6–8 (Autumn 1984), pp. 28–34.

Chapter 3: (With Arup Mallik) 'Bhāratīya ganatantra o burjoyā pratikryā', *Anya artha*, 8 (March 1975), pp. 6–25. Translated from the Bengali.

Chapter 4: '1977: Reflections on the "Second Independence" '; paper presented at the Indian Political Science Conference, Bangalore, December 1977; previously unpublished.

Chapter 5: 'Caran sim-er rājnīti prasange', *Anīk*, 15 (September 1978), pp. 104–8. Translated from the Bengali.

Chapter 6: 'Bhārate samsadīya rajnītir kayekti prakryā prasange', *Anīk*, 17, 3–5 (September 1980), pp. 9–10, 112–14. Translated from the Bengali.

Chapter 7: *Frontier*, 16, 15 (26 November 1983); 16, 20 (31 December 1983); 16, 22 (14 January 1984); 16, 40 (26 May 1984); 16, 44 (23 June 1984); 16, 48 (21 July 1984); 17, 2 (1 September 1984); 17, 9 (20 October 1984); 17, 11 (3 November 1984); 17, 12 (10 November 1984); 17, 14 (24 November 1984).

Chapter 8: 'The Writing on the Wall', *Frontier*, 17, 18 (22 December 1984), pp. 5–7.

Chapter 9: *Frontier*, 17, 28 (2 March 1985); 17, 39 (18 May 1985); 17, 40 (25 May 1985); 17, 42 (8 June 1985); 17, 44 (22 June 1985); 17, 50 (3 August 1985); 18, 2 (31 August 1985); 18, 7 (5 October 1985); 18, 19 (28 December 1985); 18, 27 (22 February 1986); 18, 30 (15 March 1986); 18, 38 (10 May 1986); 18, 40 (24

May 1986); 18, 43 (14 June 1986); 19, 5 (20 September 1986); 19, 12 (8 November 1986); 19, 14 (22 November 1986); 19, 16 (6 December 1986); 19, 18 (20 December 1986).

Chapter 10: 'The Politics of Appropriation', *Frontier*, 19, 8–10 (11–25 October 1986), pp. 30–6.

Chapter 11: *Frontier*, 19, 39 (16 May 1987); 19, 46 (4 July 1987); 19, 48 (18 July 1987); 20, 5 (19 September 1987); 20, 16 (5 December 1987); 20, 32 (26 March 1988); 20, 42 (4 June 1988); 20, 45 (25 June 1988); 21, 1 (20 August 1988); 21, 4 (10 September 1988); 21, 6 (24 September 1988); *Ānandabājār patrikā*, 27 October 1988, translated from the Bengali; *Frontier*, 21, 12 (5 November 1988); 21, 21 (7 January 1989); 21, 23 (21 January 1989); 21, 34 (8 April 1989); 21, 47 (8 July 1989); 21, 52 (12 August 1989); 22, 2 (26 August 1989); 22, 6 (23 September 1989); 22, 13 (11 November 1989); 22, 16 (2 December 1989).

Chapter 12: *Frontier*, 22, 19 (23 December 1989); 22, 48 (14 July 1990); 22, 50 (28 July 1990); *Ānandabājār patrikā*, 14 September 1990, translated from the Bengali; *Frontier*, 23, 14 (17 November 1990).

Chapter 13: *Frontier*, 23, 33 (30 March 1991); 23, 35 (13 April 1991); 23, 42 (1 June 1991); 23, 44 (15 June 1991); 23, 46 (29 June 1991); 23, 50 (27 July 1991); *Bāromās*, 18, 2 (April 1996), pp. 13–15, translated from the Bengali.

Chapter 14: 'Secularism and Toleration', *Economic and Political Weekly*, 29, 28 (9 July 1994), pp. 1768–77.

Chapter 15: 'Talking About Our Modernity in Two Languages', *Studies in Humanities and Social Sciences* (Shimla), 2 (1996), 2, pp. 153–69.

Contents

Contents

1

The Indian Big Bourgeoisie: Comprador or National?

Suniti Kumar Ghosh has written a serious and provocative book[1] which deserves to be widely discussed in political circles in India. It is a remarkable book in many respects. Suniti Ghosh does not write in the detached, academic style of professional social scientists pretending to produce 'objective, positive knowledge' for the consumption of anyone who has use for it. He writes as a partisan in the political struggle, judging historical issues from the standpoint of a committed political activist. And in this genre of political writing in India, his book is truly remarkable for the range and depth of research that has gone into the construction of its arguments. Undoubtedly, there will be much scope for debate about Ghosh's main argument, but by not shirking the laborious task of presenting a solid and well-informed thesis, he has ensured that the debate in Left circles on the character of the Indian bourgeoisie will henceforth be raised to a much higher level of theoretical precision and attention to factual details.

Ghosh's main thesis is that the Indian big bourgeoisie has been comprador in nature from its very birth. It was never hostile to foreign capital either before or after the transfer of power. It sought not independent capitalist development but development as a subordinate partner of imperialist monopolies. But in the course of arguing his case, Ghosh undertakes a wide-ranging survey of historical developments in India from the period immediately preceding British rule to the transfer of power in 1947.

In discussing the pre-British Indian economy, Ghosh uses the results of a lot of recent historical research to make an extremely useful contribution to the Marxist debate on the subject. There

[1] Suniti Kumar Ghosh, *The Indian Big Bourgeoisie: Its Genesis, Growth and Character* (Calcutta: Subarnarekha, 1985).

has been for long a great deal of confusion among Indian Marxists regarding the pre-British agrarian structure, the nature of the 'village community', the supposed 'stagnation' and 'unchangeable' nature of Indian society, and of course that inevitable problem of the Asiatic mode of production. Suniti Ghosh shows that it is grossly incorrect to assume that there were no forces of change in the economy and society before the colonial conquest. In fact, in many areas there was a considerable expansion of commodity production and the emergence of large manufacturing centres, a vast growth of internal trade and external commerce, the organization of commercial credit, a high degree of monetization of the supra-village economy, and 'an unmistakable trend towards the growth of private property in land'. Whether all these tendencies could have amounted to the creation of conditions sufficient for the historical transformation of Indian society is a question so speculative as to be virtually meaningless. Because surely, the sufficient conditions of revolutionary transformation are provided not just by structural movements in the economy, but also by the political configuration of the class struggle in the period of crisis. And on the latter question, there are no historically available means by which an answer might be attempted, because the imposition of colonial rule changed the fundamental political configuration.

But the significance of the finding that there were these tendencies of change in pre-colonial India is that it enables us to make a much clearer and unambiguous assessment of the consequences of British rule. On this, too, there has been a lot of hedging and prevarication among Indian Marxists; and, it cannot be denied, Marx himself contributed to the confusion by what he wrote in his early articles on India. In 1853, he had written:

England, it is true, in causing a social revolution in Hindostan, was actuated only by the vilest interests, and was stupid in her manner of enforcing them. But that is not the question. The question is, can mankind fulfil its destiny without a fundamental revolution in the social state of Asia? If not, whatever may have been the crimes of England, she was the unconscious tool of history in bringing about that revolution.[2]

This was a chief source of the ambivalent attitude of the

2 Karl Marx, 'British Rule in India', in Karl Marx and Frederick Engels, *Collected Works*, vol. 12 (Moscow: Progress Publishers, 1979), pp. 125–33.

'progressive' intelligentsia in India about the historical necessity of colonial rule, and helped in perpetuating the myth about the dual role of British rule — its 'destructive' as well as its 'regenerative' effects.

Marx's writings on India in the 1850s show to what extent he was still imprisoned by the stereotypes of the European Enlightenment. But his later writings, beginning with the *Grundrisse* and *Capital*, and particularly his studies from 1871 to his death which have survived in the form of draft notes, show how seriously he struggled with these stereotypes; how till his last days he unceasingly groped for a framework of world history that would go beyond the Enlightenment notion of unilineal 'progress' towards 'the destiny of mankind', that would be more universal precisely by accounting for the specifically *different* possibilities of historical development in countries such as Russia or India or China. Suniti Ghosh has forcefully made the point regarding the significant changes in Marx's thinking about the effects of British rule in India. These late writings make it abundantly clear that Marx abandoned his earlier belief in the 'regenerative' role of colonialism. In fact, time and again, in his brief remarks in *Capital*, and most unambiguously in his *Ethnological Notebooks*, Marx pointed out how by its interventions in the agrarian and manufacturing economies and by its legal and administrative actions, the colonial state had, instead of unleashing new forces of transformation, only distorted and stultified the course of social development.[3] Ghosh's survey of the historical material on pre-British India brings him to the same conclusion:

The possibility of the transition from feudalism to capitalism was forestalled by colonial rule, which destroyed the progressive elements awakening to life within the old society, allied itself with all its reactionary and benighted forces, and gave rise to retarded, misshapen, lopsided economic and social structures. (p. 81)

Was Indian Society Feudal?

In his discussion of pre-colonial Indian society, however, Suniti Ghosh also makes a formulation which seems to ignore a rather

[3] Lawrence Krader, *The Ethnological Notebooks of Karl Marx* (Assen: Van Gorcum, 1974).

basic position that Marx continued to hold even in his last writings. Ghosh's argument is that the mode of production in precolonial India was feudal, not Asiatic (as Marx characterized it) nor 'tribute-paying' (in Samir Amin's recent formulation).[4] The state in India was the chief landlord; the form in which the surplus was extracted was a land tax, but this is only a formal difference from rent in European feudalism. Not only that:

India, at least certain parts of the subcontinent like Bengal, had entered a late feudal stage at the time of the advent of colonial rule. No doubt, feudalism was on the decline and a serious crisis afflicted every sphere of feudal life. (p. 77)

Ghosh seems to think that Marx's 'early characterization of the mode of production in pre-colonial India as Asiatic' was the result of his misplaced reliance on the writings of European travellers like Bernier and of British officials. But even in his later writings on India, in which he fundamentally revised his earlier assessment of the historical role of colonialism, Marx did not give up his identification of the crucial difference between European feudalism and the social formation in India. And here the charge of over-reliance on Bernier's accounts cannot be sustained, because Marx's jottings in the *Ethnological Notebooks* show how deeply he had familiarized himself with the workings of the land revenue system and the agrarian economy in British India, particularly Bengal, in the late nineteenth century. For Bengal in particular, Marx was perfectly aware of the consequences of the Permanent Settlement: the breakdown of the old *zamindaris,* the purchase of estates by 'comprador' traders, the growth of subinfeudation, the fragmentation of *zamindari* property, its sale and mortgage, even the differentiation among *raiyati* holders.[5] In other words, Marx was well aware of the evidence on which Ghosh bases his conclusion: 'Land became a commodity — alienable private property — and the peasant's traditional right of occupancy to land was abolished.' (p. 114) But Marx did not accept this formulation: in fact, he specifically criticized British officials such as James Phear for suggesting it.

[4] Samir Amin, *Le developpement inégal* (Paris: Edition de Minuit, 1973).

[5] See my introductory comments to the Bengali translation of the sections on John Phear in Marx's *Ethnological Notebooks*: 'Bāṅlār grāmsamāj prasaṅge kārl mārks', *Bāromās*, 9, 1 (September 1987), pp. 1–22.

Why? One must not forget that Marx's chief concern in inquiring into the dynamics of pre-capitalist formations was to identify the possibilities of transition to capitalism. And here, the fundamental structural condition for transition was the separation of a large proportion of direct producers from the means of production. Marx was certain that the overall conditions of reproduction of feudal relations of production in Europe were much more favourable for such a separation than the corresponding conditions in India. In particular, Marx identified two elements: first, the existence in feudal Europe of a notion of individual proprietorship of the lord over his estate (carried over from the concept of property in Roman law), which in turn implied an individuated notion of the bondage of a serf to his lord; and second, the network of a two-way flow of commodities between town and country in late medieval Europe, which implied that with commodity production the rural economy would in no way be insulated from its transformative consequences. Neither of these elements was in general present in pre-colonial India; and, crucial for Marx's argument, neither of them was unambiguously established even after one hundred years of British rule.

The implication of British land settlements in Bengal was not to introduce alienable private property in land, but rather to transform into a commodity the different sets of revenue-collecting rights. Marx made detailed notes on the way in which *zamindari* and intermediate tenure-holding property was being subdivided and transferred in Bengal, and he especially emphasized the fact that what was being bought and sold was a specific share at a particular rung of the revenue-collecting hierarchy. Besides, such a transfer would not necessarily affect the rights of others to the same piece of land. This was hardly an appropriate legal–political condition under which an emergent capitalist, or a landlord wishing to evict small tenants in order to lease out his land to a capitalist farmer, could exercise unrestricted and individuated private property rights in land. It was also not conducive for that drastic development which was a necessary precondition for generalized commodity production: the large-scale eviction of peasants completely dissociated from their ties with the land.

In fact, it was the very political conditions of colonial rule in the nineteenth century that forced the development of a highly fragmented and ambiguous notion of property rights in land. The Permanent Settlement did confer 'proprietary rights' on landlords; the *haptam* and *panjam* regulations did fortify this with arbitrary powers of distraint, etc. But the colonial state was unprepared to endanger the political conditions of colonial extraction by allowing large-scale eviction of tenants. Thus, it was forced to curb both the 'high landlordism' of the 1830s and 1840s and the depredations of English indigo planters, by successively limiting the 'proprietary' rights of landlords by protecting the 'occupancy' rights of certain sections of tenants. The result was not the generalization of bourgeois private property in land, but rather a half-baked and distorted structure of property rights.[6] In fact, this distorted legal–political form was a specific expression of the development in eastern India of those production relations which many have characterized as 'semi-feudal.'

Specificities of Asian Societies

The historical material which Suniti Ghosh uses in his discussion of the pre-colonial and early colonial economy should lead to a much more serious enquiry into the specific character of the social formation in India. First of all, there was considerable variation in the actual form of 'possession' of land within the village. The phenomenon of 'joint ownership' was quite rare. (Incidentally, Marx too was perfectly aware of this.) Second, there were differential rights over land within the village and certainly a fair amount of inequality in the size of holdings. Further, in most parts of India there existed a sizeable portion of the labouring population, comprising the lowest castes, who were denied all rights of possession of land. Consequently, there existed exploitative class relations not only between a state nobility and the direct producers in the village, but also between sections of the village population, in particular between upper castes and landless untouchables. (Here, Marx can be faulted for not recognizing the significance of the latter set of relations.) Yet, despite the existence of exploitative relations within the village, the conditions of reproduction were maintained by a

[6] For a longer discussion, see Partha Chatterjee, *Bengal 1920–1947: The Land Question* (Calcutta: K.P. Bagchi, 1985).

comprehensive cultural–ideological system — an ethical system — which emphasized the mutual dependence of different elements within the *jati* structure of division of labour. By emphasizing the *social* obligation of guaranteeing a subsistence for all, albeit a differential subsistence according to one's place in the caste hierarchy, the ideological structure of caste expressed the overall *social* unity of the labourer with his means of labour. It was in this sense that there existed a 'community', the social unity of a class-divided collective.

Marx was keenly aware of the strength and comprehensiveness of the collective framework of social relations in the Indian village. Hence, his emphasis on the difficulties of effecting a separation of a large section of producers from the means of production. Marx did not think that the producers in Indian villages were free, but their unfreedom was of a *collective* nature, very different from the individual unfreedom of the European serf. What Marx was relatively unaware of was the continued existence of elements of resistance within this comprehensive social structure — of ideologies which did not accept the Brahmanical code, of movements which sought to defy the rules of caste. How such elements were related to changes in the economy, to what extent they contained the possibilities of overturning the ideological framework of caste, why they failed in doing this, what changes occurred in the social structure because of the impact of these movements — these are problems to which Marxists in India have paid little attention. Yet they are vital for an understanding not only of the nature of pre-colonial society, or of the specific distortions which capitalist development brings under colonial rule, but also of the possibilities of transformation which exist today. The specific problems posed in countries such as India will not be resolved by arbitrary attempts to force Indian reality into the received moulds of European history.

It is worth remarking here that the question of 'feudalism' in China, from which many Marxists in India have drawn their analogies, is by no means unproblematic. In a recent collection of essays from the Chinese Academy of Social Sciences,[7] Wu Dakun of Beijing University has shown how many of Marx's arguments on the Asiatic mode conform to the facts of Chinese

[7] Su Shaozhi et al., *Marxism in China* (Nottingham: Spokesman, 1983).

history. Even more remarkable is his clarification that the term 'feudal' used in English translations of Mao's works is meant to be a rendering of the Chinese word *fengjian*, an old Chinese term whose meaning is fundamentally different from the English term 'feudal'. Perhaps we have all been misreading Mao in poor English translations!

The Big Bourgeoisie

Let us now come to Suniti Ghosh's main thesis about the origins and character of the Indian big bourgeoisie. His arguments are fundamentally aimed against nationalist historians, including 'Left nationalists', who seek to portray the Indian bourgeoisie as a whole as struggling singlemindedly against imperialist domination. But in doing this, Ghosh sets up a straw man, because he alleges that these historians are positing 'an irreconcilable contradiction' between the Indian capitalist class and foreign capital. Now, the more sophisticated among such historians would hardly do this; they would not deny that there was some degree of collaboration between the two. But, of course, their argument is that in the end the Indian bourgeoisie came around to the cause of 'national freedom'.

Suniti Ghosh does not deny that there was '*some* contradiction' (p. 177) between the Indian big bourgeoisie and imperialist capital. But his point is that 'such contradiction was over secondary issues . . . [they] could be resolved within the framework of the imperialist system itself'. Fundamentally, '*much* of the capitalist industry that developed in India did so not in the *strongest* contradiction with the policies of imperialism but *mostly* on a comprador basis'. (p. 215) Now, all the italicized terms above (my italics) are qualifications to Ghosh's main formulation which suggest a certain *quantitative* measure of the degree of comprador or national characteristics. Can such a measure be found? Or will such a mode of argument resolve the debate?

Let us turn Ghosh's argument around by beginning from the end. In the final sentence of his book, Ghosh quotes Mao to make the point that 'in the era of imperialism the road to *independent capitalist* development of a colony or semi-colony [is] blocked'. (p. 290) If that is so, then it is hardly surprising that the Indian big bourgeoisie, inasmuch as it still exists and flourishes as a dominant class in India, should not display the signs of an *independent* capitalist class.

But, on the other hand, Ghosh also quotes Lenin to argue that it is the characteristic of national movements to strive for 'the formation of national states' since they provide the best conditions for modern capitalism. Now, it is an undeniable fact of world history since World War II that formally independent national states have been created all over Asia and Africa in many of which the indigenous big bourgeoisie is in a dominant position. What then is our theoretical problem: to identify the specific character of this bourgeoisie which remains dependent on foreign capital and yet enjoys power in its particular national state, or to reassert the general proposition that the big bourgeoisie is not a truly independent capitalist class?

An Obsolete Problem

I think it is because Suniti Ghosh restricts himself to the second problem that he is unable to bring out the most significant implications of the historical material on the growth of Indian capitalism. It is because of this again that his case against nationalist historiography is not as strong as it could have been. He summarizes the fairly well-known facts about the close connections between early Indian industrial entrepreneurs and British capital as well as the colonial government. He traces the origins of the present big industrial houses in India in their role as brokers and suppliers of British managing agencies. He notes the fact that in the period up to the end of World War I, Indian capitalists accumulated vast wealth principally by collaborating with foreign capital and the colonial government. But in discussing the relation between the big bourgeoisie and the nationalist movement, Ghosh does not quite see the economic possibilities and political strategies which the leading Indian capitalists used to explore their prospects in a rapidly changing historical situation.

Once again, to turn his argument around, Ghosh recognizes that formal political independence has now given the Indian bourgeoisie the freedom to woo several imperialist powers instead of one, and to bargain between them. (p. 278) He also notes (pp. 130–4) that a formally independent state has given the bourgeoisie the added option of harnessing public resources in the cause of private accumulation by instituting a structure of state capitalism.

But all this *required* the creation of a formally independent state, and this was a principal political objective of the Indian big bourgeoisie, certainly by the late 1930s. Ghosh also ignores the fact that it was from this time that Indian capitalists, particularly those based in Calcutta, launched a major onslaught on British-owned companies in the jute and coal industries. They used their financial links with British capital to actually take over British companies, not in the way in which lackeys like the Maharaja of Burdwan or Lord Sinha or Sir B.P. Singh Roy would be made directors, but in the face of fierce opposition from British expatriate businessmen. (The evidence contained in the papers of Sir Edward Benthall is quite revealing on this point.) It is in this perspective that the ideas contained in the so-called 'Bombay Plan' can be understood. The state which the Indian big bourgeoisie visualized was not based on a revolutionary transformation of the colonial economy. It was a state which would in fact carry over almost wholesale the framework of colonial government; the changes it would bring about would be in small doses, in a reformist manner. But it would be *their* state.

Ghosh is not incorrect in stating that 'instead of coming into conflict with each other, British monopoly capital and Indian big capital looked forward to playing complementary roles in the post-war period'. (p. 234) But what is crucial is that Indian big capital was looking towards changing the *political terms* on which such bargaining and collaboration would be made. It was seeking to collaborate not under the aegis of a colonial state, but of an independent state operating in the world economy.

To a large extent, the old problem of comprador/national capital developed in the context of the pre-World War II situation is now obsolete. The political significance of the concepts at that time was to identify enemies and allies in a revolutionary struggle of national liberation. It was not presumed that this struggle would remain under the leadership of the bourgeoisie. For whatever historical reasons, the leadership of the national movement in India remained firmly in the hands of the bourgeoisie, and so have the central organs of the Indian state since independence. It is now futile to speculate on what might have happened if a genuine revolutionary force had seized the leadership of the national struggle, and whether in that case a section of the bourgeoisie might have been mobilized in the cause of independent capitalist development. Since that did not happen, simply to reassert the truism that the Indian big bourgeoisie remains dependent on foreign capital will not get us very far in understanding the specific forms of capitalist development in India or of the role and nature of the contemporary Indian state.

2

The Nehru Era

The Decade after Freedom

The publication of the first volume of Professor Gopal's biography of Jawaharlal Nehru[1] was an important event in the writing of the history of modern India. Despite the many criticisms one could make of that book, there was no denying the importance of the historical material presented in it, or the unmistakable sensation of a massive turmoil overtaking the leaders of the nation as they tried to make sense of those events and to control them as best as they could. One was frequently moved by the warmth and sensitivity of Gopal's portrayal of a leader in the making, urged on by what was basically an intellectual appreciation of the ideals of national freedom on the one hand and an unquestioning emotional loyalty to the Mahatma on the other; a man wanting desperately to plunge headlong into the currents of mass upsurge, yet forced by his intellect and temperament to remain aloof. Gopal's first volume on Nehru was a sincere study of the hero in his youth, for those were days of sacrifice and idealism. The many indecisions, vacillations, irresolutions of purpose, the compromises on principles, could with justification be ignored in the face of the overwhelming onward march of history.

Gopal's second volume[2] leaves much to be desired. In the first place, it deals with a period that is less obviously dramatic. It is a period of slow reconstruction, of long-range planning, of a gradual evolution of relations and structures; a period in the country's recent past which saw few open confrontations in the political battlefield between the great forces of history.

[1] Sarvepalli Gopal, *Jawaharlal Nehru: A Biography, volume 1, 1889–1947* (Delhi: Oxford University Press, 1976).

[2] Sarvepalli Gopal, *Jawaharlal Nehru: A Biography, volume 2, 1947–1956* (Delhi: Oxford University Press, 1979).

It is a period that requires the cold ray of analysis to penetrate the deceptive layer of contemporary perceptions, and bring to light the more latent social processes which worked to change the various structures on which our society is built. If there is any drama at all in this history, it can only emerge out of an analysis of the interaction of those more imperceptible forces. Gopal, unfortunately, does not attempt this analysis. Secondly, because politics during these years could no longer be seen as the clash of great ideals, manoeuvres and machinations necessarily seem more naked, unabashedly prompted by narrow considerations of personal, sectarian, or organizational power. This was the sort of politics that must have been quite disasteful to Nehru himself, or at least to that part of him which was a Fabian liberal. Gandhi, too, was no mean practitioner of the art of realpolitik; yet a total clarity of commitment to his own ethical norms freed him completely from any feeling of guilt on this score. Nehru, on the other hand, is tormented by guilt. Again unfortunately, lacking the scientific apparatus to situate the activities of a political leader in the more impersonal context of structures and processes and thus, in a sense, to 'objectify' the problem, Gopal is hard put to it to explain Nehru's crisis. Much of what he says in the book by way of comments on Nehru's actions seems like special pleading.

I will suggest that both these shortcomings arise because of certain methodological problems inherent in the very project which Professor Gopal has set out for himself: namely, to write as biography the history of Indian politics in the very recent past, using the conventional techniques of the historian. Gopal uses Nehru's letters as his principal source. One result is that each event takes on a structure dictated by the contents and tone of the letters. This is not so much of a problem in the case of conventional histories which use the biographical form, for there the broad structural features of society or the basic historical processes are usually reasonably well understood and have already become part of the standard historical literature for the period. Biases, distortions or angularities in the biographical material can, therefore, be set against the more 'objective' constructions of the economic, political, or social histories of the period concerned. In fact, in the hands of a skilful historian, the distortions themselves can become material for the study of social ideology. This procedure, however, is not adequate for periods which are still, in important ways, contemporary. For here, our perceptions have not yet been sufficiently clarified by theoretical understanding; they are still subjects of current research and debate within the various social science disciplines. Biographical material in what these days is called 'contemporary history' must, therefore, be placed against these tentative findings of the social sciences and interpreted as best as possible in the context of their still-inconclusive debates.

Gopal, however, does not go beyond the conventional methods. The text is constructed very largely out of direct quotes from or paraphrases of Nehru's correspondence, with occasional references to contemporary newspapers and published reminiscences on Nehru. Even the narrative follows in the main a sequence determined by the letters. Nehru's views on the Soviet Union, to take one example, seem to undergo inexplicable changes. In September 1948, he thinks there is 'not the least chance of India lining up with the Soviet Union in war or peace'. (p. 45) In February 1949, he is 'anxious, despite Soviet criticism of his government and support for the Indian Communist Party, to be as friendly as possible and develop contacts in such non-political matters as exchange of films and cultural delegations, to continue talks on a possible trade agreement and offer to buy petrol'. (p. 57) In July 1950, 'his suspicions of the Soviet Union were unchanged . . . "we face today a vast and powerful Soviet group of nations, which tends to become a monolithic bloc, not only in pursuing a similar internal economic policy but a common foreign policy. That policy is an expansionist one. . . . It is expansionist not only in the normal political sense but also in encouraging internal trouble in other countries" '. (p. 102) In August 1957, however, Nehru is writing to Katju: "At the present moment, I would almost say that owing to various circumstances, we have rather undermined the Communist position in India." (p. 277) Nevertheless, during his Moscow visit in August 1955, he 'was concerned to put forward the case for the United States and to make clear that his independent thinking could not be submerged by cordiality and the current coincidence of his outlook with the Russians'. (p. 247) And yet, it is clear by this time that 'from the summer of 1954, the drift away from the United States and towards the

Communist Powers continued steadily'. (p. 226) From Gopal's account, it is quite impossible to know how one should interpret these sudden changes in Nehru's thinking. And as for the larger question of the reasons behind the slow but decisive shift in official Indian foreign policy, Gopal can find no explanation in his sources other than certain irritating communications from the US State Department.

To take another example of how the narrative is shaped by the contents of the Nehru papers, there occurs more than one digression on relations between Nehru and Krishna Menon. Menon, incidentally, comes off very poorly: 'fawning hysteria and plaintive self-pity' is Gopal's comment on Menon's attitude. (p. 142) But one can see no better reason for these extensive digressions than the existence of a few quotable letters.

To the extent Gopal uses any explanatory concepts at all, they are the usual poorly defined catch-all phrases of Indian political journalese, many of them used by Nehru himself to order his own thinking on politics and society. There is that ubiquitous force of communalism which seems to explain so much that is complicated and difficult in Indian politics. This, for instance, is how Gopal handles the Abdullah episode. To start with, Nehru has complete confidence in Abdullah, 'a close friend and comrade' from the days of the freedom struggle. 'The only person who can deliver the goods in Kashmir is Abdullah. . . . No satisfactory way out can be found in Kashmir except through him.' (p. 117) But then Abdullah begins to complain about Hindu communal forces in India who believed in surrendering Kashmir to Pakistan: ' . . . there are powerful influences at work in India,' wrote Abdullah to Nehru, 'who do not see eye to eye with you regarding your ideal of making the Union a truly secular state and your Kashmir policy.' (p. 119) Nehru plays down Abdullah's fears about Hindu communalism. Abdullah, remarks Gopal, is 'obsessed with Hindu communalism and the fantasy of independence'. (p. 124) Nehru sought to 'explain away' Abdullah's fears by saying: 'He is not a very clever thinker. . . . He is of course obsessed with the idea of meeting the challenge of Pakistan and keeping his own people from being influenced by Pakistan's propaganda.' (p. 117) But Nehru's efforts to support Abdullah are upset by a communalist combination of the Jana Sangh, Akali Dal, Hindu

Mahasabha and the RSS. There were communalists in the bureaucracy too: 'The Home Ministry was at this time in the hands of Kailas Nath Katju . . . and his doddering ineptitude was accentuated by the tardiness of many officials whose communal sympathies were barely concealed.' (p. 123) One thing led to another and the episode culminated in Abdullah's dismissal and arrest. One cannot but conclude from this that either Abdullah was fully justified in his alleged 'obsession' with the influence of Hindu communal forces, or else what shaped the course of these events were forces much more complex and variegated than what is suggested by the term 'communalism'.

Caesar?

The lack of theoretical reasoning in Gopal's presentation is particularly painful because there is a wealth of material in the Nehru correspondence quoted by Gopal which could be used to illuminate many crucial but not very well understood problems of Indian politics. Consider, for instance, the question of Nehru's role in the building up of the Congress party organization in a situation where the party was in power and had to remain in power by winning elections. From all that we know of this process, the role of a Caesarist leadership is vital; for, the delicate balancing of contending interests within the broad coalition of ruling forces requires a leader who is not identified with any specific group and yet has the charismatic power to reach the people directly. How far was Nehru this sort of a Caesarist leader? We have some clues in the correspondence which Gopal quotes. Nothing is more distasteful to Nehru than the business of selecting Congress candidates for the elections. That is where there is the most unbridled bickering and infighting among the various groups in the ruling party. But Nehru feels himself a complete outsider at these proceedings: 'I have felt recently as if I was in a den of wild animals.' (p. 161) When a whole spate of agitations break out in 1955–6 on the question of linguistic provinces, Nehru is at a complete loss to understand the reasons behind the trouble. 'This is a terrible job, and I do not see much light yet. Passions have been roused and old friends have fallen out.' He is hesitant, unsure of himself. He does not have a clear stand. As he stated:

I have been greatly distressed about the Bombay and Maharashtra matter and the fact that practically the entire people of Maharashtra feel almost unanimously and strongly on this subject, is rather an overwhelming one. Nobody can deny that there is a good deal of logic in what they say, although there is some logic for the other view too. Anyhow, we have landed ourselves in a position where we are doing something which intimately hurts the whole people of Maharashtra and their representatives. That is a bad position. (p. 269)

In all these squabbles about language, religion, caste, region, and such other parochial loyalties, Nehru is never a partisan; he is always the distant observer, quite alienated from all those concerns which to the rest of his colleagues in the party and to his countrymen are the very stuff of politics.

Yet it was not as though Nehru was not conscious of the need to gain organizational power within the party. He did not think of his own role as that of an outsider co-opted into the leadership. He worked with conscious deliberation towards acquiring a position of unchallenged personal authority in government as well as in the party. The most crucial episode here is that of Tandon's election to Congress presidentship and his subsequent resignation. Unfortunately, Gopal can see no more in this than Nehru's attempt to 'wage full war against all communal elements in the country'. (p. 155) The whole question of how Nehru succeeds in building, step by step, a complex and intricately balanced political structure so as to organize the power of the state within a political process of electoral democracy, is missed entirely.

There is a similar inability to see the crucial importance of socialist phrase-mongering in an ideology of populism which goes hand in hand with this kind of political structure and process. The questions of the electoral non-viability of an independent Socialist Party, and the appropriation of most parts of the Socialist platform by Nehru and his Congress, are reduced essentially to personal relations between Nehru and Jayaprakash Narayan (Jayaprakash was 'cross-grained, wolly-minded and exasperatingly self-righteous') (p. 66) or to the 'escapist mood' of the Socialists who 'had no positive alternative to offer and contented themselves by giving petty trouble on minor issues to the government'. (p. 68) No significance is attached to Nehru's persistent efforts to secure support for his programmes from the

Socialists, his employment of Kidwai for this purpose (p. 153), and his concern, despite all this, that the Socialists should maintain an independent organization outside the Congress. 'The resolution of the Congress in January 1955 to build a "socialistic pattern" of society,' Gopal himself notes, 'blurred differences between the Congress and left-wing parties. . . . Most Socialists felt there was now no basic reason why they should not return to the Congress fold, but Nehru dissuaded them. He claimed to have done so because of his belief that the Socialists still had a role to play as a responsible opposition party; but he was probably also influenced by the desire not to hurt Jayaprakash.' (p. 235) Rather a naive view of politics, this!

Take, again, the decision to retain the ICS cadres in the highest echelons of the bureaucratic machinery. This too was a vital decision in the construction of the new state apparatus under Nehru. It is the unbroken tradition of a colonial bureaucracy, originally built around intricate rules and procedures enshrining unfettered executive power, which provided in the governmental system of independent India an effective mechanism for country-wide control. It is above all the upper bureaucratic structure which protects, in a well-ordered, recurrent and continuous process, those sections of the ruling classes which have interests of an all-India character. Nehru took a conscious decision to retain the ICS. 'Before independence,' says Gopal, 'none had been severer than Nehru in criticism of these officials; but he did not, when the chance came, promptly retire them. Their retention was,' and this is Gopal's principal explanation, 'in a sense a concession to his basic generosity. . . . But perhaps also,' and this is a second, more contingent, explanation, 'in the pressure of post-partition events, there was no alternative to reliance on the Indian Civil Service if the administration was not to break down completely.' (p. 35) But Gopal does not stop here. The consequences of retaining the ICS were not entirely happy. These officers were 'conservative by training and temperament'; in course of time 'they gradually encroached on the making of policy'. But, of course, it was not Nehru who was at fault, because 'Nehru never, like Patel, became the unqualified champion of these officials . . . they were encouraged in this not only by Patel, who approved of their traditional attitudes, but also by Mountbatten, who though temperamentally close to Nehru, was in ideology akin to Patel'. It is true that the civil servants became increasingly powerful, despite Nehru. 'Nehru realized and regretted this; but he also recognized that there seemed little he could do about it. . . . It should have been easier to have changed the over-bureaucratized system of government at the time of the transfer of power, but the nature and context of that occasion had prevented it; and now the system, even though it lacked intrinsic strength, had succeeded in perpetuating itself.' (pp. 36–7)

Compromises

Substantial doubts also arise about the way Gopal has used secondary material to buttress his arguments at crucial points. Let me give just two instances which I have checked. On the question of Kashmir, Gopal is greatly concerned to show that what Nehru did had nothing to do with any romantic attachment he might have felt towards the land which his family had called home. As an argument, Gopal says that when the first request came from the Prime Minister of Kashmir for Indian troops, 'Nehru declined and was only persuaded by Patel and Abdullah to agree'. (p. 19) In support of this, Gopal cites M.C. Mahajan's account of this meeting in his memoirs.[3] Now, reading the relevant passage in Mahajan's book, one finds there were many more dimensions to the context in which this meeting took place than would warrant the rather straightforward conclusion that 'Nehru declined and was only persuaded by Patel and Abdullah to agree'. Mahajan, for instance, had only a few weeks earlier been appointed Prime Minister by the Maharaja of Kashmir with the clear intention of preventing Abdullah from staking a claim to that office. Nehru was always unenthusiastic about Mahajan's appointment because he wanted a popular government in Kashmir under Abdullah. It was at Patel's urging that Mahajan went to Kashmir.[4] Only the day before, Mahajan had rebuffed an emissary from the Pakistan government who was threatening him with dire consequences if Kashmir did not immediately join Pakistan, by telling him that such threats would 'throw the state

---

[3] M.C. Mahajan, *Looking Back* (Bombay: Asia Publishing House, 1963).
[4] Ibid., p. 127.

into the lap of India'.[5] The next day, Mahajan was in Delhi requesting Nehru for immediate military aid to save the town of Srinagar.

the Prime Minister said that even if the town was taken by the tribesmen, India was strong enough to retake it. Its recapture, however, could not have undone the damage that would have resulted. I, therefore, firmly but respectfully insisted on the acceptance of my request for immediate military aid. The Prime Minister observed that it was not easy on the spur of the moment to send troops as such an operation required considerable preparation and arrangement, and troops could not be moved without due deliberation merely on my demand. I was, however, adamant in my submission; the Prime Minister also was sticking to his own view. As a last resort I said, 'Give us the military force we need. Take the occasion and give whatever power you desire to the popular party. The army must fly to save Srinagar this evening or else I will go to Lahore and negotiate terms with Mr Jinnah.'

When I told the Prime Minister of India that I had orders to go to Pakistan in case immediate military aid was not given, he naturally became upset and in an angry tone said, 'Mahajan, go away.' I got up and was about to leave the room when Sardar Patel detained me by saying in my ear, 'Of course, Mahajan, you are not going to Pakistan.' Just then, a piece of paper was passed over to the Prime Minister. He read it and in a loud voice said, 'Sheikh Sahib also says the same thing.' It appeared that Sheikh Abdullah had been listening to all this talk while sitting in one of the bedrooms adjoining the drawing room where we were. He now strengthened my hands by telling the Prime Minister that military help must be sent immediately. This came as a timely help for the success of my mission to New Delhi. The Prime Minister's attitude changed on reading the slip.[6]

Take another instance. In course of describing Nehru's role in the making of the Constitution, Gopal says, 'Nehru had opposed the listing of the right to property among the fundamental rights, but had to give in.' (p. 79) He cites K.M. Munshi's description of this event.[7] Gopal then goes on to say:

From this arose the question of the right to compensation in case of

[5] Ibid., p. 142.

[6] Ibid., pp. 151–2.

[7] K.M. Munshi, *Indian Constitutional Documents, volume 1: Pilgrimage to Freedom (1902–1950)* (Bombay: Bharatiya Vidya Bhavan, 1967), pp. 79–80.

expropriation of private property. . . . But Nehru, Pant and others who were eager to press forward with the abolition of the *zamindari* system wished to make it clear that it was for the legislature and not the courts to lay down the principles on which compensation should be paid. So Article 31 stipulated that the law must specify the compensation or the principles on which it should be paid. (pp. 79–80)

But in Munshi, the context is quite the opposite. The immediate context of discussion in the Advisory Committee was the issue of *zamindari* abolition. There was strong opposition to the draft clause on Fundamental Rights from 'the representatives from the U.P. and Bihar. . . . Govind Ballabh Pant, the Chief Minister of the U.P., led the attack on the right to property'. The issue was the question of fair compensation and who should decide what was fair. A large section, including Nehru, Pant and others, thought the legislatures should have unfettered discretion in this matter, while others, notably Munshi and T.T. Krishnamachari, argued for the right of property to be included in the Constitution so that the courts could act as final arbiter. As Munshi states:

Finally, the controversy came to a head at the Party meetings when the right to property (ultimately numbered Article 31) was being discussed. Jawaharlal Nehru thundered against its inclusion; he urged that in the history of man notions of property had changed from time to time; the right to property, therefore, should not be included as a Fundamental Right.

During the discussions, the final blow was struck in defence of the right to property by John Mathai, the then Finance Minister of the Union Government, who fought back vigorously. . . .

A compromise was ultimately effected. An amendment implementing the compromise formula was moved in the Assembly which stood in the name of Jawaharlal Nehru, Govind Ballabh Pant, Alladi Gopalaswamy Ayyangar and myself.

Clearly, then, the context was one of a generalized debate springing from the specific issue of *zamindari* abolition and payment of compensation, not an abstract philosophical position on the right to property giving rise to a specific debate. There were many others in the Congress leadership who shared Nehru's position on this matter all down the line. Yet, the subtle shift in context which occurs in the course of Gopal's use of this evidence produces the impression of a majestically lonely figure, wanting to stand firmly by his cherished principles of socialism, but forced by the pressure and machinations of those he must work with to compromise on each one of them.

The Unexamined Hero

This may seem like quibbling on minor matters, but it is not. It is closely related to the question of the difficulties of using the biographical method when writing 'contemporary history'. There is, for one thing, the matter of the historian's biases and prejudices, which can be intense as well as inconsistent when personalities from within one's own life-experience are involved. Gopal is particularly guilty on this score. His adulation of Nehru is frank. But his penchant for invective against those he does not like is equally unrestrained. We have already noted his remarks on Jayaprakash Narayan and Krishna Menon. Rajendra Prasad was a man 'of inferior intellectual quality and with a social outlook which belonged to the eighteenth century', (p. 77) Bidhan Roy was 'reactionary', (p. 72) but the choicest epithets are reserved for Nehru's special assistant, M.O. Mathai. In four long paragraphs towards the end of the book, Gopal lambasts Mathai, 'an illiterate upstart', 'disloyal, avaricious and opportunistic' who 'revived in Delhi the atmosphere of a decadent court'. (pp. 310–12)

But this matter of biases is not necessarily all that much of a shortcoming. In fact, there is much to be said in favour of the view that a good biography requires a sympathetic biographer, just as a good portrayal on stage or screen requires an actor who can empathize with the character he portrays. The important thing is to probe deeply into a personality, to search for those compelling inner motivations which keep a man going, to discover the logic and ideological consistencies of an active and imaginative mind, to see him in a certain social context, a context which moulds his life and personality, changes it with time, and which in turn is affected by his activities as a leader of society. One is not necessarily asking for a psycho-history, although some forays into the terrain of psychology are unavoidable for any biographer. In any case, the whole field of the working of the human mind, whether individual or collective, is still only vaguely charted by science, so that almost anything that an intelligent, sensitive and courageous writer — novelist, playright or biographer — may say on the subject is likely to be of some value.

The trouble with Professor Gopal as a biographer is that his courage seems to fail him whenever he comes up against the problematical or contradictory aspects of Nehru's personality. It is almost as though he is afraid of finding something unpleasant and so stops probing any further. Yet the contradictions in Nehru's personality are so fundamental and glaring that one cannot but ask: What kept the man going? Why didn't he chuck it all up? His disillusionment with what the Congress had become was acute.

If I chose according to my own inclination, I would like other people to carry on the business here and to be left free to do some other things that I consider very important. Yet with all modesty, I think that my leaving might well be in the nature of a disaster. No man is indispensable, but people do make a difference at a particular time. (p. 75)

This was not something Nehru wrote in a sudden fit of depression; quotes of this kind occur throughout Gopal's book.

I have an increasing feeling that such utility as I have had is lessening and I work more as an automaton in a routine way rather than as an active and living person. . . . Functioning in such a way ceases to have much meaning. Many of our policies, economic and other, leave a sense of grave uneasiness in me. I do not interfere partly because I am not wholly seized with the subject and partly because of myself being entangled in a web out of which it is difficult to emerge. . . .

I feel that if I have to be of any real use in the future, I must find my roots again. I do not think I can do so by continuing for much longer in my present routine of life. I am prepared to continue for a while, but not too long. I do not think that my days of useful work have ended, but I feel sure that my utility will grow less and less in existing circumstances. (pp. 158-9)

Yet he kept at it till the end of his life, 'putting in,' as Gopal testifies, 'a twenty-hour day with hardly even breakfast as a private meal.' (p. 309) What kept him going? An ideological commitment? A vision of the India of the future? Yet there is little to show that Nehru had clear ideas about what he wanted India to be in the years ahead. He wanted industrialization, modern technology, the building up of infrastructure on a massive scale. When the great river valley projects were inaugurated, Nehru wrote: ' . . . a sense of adventure seized me and I forgot for a while the many troubles that beset us.' (p. 35) Yet, four years later, 'a sight of the hovels in which the workers of Kanpur lived caused him such intense shame that he developed a sort of fever. "I have no need for any industrialization which degrades a human being and sullies his honour." ' (p. 199) Confusion? Or hypocrisy? Self-deception? He compromised repeatedly on his principles of socialism. When Jayaprakash pointed this out to him — 'You want to go towards socialism, but you want the capitalists to help in that. You want to build socialism with the help of capitalism. You are bound to fail in that' — his defence was: 'I cannot, by sheer force of circumstance, do everything that I would like to do. We are all of us in some measure prisoners of fate and circumstance.' (p. 67) The arrest and detention of Abdullah rankled in his conscience. He wrote to Abdullah: 'We, who are in charge of heavy responsibilities, have to deal with all kinds of forces at work and often they take their own shape. We see in the world today great statesmen, who imagine they are controlling the destinies of a nation, being pushed hither and thither by forces beyond their control.' (p. 303) Was there, underlying the moral conflicts, a compelling ruthlessness which pushed him repeatedly towards the decisive use of the instruments of power?

Professor Gopal unfortunately does not help us find an answer. In fact, the sad thing is that he seems to prefer not to know the answer.

The Last Years

For Nehru fans, the last five or six years of the hero's life clearly pose the greatest problems. In domestic politics, there was in those years a sudden resurgence of linguistic, regional and communal strife; the ruling party organization began to show signs of widespread corruption, ineptitude and factionalism; and of course there was the inglorious episode of the ouster of the communist ministry in Kerala. On the economic front, the heady enchantment of planning began to wear off and a massive crisis loomed on the horizon. Internationally, there was the inexplicable dithering on Goa, a growing resentment voiced by African countries over India's role in the Congo, isolation from her neighbours nearer home, prevarication over the very foundations of non-alignment, and above all the shattering experience of the China War. Clearly, the hero had lost his magic touch; he was old, tired, disillusioned, embittered, no longer in control of things. It is not an easy period for an admiring biographer to write about.

To be fair to Sarvepalli Gopal, he has faced up to the task with considerable courage.[8] He decided that he would criticize Nehru where criticism was due. He has also attempted a general stock-taking of the economic and political conditions in India at the end of the Nehru era, and has taken note of the many criticisms that have been made of Nehru's policies from positions entirely at variance with Nehru's own. And yet, it all ends up with a 'despite these drawbacks his achievements were substantial' kind of conclusion. The criticisms remain on the surface. They do not lead Gopal to ask questions about the very nature of the economy and polity in which a leader such as Nehru could flourish — and flounder — and whether that is necessarily the kind of economy and polity which the Indian people must have.

Besides this superficial readiness to be critical, Gopal's style remains much the same as in the two earlier volumes. The narrative is primarily built upon Nehru's correspondence and other official papers to which Gopal has had privileged access. For the main part, he proceeds by paraphrasing large chunks of Nehru's prose and recorded speech. This is not of very great advantage to him. There are long passages with sentences such as these:

Obviously every country should evolve its own policies to fit in with its own conditions, as the best of theoretical approaches might not fit with the objective situation . . . one should change with the times and not be the prisoner of phrases. Socialism for India was not just an emotional commitment or an ideological preference; it was the only scientific way of solving social problems, the pragmatic means of achieving quickly higher standards of living for all. . . . Such material progress could also be achieved without divorce from values if the

8 Sarvepalli Gopal, *Jawaharlal Nehru: A Biography, volume 3, 1956–1964* (Delhi: Oxford University Press, 1984).

people absorbed the right ideals and acted up to them. India had thought a great deal about these values through hundreds and thousands of years and it would be a misfortune if she forgot them in the pursuit of material well-being. . . . (p. 116)

Such paragraphs go on and on, over and over again, endlessly. Whatever meaning these sentences may have carried in the 1950s has been washed away by years of Nehruvian didacticism; today it is frothy verbiage — long-winded, hollow and painfully boring.

To come to the main events, the one most easily disposed of is Goa. It has always been a mystery why Nehru took such an interminably long time to decide on what to do about the wholly anachronistic obduracy of Salazar's government on the subject of Goa. On cultural, political and moral grounds, India's case was as perfect as it could ever be. Nehru's hesitation was about the use of force, and not, as Gopal points out at several places, because of any basic moral qualm. Nehru was not, he asserts, a pacifist. (Rather, he was a 'pacificist', says Gopal on the basis of a quite trivial distinction picked up from a book review by the redoubtable A.J.P. Taylor — the argument is that Nehru was prepared to abandon peaceful methods 'in the last resort'.) (pp. 190–1) Specifically, Nehru was worried about what 'the friends of India' would say if she was to use force in liberating Goa. Which friends? Nobody in the colonial or post-colonial world, or in any of the socialist countries, was likely to raise an eyebrow. The friends Nehru was bothered about were in Britain, France and the United States, and Nehru 'boxed himself in' by preaching to them so often about the absolute sanctity of peaceful methods. After the Goa operation was finally over — with, as it turned out, virtually no bloodshed at all — these 'friends' came back at him with a vengeance, accusing him of hypocrisy and jingoism. Strangely enough, Gopal himself shows extraordinary sensitiveness towards these charges, and seems to suggest that it would have done Nehru's image a lot of good if he had been able somehow to avoid 'shocking' his friends in this manner. The agonies of the liberal soul are often beyond comprehension.

Kerala 1957–9

Kerala 1957–9 is a much trickier subject for Gopal to handle. He seems to concede in a roundabout sort of way that wrong was done. But there were, he argues, extenuating circumstances which justified Nehru's action. In the first place, the communists themselves were to blame by their hasty and dogmatic decisions which alienated a lot of powerful interests in Kerala. Gopal approvingly quotes Nehru's judgement that the 'bookishness' and 'extra-territorial loyalties' of the Indian communists made it difficult for them to 'fit into the Indian context'. (p. 53) (There is an element of the ridiculous in a Jawaharlal Nehru accusing E.M.S. Namboodiripad or A.K. Gopalan of failing to 'adapt themselves' to Indian conditions, but Gopal does not see this.) Second, the Congress in Kerala, and subsequently several important central leaders like Pant, Indira Gandhi and even Krishna Menon, were pushing Nehru to dismiss the communist ministry. The crucial swing in Nehru's thinking came in July 1958, following the execution of Imre Nagy in Hungary. Holidaying in Manali, he suddenly saw civilization as

mentally exhausted and unable to cope with the rapid pace of change in human life . . . Rationalism too seemed inadequate . . . Communism . . . ultimately failed partly because of its rigidity but even more because it ignored certain essential needs of human nature . . . India had to evolve her own peaceful approach . . . perhaps we might also keep in view the old Vedantic ideal of the life force which is the inner base of everything that exists. (pp. 61–2)

This flight into metaphysics acquired a somewhat macabre significance, because Nehru returned from Manali to deliver a virtual charge sheet on Namboodiripad. 'Against this Nehru,' Gopal writes, 'Namboodiripad had little chance.' (p. 62) Nehru had now ceased to listen, though the communist Chief Minister continued to plead with him until the day before his dismissal, expecting a 'non-partisan and rational approach'. In the end, Gopal's judgment is that

Nehru was driven into a decision by the communists who passed on the initiative to him so that they could appear as victims and by the Congress who looked for undeserved and undemocratic advantages from a contrived crisis. . . . It could be faulted in theory and could be interpreted as inspired by narrow party advantage; but it appeared to him to be required in the public interest. He finally arrived at a decision which he knew to be wrong for what he believed were the right reasons. (p. 73)

What were the implications of this decision for Indian politics? Gopal thinks that it tarnished Nehru's reputation with the Indian Left: 'This made it more difficult for him, in the penultimate stage of his career, to achieve the goals of his economic and social policies.' (p. 74) A dubious conclusion. On the contrary, what the experience of Kerala achieved — something that was subsequently confirmed by the experience of the two United Front governments in West Bengal in 1967 and 1969 — was to define within the Indian state system the limits of communist political activity. This was Nehru's political achievement on behalf of India's ruling classes. The communists' reading of this experience could conceivably have been quite different. The rulers had given them the rules of the game; they could have thrown them aside. As we know, however, the main part of the communist movement decided henceforth to play within the rules.

War with China

The boundary dispute and the war with China naturally take up the largest part of this volume. On this, the reader is placed in considerable difficulty. Gopal's account is almost entirely a reiteration of the official stand of the Nehru government (which is not surprising because Gopal himself played an important part in preparing the historical documentation on behalf of that government). Gopal's evidence on the history of the dispute, the course of negotiations, and the series of border clashes leading up to the war in October 1962 and the unilateral Chinese withdrawal in November are mainly based, apart from published accounts by various Indian generals, on Indian official sources to which the ordinary scholar has no access. It is therefore impossible to judge whether Gopal's construction of the case is fair. His main argument on the border dipute is that the Indian claim was based on the 'traditional' demarcation. He does not even consider the argument as to whether a government which had come to power after struggling against a colonial regime was right in attributing such overwhelming sanctity to a border clearly drawn up according to the strategic interests of an imperial power, in a virtually unpopulated area with no complicating ethnic or national questions. Gopal argues that while holding firmly to this 'traditional' claim, Nehru was prepared to negotiate, but the Chinese kept changing their demands. Once again, without access to the relevant documents, it is hard to judge whether Gopal is right.

Gopal's explanation for the war itself is, expectedly, Chinese ambition and perfidy. He quotes Nehru with approval in laying the blame squarely on China's 'tradition of expansionism and its conceit and faith in its mission of world domination by force and revolution'. Gopal even goes into an assessment of Mao's legacy to China:

A hard-headed nationalist, he was determined to regain for his country not only equality among nations but a prime position in Asia . . . the permanent legacy of Mao to his country has been not continuous social and economic upheaval but a powerful state and army. China has become, under Mao's inspiration, an ambitious nation and a skilled practitioner of realpolitik. . . . In this as in most other issues of world affairs demanding a long perspective, Nehru was among the clear-sighted statesmen of his time. (pp. 238–9)

Let us ignore the utter imbecility of this political judgement on Mao which would have done credit to Ronald Reagan's speech-writers. But 'China's traditional expansionism' strengthened by the resurgence of Chinese nationalism? Whose expansionism? Of the country? The nation? Its imperial rulers? Would it not be ridiculous to suggest, on the basis of Indian history for instance, that Uzbekistan or Afghanistan has a 'tradition of expansionism?'

What does emerge from Gopal's recounting of the events of 1961 and 1962 is a picture of utter confusion in the political handling of a military situation. It does not put Nehru in a very favourable light. Gopal explains this in terms of an 'incompatibility between character and role' (buttressed by a bizarre citation of a scholarly work on Shakespearean tragedy): 'Forced to lead his people in resistance to aggression, he did his best without enthusiasm and seeking always to secure India from the corruption of battle.' The much-discussed 'forward policy', (p. 227) for instance, was in Nehru's mind one of establishing patrols and posts as close to the border as possible, with intermediate and near bases to support the forward positions.

But in the orders issued by Army Headquarters in furtherance of

Nehru's decision, the stipulation about strong bases in the rear was omitted. No explanation for this lapse is available, though the later justification of General Thapar . . . suggests that the omission was deliberate . . . the decision to push ahead with patrols and posts without supporting bases clearly was a departure from Nehru's policy and apparently not known to him. (pp. 208–9)

Nehru, it seems, was content only to lay down broad policy.

However, the army commanders were unable to take the right decisions within the ambit of the broad policy laid down by the Prime Minister and to utilize properly the discretion which he had vested in them . . . the officers in local command produced a scheme for evicting the Chinese which, incredible as it sounds, was apparently a make-believe plan which was not intended to be taken seriously but on which Kaul seized as the appropriate tactics. (p. 220)

In fact, Gopal's account does not contradict the interpretation that the Chinese read these ham-handed military moves as signs of the aggressive intent of the Indian government. Whether Nehru is to be blamed for warmongering is not quite relevant; the fact that political control was lax enough to allow the 'considerable personal distrust' among the generals to get on top at such a critical moment points to a political failure, and the Prime Minister cannot be absolved of ultimate responsibility.

Request for US Aid

Gopal's account also produces one or two startling facts about Nehru's reaction to the crisis. After the fall of Bomdila on November 19, he wrote to Kennedy requesting the immediate despatch of American fighter squadrons manned by American personnel; but he did this on his own, without consulting his Cabinet, and when S.K. Patil asked him about this, Nehru blandly replied that no policy decision had been taken without reference to the Cabinet. Gopal's comment on this case, of a Prime Minister misleading his own Cabinet on a major question of foreign policy in the middle of a war, is a model of understatement: 'Clearly Nehru's memory was not at this time at its best.' (p. 228n) One also reads with astonishment about Nehru's correspondence with Mountbatten in January 1961 on whether a post of Chairman of Chiefs of Staff should be created, and the latter's suggestion that Thimayya would suit the job because he was 'one of the most outstanding generals that I have ever come across in any country'. (p. 132) The reason why Mountbatten's suggestion was rejected was not the obvious impropriety of a former Viceroy advising the Prime Minister of an independent republic about appointments in its army, but because Nehru at this time had developed a distrust of the officer corps as a whole and was apprehensive of a military coup!

Nehru's overtures to the United States in the wake of the China war clearly spelled doom for the much-vaunted policy of non-alignment. Gopal does a lot of hair-splitting about what the principles of non-alignment really mean: 'War has its own momentum, and non-alignment cannot be at the cost of national survival . . . ' and so on. As far as Nehru was concerned, he was much more forthright: there can be no non-alignment *vis-à-vis* China, he said. (p. 229) Ironically, it was the Chinese themselves who saved India's non-alignment from an inglorious death, by withdrawing unilaterally.

Economy and Polity

Gopal also spends some time discussing the economy and the policy of development. He agrees that 'after years of planning, development in India is associated as much with an overall increase in poverty, inequality and unemployment as with a steady growth. All the measures introduced by Nehru were found compatible with the maintenance of capitalist relations of production and the preservation of middle-class hegemony.' (pp. 295–6) But this is not how it was meant to happen. Nehru had visualized a private sector helping to increase the national wealth, but the public sector would expand and ultimately overwhelm private capitalism and establish a socialist society. 'A rich business class,' pronounces Gopal, 'nullified the intentions of the Government.' (p. 291) Is this not infantile? What did one expect the business class to do? Happily cooperate with a 'socialist' policy in order to dig its own grave?

Gopal also says a lot of things about Nehru's belated realization that something had to be done about agrarian reform. The scheme of village cooperatives and panchayati raj, says Gopal, was meant to be a revolutionary step — not a 'passive revolution' in Gramsci's sense, but 'an active, democratic revolution carried out by the masses themselves'. (p. 168) This is another instance of Gopal's inept use of theoretical concepts. Had he understood Gramsci's concept correctly, he would have identified Nehru's panchayati raj and village coperatives as a classic instrument of the passive revolution. In the end, Gopal would have us believe, the policy failed because of lack of support from the bureaucracy. If indeed it was an 'active' revolution launched by the people themselves, one wonders how the bureaucracy came to have anything to do with it.

In fact, as author of a major political biography such as this, Gopal's lack of any kind of systematic understanding of the nature of the Indian polity and its balancing processes is painfully obvious. On the significance of such a crucial event as the Kamaraj Plan, all Gopal does is quote Rajni Kothari's debatable proposition that in place of the Prime Minister's overarching authority, it gave more power to influential party bosses and weakened the central government. What Gopal has to add by way of his own comment is a flippant remark: the Kamaraj Plan had the effect of barring Morarji Desai from succeeding Nehru as Prime Minister, 'and who, having seen Desai in the office of Prime Minister many years later, can say that Nehru was wrong?' (p. 245)

In the end, Gopal continues to maintain an undiminished admiration for the personality of Nehru. He does not find it odd that someone who preached so much about the need to adapt to the real conditions of India, about being pragmatic and not dogmatic, should have felt so alienated in his intellectual make-up from the beliefs and practices of the people of his country. All his life, he never stopped complaining that the people were not behaving the way they should. When regional or communal riots broke out, he complained that people 'were forgetting major issues and getting excited over minor matters'. (p. 175) When the Nagpur resolution did not appear to rouse much enthusiasm about agrarian reform, he complained about 'the general sense of depression among our people'. (p. 117) When charges were made about corruption in high places, he complained about 'this kind of underground, over-ground and middle-ground propaganda of every type. . . . We are a gossipy people'. (p. 123) When caste and class differences appeared unlikely to vanish, he complained: 'What is wrong with us? We have no sense of equality?' (p. 280) During his momentous sojourn in Manali, he even thought the whole world was out of step with the kind of thinking that was required for the progress of human civilization. (p. 61)

Gopal finds in all this confirmation of the vast intellectual superiority of his hero:

... the Prime Minister was really looking far too ahead; and his images of maintaining and coordinating the rhythms of life between the individual and society and the past and the present and getting the Indian peasant in line with the rhythm of the modern world, all by means of the cooperatives, the panchayats and the schools, were well beyond the understanding, let alone the reach, of his officials and party men. (pp. 169–70)

He does not stop to consider the paradox of a 'pragmatic' leader, impatient of rigid theoretical schemes, always thinking 'far too ahead' of those who were meant to implement his policies, not to speak of those on whom they were to be implemented. Theoretically, Gopal tells us, Nehru shared a 'spirit of over-confident Benthamism'. (p. 280) Gopal admits that this showed a 'capacity for self-delusion,' even if not 'amounting almost to deliberate self-deception.' Basically, we are told again, Nehru was 'in the line of William Morris;' his socialism, 'as that of the French socialists, Jaurès and Blum, was above all "a humanistic creed, placing its major emphasis on the fulfilment of the individual." ' (p. 285) Why this unprecedented amalgam of Benthamism, William Morris and French socialism should appear to anyone as being suited to Indian reality defies comprehension.

Finally, a minor point. Reviewing in his last chapter some of the arguments put forward by Nehru's critics, Gopal writes: 'The angry prejudice which insinuates that he was a hypocrite or no more than an ambitious politician does not merit serious treatment.' (p. 298) I read through the line and then the whole page until I discovered from the footnote at the bottom that Gopal was referring to a review I had written of the second volume of his book. I found it hard to believe that anything I had written on Nehru could be reduced to something as crass as this. I hunted up a reprint of the review and found that the offending lines were in the penultimate paragraph which ran as follows:

What kept him [Nehru] going? An ideological commitment? A vision of the India of the future? Yet there is little to show that Nehru had clear ideas about what he wanted India to be in the years ahead . . . Confusion? Or hypocrisy? Self-deception? He compromised repeatedly on his principle of socialism. When Jayaprakash pointed this out to him — 'You want to go towards socialism, but you want the capitalists to help in that. You want to build socialism with the help of capitalism. You are bound to fail in that' — his defence was: 'I cannot, by sheer force of circumstances, do everything that I would like to do. . . . ' The arrest and detention of Abdullah rankled in the conscience . . . Was there, underlying the moral conflicts, a compelling ruthlessness which pushed him repeatedly towards the decisive use of the instruments of power?

That is what I wrote. Does this amount to an insinuation that 'he was a hypocrite or no more than an ambitious politician?' I do not have the temerity to question Professor Gopal's knowledge of the English language. Gopal has now conceded, in the final volume of his biography, Nehru's self-deception and the impossibility of building socialism with the help of capitalism. About the rest, what can one say except that Sarvepalli Gopal twists what he reads in order to suit his purpose, even to mislead?

Gopal's biography ends dramatically. Nehru, he announces, 'is India's once and — we may hope — future king.' (p. 302) No, Professor Gopal. The freedom of the Indian people lies in the steadfast rejection of all such pretenders to the throne.

3

Indian Democracy and Bourgeois Reaction[*]

There has been much talk in recent months about the rise of fascism in India. Some are arguing that the government, bent upon crushing the opposition movement by the use of 'semi-fascist' methods, is turning the country into a 'police state'. Others are claiming that it is not the government but various reactionary forces outside it that have launched a movement with a view to destroying democracy and installing a right-wing regime. All these discussions, however, seem to assume a notion of ideal bourgeois democracy at one extreme and of pure fascism at the other; the problem is seen to be one of judging how much Indian politics has moved away from the former and towards the latter. What is forgotten is that bourgeois reaction can take many different political forms. These forms depend upon the nature of the resistances which the bourgeoisie faces in its attempt to generalize its particular mode of production throughout society.

Consequently, before we decide how much we have deviated from the ideals of bourgeois democracy or what are the possibilities of fascism in India, we first need to have a clearer idea of the political resistances faced today by the Indian ruling classes. It is on the basis of their understanding of these resistances that the ruling classes will weigh the various economic strategies open to them. The specific choice of strategy, and the subsequent forms of political movement conducted by the opposition forces, will determine the kind of political regime the ruling classes will seek to impose.

In this essay, we will first present a brief description of the social conditions necessary for establishing bourgeois rule within

---

[*] This essay was written, jointly with Arup Mallik, three months before the declaration of internal Emergency in June 1975.

a democratic structure, i.e. the 'first way' of capitalist development. We will then discuss the historical possibilities of a 'second
way' of capitalism which dispenses with democracy.

Capitalism and Democracy

Three conditions are necessary for the 'pure' (or more precisely,
the English) way of capitalism. Following Adam Smith's classic
analysis, these can be enumerated as follows: (1) the abolition of
rent as the principal mode of surplus extraction from agriculture;
(2) small units of industrial production; and (3) a general preference for productive over unproductive labour. These conditions
make for a social dynamic leading towards an industrial revolution.

When a bourgeoisie generalizes its mode of production in
society, it establishes its leadership not only over the economy
but over all structures of society, including its ideological–cultural superstructure. Most notable here is the split between state
and civil society. Bourgeois social philosophy depicts the state as
an abstract and neutral arbiter situated above all social conflicts.
By doing this, the bourgeoisie can separate the sphere of production from the domain of the state, and can keep the state from
getting entangled in social conflicts emanating from the domain
of production. This is a major political significance of the doctrine of *laissez faire*.

Where the political state has achieved its full development, man leads
a double life, a heavenly and an earthly life, not only in thought or
consciousness but in *actuality*. In the *political community* he regards himself as a *communal being*; but in *civil society* he is active as a *private individual*,
treats other men as means, reduces himself to a means, and becomes
the plaything of alien powers. The political state is as spiritual in relation
to civil society as heaven is in relation to earth. . . . In the state where
he counts as a species-being . . . he is an imaginary member of an
imagined sovereignty, divested of his actual individual life and endowed
with an unactual universality.[1]

What is most significant about this process is not so much the
capture of state power, but rather the success of the bourgeoisie

[1] Karl Marx, 'On the Jewish Question', in Lloyd Easton and Kurt Guddat,
eds, *Writings of the Young Marx on Philosophy and Society* (Garden City, N.Y.:
Doubleday, 1967), pp. 225–6.

in diffusing its own world-view into the practices and beliefs of the overwhelming majority of the people. By abolishing the directly political character of civil society in feudalism, the bourgeoisie separates it from the state, and by achieving hegemony over civil society, legitimizes its political rule. The state, it can argue, is neutral; the state stands above all social conflicts. No single group or class has control over the state; even when particular governments come and go, the framework of the state remains unaltered.

By splitting man into public and private, and by granting public political rights to the individual as citizen, the bourgeoisie secures recognition of the private nature of the individual in civil society.

The state abolishes distinctions of *birth, rank, education* and *occupation* in its fashion when it declares them to be *non-political* distinctions, when it proclaims that every member of the community *equally* participates in popular sovereignty without regard to these distinctions, and when it deals with all elements of the actual life of the nation from the standpoint of the state. Nevertheless the state permits private property, education and occupation to *act* and manifest their *particular* nature as private property, education and occupation in their *own* ways. Far from overcoming these *factual* distinctions, the state exists only by presupposing them; it is aware of itself as a *political state* and makes its *universality* effective only in opposition to those elements.[2]

The bourgeoisie grants political liberty to all citizens, i.e. gives every citizen as a private individual the right to do anything which does not harm other private individuals. By granting this right of liberty, it secures the legitimation of the right of private property. By granting to each citizen the security of his person and property ('the supreme social concept of civil society, the concept of the police'), it guarantees the basic egoistic principle of bourgeois economy and law.

At the same time, the bourgeoisie, through various civil–social institutions — the family, the cultural associations, the communications media, and particularly the educational system which, in bourgeois society, becomes the most influential part of the ideological state apparatus — seeks to diffuse its own individualistic world-view over the rest of society; an individualistic world-view

[2] Ibid., pp. 224–5.

which again seeks to de-emphasize cultural distinctions in the realm of political life. This ideological–cultural programme of bourgeois society is linked very closely with the process of universalization of the capitalist mode of production in first-way capitalism. For, this facilitates the creation, on the one hand, of a homogeneous consumer market with relatively similar tastes and cultural values; and on the other, of a free capital and labour market with relatively unrestricted movements of finance and population within the country. A uniform legal code and a gradually broadening education system through the medium of a common and popularly understood language creates the conditions for a relative cultural homogeneity among the peoples of the nation. Indeed, once these conditions are ensured and civil liberties are given universal recognition by the state, only to guarantee the continued existence of inequality and exploitation, the bourgeoisie can continue to grant political rights to the working class. It gives the working class the right to vote, and thereby legitimizes the false concept that by being able to express one's opinion as an individual one acquires a part of the popular sovereignty. It allows the workers the right to form unions, but the sway of the principles of egoism in civil society virtually ensures that these remain bogged down in the mire of economism.

It is worth noting that bourgeois democracy achieves its complete political form only *after* the bourgeois revolution, *after* the industrial revolution and *after* the conquest of social hegemony by the bourgeoisie. In the countries which were latecomers to capitalism, which were left behind in the race for overseas colonies, the conditions for 'normal', i.e. first-way capitalist development did not exist. In countries like Germany, the industrial bourgeoisie was weak as a social class, and it required an authoritarian state to take the initiative for capital accumulation and economic growth and thereby carry through the programme of industrialization. The state, by imposing protective tariffs, guaranteed the domestic market for German industrialists. The Prussian landlords emerged as capitalists in agriculture and the eviction of tenants from land supplied the industrial reserve army. With the expansion of productive capacity, the industrialists soon had to come up against a restricted domestic market; the solution to this problem was sought in increasing militarism and an aggressive foreign policy.

The second way of capitalist development thus requires from the start an absolutist, centralized and undemocratic state. The bourgeoisie there cannot afford to grant civil liberties — its programme of industrialization must be carried through with maximum speed and efficiency, involving a forced mobilization of resources imposed from above. Consequently, in second-way capitalism, because of the direct participation of the state in the system of production, the bourgeoisie is unable to achieve an effective separation between state and civil society.

We are now in a position to make two formulations for our subsequent discussion. In countries where the bourgeoisie is able to establish its hegemony in the classical form, it is possible for it to contain political opposition by using normal legal methods — such as, for instance, the police. Where the bourgeoisie does not exercise such hegemony, its authority can be so weak as to make it impossible for it to rule within the normal legal limits of coercive powers. In such cases, bourgeois reaction will take a different political form.

India: Economy and Polity

Before 1947, much of the industrial sector which existed around the metropolitan centres of India was dominated by foreign capital. However, particularly after World War I, indigenous Indian capitalism on a modern industrial scale developed significantly in engineering, textiles, cement, jute and paper. Nevertheless, this indigenous industry relied heavily on selling its products to government establishments and to foreign exporters and manufacturers. Even before independence, industrial capital in India tended to be highly monopolistic in character.[3] Apart from the bourgeoisie, urban life and politics in India were dominated by the upper petty bourgeoisie — successful professionals, Westernized, articulate. In their role as professionals, they had developed a range of interests that was all-India in scope: in this role, therefore, professionals from Bombay could associate with those from Calcutta or Madras or Allahabad in an all-India forum such as the Indian National Congress.

[3] On this, see Amiya Kumar Bagchi, *Private Investment in India, 1900–1939* (Cambridge: Cambridge University Press, 1972).

As far as the organization of agricultural production was concerned, this was where colonialism left its most crucial impact. Colonial revenue policies had the effect of forcing the peasant to produce cash crops; if he did not have adequate capital, or if his produce or its price was insufficient, he was forced to borrow. As a result, usury and speculative trading in cash crops became lucrative occupations for those who had any funds. One consequence was the rapid expansion in commercial crop production at the cost of food crop production.

The root of the problem of stagnation in Indian agriculture was lack of investment. With the introduction of commercialization in a labour-surplus economy with low levels of irrigation, it was decidedly more profitable for landlords to turn to rack-renting, usury and speculative trade than to invest in the improvement of the land or its output. Thus, while rent exploitation was extended over lands transferred from an immiserized peasantry, the landlords did not turn to intensive exploitation through capitalist farming. That remained the crux of the agrarian problem in colonial India.

The Legacy of the National Movement

The national movement as it developed during the first half of the present century was supported by the Indian business houses at the highest levels of the organizational structure of the movement. Clearly, the objective was to achieve an influence over the emerging national state-power in order to further expand and consolidate their monopolistic command over various sectors of domestic production and trading. However, as we have already mentioned, by the very nature of the commodities they produced, these industries were heavily dependent upon the foreign market and upon orders from the government at home. With the possible exception of textiles, which too were rapidly tending towards the manufacture of finer varieties, these monopolistic industries did not produce commodities of mass consumption. Their markets were consequently limited from the very beginning.

While the Indian industrial and commercial classes provided the bulk of the financial support to the national movement and sought to further their programmes through the Congress organization, the personnel of the Congress came overwhelmingly from the urban middle classes. They usually manned the various provincial Congress committees and many district committees as well, represented the Congress party in the provincial legislatures, and were the acknowledged public leaders of the party.

The mass organization of the Congress, however, brought into the national movement much broader sections of the people. From recent researches into the social bases of mass movements led by the Congress,[4] it seems clear that these localized but prolonged rural movements were invariably led by the upper and middle strata of the *raiyat* peasantry. While the broader issues of anti-imperialism and the Gandhian programme were always reiterated, it is also clear that what actually served to mobilize a broad-based participation were local issues affecting the lot of the common peasantry, issues that often had strong anti-landlord or anti-moneylender overtones. In many cases, 'no-tax' campaigns of the Congress were pushed ahead towards a refusal to pay rent to the *zamindar*. These local issues reflected clear, and often quite specific, class demands, and thus succeeded in making the Congress popular with large masses of the lower peasantry.

However, the notable feature of the organizational structure of the national movement, especially that of the Congress, is that it became differentiated into several levels. The leadership at each territorial level — village, *thana* or *taluka*, subdivision,

---

[4] See, for instance, Hitesranjan Sanyal, ' Arāmbāger jātiyatābādī āndolan', *Anya Artha*, 6 (September 1974) and 7 (November 1974); Hitesranjan Sanyal, Bāṅkuḍā jelār jātiyatābādī āndolan', *Itihās*, 1975; Hitesranjan Sanyal, 'The Sociopolitical Roots of Nationalism: A Case Study of Political Movements in Eastern Medinipur', paper presented at the Indian History Congress, Chandigarh, 1973; Hitesranjan Sanyal and Barun De, 'Background of the 1942 Uprising in Eastern Medinipur', paper presented at the Indian History Congress, Jadavpur, 1974; Gyanendra Pandey, 'A Rural Base for Congress: UP 1920–39', unpublished paper; Majid Hayat Siddiqi, 'Peasant Movements in Western UP', paper presented at the Indian History Congress, Jadavpur, 1974. [These researches, ongoing in early 1975, have since appeared as monographs (in Hitesranjan Sanyal's case, posthumously): Hitesranjan Sanyal, *Svarājer pathe* (Calcutta: Papyrus, 1995); Gyanendra Pandey, *The Ascendancy of the Congress in Uttar Pradesh, 1926–1934* (Delhi: Oxford University Press, 1978); Majid Hayat Siddiqi, *Agrarian Unrest in North India: The United Provinces, 1918–1922* (New Delhi: Vikas, 1978)].

district, province — enjoyed fairly large areas of relative autonomy, varying naturally with the strengths of the organization
at each level and locality, as also with the personalities involved.
However, this meant that while a broad-based mass support
could be achieved and maintained at the lower levels by means
of radical rhetoric and marginal concessions touching upon local
issues, the necessary political compromises could be made at
the higher levels of the political structure. There are numerous
instances again of the village and *taluka* Congress committees
carrying on vigorous propaganda against the local landlords or
moneylenders, while these same landlords and moneylenders
would make marginal concessions but still maintain a large
degree of political effectiveness by influencing the district or
provincial Congress committee. An appreciation of this differentiated and flexible structure of the Congress political organization is important for an understanding of how the later
ruling class alliance, based upon a major political compromise
and containing within itself several crucial contradictions, could
be forged and maintained for decades after independence.

Constraints on Indian Capitalist Development

Immediately after independence and during the framing of
the Constitution, the future ruling alliance was still in the
process of formation. The various constraints and social forces
to be reckoned with had still not clearly emerged. Domestic
capital, under the unquestioned domination of the big houses,
at this time made an effort to push forth its programme.
A crucial part of this programme was the integration of the
princely states with the Indian Union and the abolition of
zamindari. This programme was reflected quite clearly in Val-
labhbhai Patel's speeches in the Constituent Assembly and in
his major political acts of the period.[5] Of course, the price
was the payment of compensation to landlords (which in fact
strengthened the concept of property in the legal institutions
of the country) and sizeable representation to princes and *zamindars* in the Constitutent Assembly. Nevertheless, an important

---

[5] On this point, see S.K. Chaube, *Constituent Assembly of India* (New Delhi:
People's Publishing House, 1973).

step towards clearing the ground for capitalist development was accomplished.

It was largely this programme which was pursued in the First Five-Year Plan. The First Plan was extremely modest in scope. It soon became apparent that any rapid capitalist development towards an independent industrial revolution was structurally impossible. The basic problem was one of increasing capital accumulation. None of the basic conditions for 'normal' capitalist development along English lines existed in post-colonial India. Theoretically, of course, there was a possibility of Indian capital using its newly gained control over the state apparatus to erect protective barriers against foreign competition, and then mopping up the surpluses from the agricultural sector to promote capitalist development along the 'second' way.[6] However, given the specific historical conditions, the second way was closed.

For one thing, capitalism in agriculture, even if it could be promoted over large areas of the country through government support policies, was unlikely to solve the marketable surplus problem in a land-scarce, labour-surplus economy like India's.[7] Further, the big bourgeoisie in India is not exactly comparable to its German counterpart. Though German industry developed under tariff protection, its ultimate aim was to compete with English and French industry in the international market: further ideological motivation was provided by the frenzy of *Weltpolitik*. This element of competition was the main stimulus for technical advancement. Coming in the post-colonial era when the historical gap between the developed and the underdeveloped world is enormous, Indian capitalists have neither the aspiration nor the ability to compete independently in the international market. On the contrary, they operate by borrowing obsolete foreign technology in the protected domestic market. Competition in the export market for sophisticated manufactured goods only takes them into further dependence on foreign technology. Even offical reports admit that Indian firms with foreign technical collaboration spend very little on research

[6] The theoretical conditions are outlined in Karl Marx, *Capital*, vol. 3, ch 20.

[7] Amiya Kumar Bagchi, 'Notes Towards a Theory of Underdevelopment: In Memoriam Michal Kalecki', *Economic and Political Weekly*, 6, 3–5 (January 1971).

and development activities with a view to future technological independence.[8]

These points of difference are crucial in understanding the different evolution of state capitalism and the associated political forms in the two situations. What was most important was that the new political structure of independent India was overtly based upon the principles of liberal bourgeois democracy, with unrestricted party competition at the elections, and universal adult suffrage. The consensus on these basic constitutional issues had been created in the minds of the nationalist leadership almost from the very beginning of the movement, and reflected the profound, though often purely formal, liberal ideology of the colonial upper petty bourgeoisie from which the leading person- nel of the Congress party was drawn. The very form of the national struggle, with a very strong legal constitutional bias, made it virtually inevitable that a formal structure of electoral democracy be created under the new Constitution. In the ab- sence of the necessary social bases, of course, the Constitution could never attain a true liberal democratic content. From the very start, therefore, the Indian bourgeoisie was faced with a challenge which no bourgeoisie in the world has ever tackled successfully: to make an industrial revolution under capitalism within a political structure of electoral democracy and universal adult suffrage.

As a consequence, any programme of rapid capitalist develop- ment with active intervention by the state presupposed the con- tinued dominance of the bourgeoisie within the structure of state power, in a system which required periodic general elections. For this, an alliance with other powerful social forces was in- evitable. The most crucial element in the coalition became the rural gentry, possessing varying amounts of landed property and wielding varying degrees of local political influence. The highly differentiated and flexible political organization of the Congress, developed during the period of the national movement, was now streamlined into an efficient vote-getting machinery. Again a measure of autonomy was granted to the leadership at each level of the Congress organization, and a tendency towards the main- tenance of the status quo was thereby built into the structure of

[8] *Reserve Bank of India Bulletin* (June 1974).

the party. Given the socio-economic formation in post-colonial India, politics made it inevitable that only a class coalition would rule and that the interests of none of the constituents of this coalition would be seriously disturbed.

Nehru, Populism and State Capitalism

To appeal to the voters, however, it was clearly unwise for the Congress party to appear publicly as a party of the status quo; for it was evident that, to the overwhelming majority of the population, the status quo was intolerable. For an acceptable popular image, it was necessary for the ruling party and the government to appear to be responsive to the general popular desire for change, and not to appear to be too closely identified with any of the forces of exploitation in society. This was necessary not only to present a populist image to the mass of the peasantry, but also to pre-empt those issues on which the more organized opposition forces, that is to say, the working class and the lower petty bourgeoisie, could agitate.

It was Nehru who accomplished this facelift for the party. Patel's death perhaps facilitated the process, but Nehru assumed virtually dictatorial powers on all important policy matters within the government, and himself took over the office of Congress Presidentship by removing Purushottam Das Tandon. In economic policy, the Second Plan called for an ambitious programme of economic development through a strategy of partial state capitalism, and politically, slogans of 'socialism' were voiced with increased frequency and fervour. Nehru's image was suited to this populist role, wielding as he did enormous executive powers, yet appearing to stand above the mundane battle of classes to intervene decisively in favour of the weak and the oppressed.

Nehru's emergence at the helm of the government and the Congress party at this juncture was, in fact, an example of the classic phenomenon of Caesarism.

Caesarism can be said to express a situation in which the forces in conflict balance each other in a catastrophic manner; that is to say, they balance each other in such a way that a continuation of the conflict can only terminate in their reciprocal destruction. When the progressive force A struggles with the reactionary force B, not only may A defeat B or B defeat A, but it may happen that neither A nor B defeats the other — that they bleed each other mutually and then a third force C intervenes from outside, subjugating what is left of both A and B.[9]

In other words, the situation is one where neither of the principal contending forces is able to decisively clinch the issue in its favour. In such conditions, it is possible for a third force, or a great 'heroic' personality, professing to be independent of the main contenders, to emerge and take charge of the situation as a neutral party.

As in all such compromises, Nehru's assumption of the role of Caesar had mixed virtues. The Indian bourgeoisie was itself clearly in no position to assume complete control over state power. By the very nature of the existing structure of economic and political power, it was forced to accept a compromise. The legacy of the national movement dictated that the majority of the petty bourgeoisie be kept in the alliance. This meant an increased reliance on state capitalism in the programme for economic growth, an expansion of the governmental apparatus and continuance of formal liberal democracy. Insofar as the bourgeoisie was required by the circumstances to accept this compromise, it constituted (as it does in all Caesarist compromises) a progressive potential to be utilized by the progressive forces in this continuing war of position. On the other hand, the political process itself made the rural gentry a crucial element in the ruling party's electoral strategy, and this was clearly the element of restoration in the compromise. At the same time, the existence of universal franchise afforded some protection, however fragile, to peasant proprietorship; and in a land-scarce, labour-surplus economy, this constituted a progressive potential for resisting the pauperization of small peasants that would inevitably come in the wake of capitalism in agriculture.[10] Of course, the realization of this progressive potential in Nehru's populism depended entirely on a rational resolution of the agrarian question. Finally, the very

---

[9] Antonio Gramsci, *Selections from the Prison Notebooks*, tr. Quintin Hoare and Geoffrey Nowell-Smith (New York: International Publishers, 1971), p. 220.

[10] See in this connection, Lenin's evaluation of Sun Yat-sen's programme: V.I. Lenin, 'Democracy and Narodism in China', *Selected Works*, vol. 4 (London: Lawrence and Wishart, 1943), pp. 305–11.

strategy of state capitalism, coming up against the resource problem, made external assistance inevitable, thereby strengthening neocolonial interference in the economy.

The Second Plan emphasized the development of heavy industry. The linkage effects of the public investment programme were likely to create opportunities for the big capitalists. Besides, the growth of the public sector and the imposition of government controls expanded considerably the channels of profits from circulation. To the middle class, the Plan opened up new opportunities in areas of administration, education and white-collar employment. The landed gentry knew that the land reforms would not pose any serious threat to them: having retained or acquired considerable political power at the local level, they were sure to scuttle even the modest land reforms which were undertaken. Besides, the Plan also had a mass appeal in creating the impression that, by emphasizing the development of heavy industries first, India was following the socialist path of economic development.

In actual fact, of course, the policy followed with respect to the private sector was hardly unfavourable to it. In order to boost private investment, a multitude of credit institutions were opened to offer loans to the private sector at low rates of interest. This effectively helped in strengthening the grip of big business or monopoly houses over the economy. Their assets increased much faster than the growth in national income, while their own savings increased at a much slower rate. Needless to say, the development of monopoly or oligopoly capital is hardly consistent with socialism; there was not even a valid growth argument. The oligopolistic sellers increase their profit margins by charging a higher price in relation to cost of production. With investment of profits, however, the industry soon comes up against the constraint of the overall growth rate of the market. Indeed, it can be shown that oligopoly slows down the growth of the economy. This factor is, in fact, the most important in explaining the stagnation problem in mature capitalism.[11] The Indian government, by encouraging monopoly, brought into an economy at an early stage of capitalist development the problems of mature capitalism.

[11] Josef Steindl, *Maturity and Stagnation in American Capitalism* (New York: Monthly Review Press, 1978).

As the Plan progressed, the economy came up against bot-
tlenecks which, in technical terms, are summed up under three
heads: the savings gap, the foreign exchange gap and the food
gap. The institutional factors behind these so-called gaps are now
well known.[12] The main component of the economy's savings is
government savings, for the fate of the private sector depends on
the public investment programme. The amount of government
investment depends on the sustainability of the drive to raise
larger fiscal revenues and the proportion of capital formation
expenditure in the government budget. The government cannot
impose any tax on the rural gentry; it cannot introduce tax reform
measures to plug the various loopholes through which the tax
burden in evaded by the urban propertied classes.[13] The only
instrument available to the government is a system of indirect
taxes. On the expenditure side, the government cannot but continue high-level defence expenditure and a top-heavy education
expenditure. The basic point, again, was that the progressive
potential of public expenditure depended entirely on a corresponding broad-based expansion of the home market. Failing this,
domestic industry was bound to retain its character of luxury
commodity production for an extremely narrow market; even a
prolonged period of public investment was not likely to change
this 'enclaved' character of industrial production. But then a
large-scale expansion of the home market could only follow a
rational solution to the agrarian problem, and this the government could not attempt.

The argument that the public investment programme is at the
root of the foreign exchange problem is not wholly correct. In

[12] A.K. Bagchi, 'Long-term Constraints on India's Industrial Growth, 1951–
68', in E.A.G. Robinson and Michael Kidron, eds, *Economic Development and
South Asia* (London: Macmillan, 1970), pp. 170–92; A.K. Bagchi, 'Aid Models
and Inflows of Foreign Aid', *Economic and Political Weekly*, 5, 3–5 (January 1970);
N.K. Chandra, 'Western Imperialism and India Today', *Economic and Political
Weekly*, 8, 4–6 (February 1973); Ranjit Sau, *India's Economic Development: Con-
straints and Problems* (Madras: Orient Longman, 1974); Prabhat Patnaik, 'On the
Political Economy of Underdevelopment', *Economic and Political Weekly*, 8, 4–6
(February 1973); Prabhat Patnaik, 'Imperialism and the Growth of Indian
Capitalism', in Roger Owen and Bob Sutcliffe, eds, *Studies in the Theory of
Imperialism* (London: Longman, 1972), pp. 210–29.

[13] Nicholas Kaldor, *Indian Tax Reform: Report of a Survey* (New Delhi:
Ministry of Finance, Government of India, 1956).

India, the import intensity of consumption is high enough to cover 40 per cent of total imports.[14] Almost 40 per cent of these industrial consumption goods are consumed by the top 10 per cent of the rural and urban population. Most of this urban population is employed as unproductive labour. In line with the old colonial pattern, the rate of employment in the tertiary sector has been much greater than the rate of factory employment in independent India.

The problem of the food gap can be analysed from the supply as well as the demand side. The elimination of a few big *zamindars* did not mean that the rentier class and the semi-feudal mode vanished from rural India. In some of the areas previously under the Permanent Settlement, like West Bengal, even recent surveys reveal the proportion of sharecroppers in the agricultural labour force to be as high as 30 per cent.[15] In fact, as has been argued earlier, even capitalism in agriculture cannot be a solution in a land-scarce, labour-surplus economy. A possible solution might be to build up a broad base of small and middle peasants together with a public distribution scheme for the supply of agricultural inputs and the procurement of the output. But that obviously hurts the interest of the landed gentry, one of the chief components of the ruling coalition.

The food problem was aggravated by factors on the demand front also. In the period 1951–67, if everyone could be kept on a minimum nutritional requirement, India needed to import 20 million tons of foodgrain, whereas the actual imports were 60 million tons.[16] Here too, unproductive consumption played the crucial role.

In a framework of partial state capitalism, the real problems were: (1) how to solve the agrarian question in a land-scarce economy without hurting the landed gentry; (2) how to sustain accumulation and technical dynamism through the monopoly houses without ever hoping to become competitive in the international market; and (3) how to contain unproductive labour and provide for the urban middle classes at the same time.

[14] Bharat R. Hazari, *The Structure of the Indian Economy: An Analysis* (Delhi: Macmillan, 1980), ch. 3, pp. 27–50.

[15] N. Banerjee, '*Bargadars* and Institutional Finance', Directorate of Land Records and Survey, Government of West Bengal, 1973.

[16] Chandra, 'Western Imperialism and India Today'.

The problems were beyond solution. Given the configuration of social forces and the relations between them, it was a foregone conclusion that a strategy of partial state capitalism which shied away from disturbing the existing political-economic structure was not going to produce a decisive breakthrough.

The weakness of state capitalism lay in the fact that the nature of the state, while apparently giving it enormous strength, made it fundamentally weak. While on the one hand it had to maintain the balance of the class coalition (by effectively curbing any constitutent group that became too strong), and to make periodic concessions to the exploited, on the other hand it could not change the position of any constituent group too strongly, for that would affect the collective strength of the coalition. . . . The limits of state action were sharply drawn and any radical structural reform was ruled out.[17]

In the absence of radical structural reform, the Indian state did not possess the strength to mobilize sufficient resources internally. External aid, consequently, became inevitable for the development of state capitalism. The amount of aid nearly doubled in the Third Plan compared to the Second. Western aid, including aid from the World Bank, was sought and received in infrastructural projects, particularly fertilizers and seeds, and in the form of shipments of American agricultural surpluses, mainly wheat. At the same time, aid from the Soviet Union and the Eastern European countries also increased considerably. The high point of Western aid was reached around 1966 when virtually the entire IMF policy package to aid-receiving countries had to be accepted by India: the rupee was devalued in the hope of greater exports, imports were liberalized, agriculture was to be developed through the market mechanism, and for all practical purposes the five-year plan was suspended.

On the other hand, foreign private capital in the Indian economy increased phenomenally after independence — sixfold, from Rs 2,644 million in 1948 to Rs 15,428 million in 1968. Further, imperialist penetration of the Indian economy also increased in another form — foreign collaboration with Indian industries, which reached a peak in the early and mid-1960s, declined in 1968 and 1969 because of the recessionary situation, but shot up again after 1970.[18]

[17] Patnaik, 'Imperialism and the Growth of Indian Capitalism'.
[18] Chandra, 'Western Imperialism and India Today'.

The Restoration of Caesarism

Industrialization within a framework of partial state capitalism reached a virtual dead end by the second half of the 1960s. At the same time, the election reverses suffered by the Congress party in 1967 landed the ruling classes in a political crisis as well. The reverses were caused not so much by an actual fall in Congress votes, but rather by a series of effective electoral alliances between opposition parties. However, the Congress machinery had taken a highly oligarchic form in most states, and had become quite openly linked with its financiers and supporters among the business and landowning groups. On the other hand, in states like West Bengal, the ruling circles faced a more organic challenge in the form of the increased strength of the organized working class.

The Congress split of 1969 and the reorganization of the party machinery under Indira Gandhi represented a Caesarist restoration. In common with Nehruvian Caesarism, the tempo of socialist rhetoric was increased, and certain economic steps were taken to highlight the claim of a 'leftward' swing in official policy. The failure of the rightist policies of the mid-1960s, leading to the colossal dependence on Western aid even on the food front, reduced the dominance of the big bourgeoisie within the ruling alliance. This facilitated the apparent leftward swing, both in domestic policy and in international alignments involved in the new equilibrium.

However, the restoration also brought into the party certain new, and hitherto untapped, sources of support. As Gramsci has noted about modern Caesarist phenomena, they often 'shatter stifling and ossified state structures in the dominant camp as well, and introduce into national life and social activity a different and more numerous personnel'.[19] Particularly in those states where the bourgeoisie faced a more organic crisis of authority, the ruling party consciously sought to create activist cadres from among unemployed petty bourgeois youth and the backward sections of the working class. These were precisely the sections which, supported by the ample financial resources of the ruling party and unencumbered by fixed hours of work, could make use of illegal

[19] Gramsci, *Prison Notebooks*, p. 223.

means to strike at the cadres of the organized opposition, while the state itself could maintain its facade of legality. This is a feature peculiar to modern Caesarism.

In the period up to Napoleon III, the regular military forces or soldiers of the line were a decisive element in the advent of Caesarism and this came about through precise *coups d'état*, through military actions, etc. In the modern world, trade-union and political forces, with the limitless financial means which may be at the disposal of small groups of citizens, complicate the problem. The functionaries of the parties and economic unions can be corrupted or terrorised without any need for military action in the grand style — of the Caesar or 18 Brumaire type.[20]

This method of reactionary political warfare is unavoidable for a weak bourgeoisie operating within a fundamentally weak state structure. When the ruling classes lack legitimate authority in crucial sectors of society (as must be the case with a non-hegemonic bourgeoisie), the indiscriminate use of state power, i.e. the police or the military, can only erode its authority still further. The use of police methods must be selective, but where used, ruthless and decisive. Specifically, they are used to create divisions within the organized opposition and thereby to maintain their combined weakness.

. . . a social form 'always' has marginal possibilities for further development and organizational improvement, and in particular can count on the relative weakness of the rival progressive force as a result of its specific character and way of life. It is necessary for the dominant social form to preserve this weakness: that is why it has been asserted that modern Caesarism is more a police than a military system.[21]

If one compares the economic consequences of the present phase of Caesarism in India with the previous phase, certain differences are apparent. Agricultural production in the decade of the 1950s had increased mainly by bringing new lands under cultivation and through some improvements in irrigation. It is true that there were no significant efforts to mobilize the owner peasantry for cooperative ventures to increase production. Yet, it is also true that the destructive effects of the encroachment of capitalism in agriculture were to some extent resisted. Capitalism

[20] Ibid., p. 220.
[21] Ibid., p. 222.

of a sort made rapid inroads into Indian agriculture from around 1966 under the banner of the 'green revolution'. In spite of this much-heralded 'breakthrough', it turns out that per capita production of foodgrains grew at a slower rate in the 1960s than in the 1950s.[22] And whatever growth did occur was for a limited period (the output having reached a plateau in the years 1972–4 in Punjab and Haryana), in specific regions and among owners of large holdings. As a result, a major part of the marketable surplus of foodgrains in the country is now controlled by a few persons in a limited region of the country. Indeed, a convincing argument can be made that it is the uneven development of capitalism in agriculture, together with the government procurement policy, which is at the root of the chronic inflationary situation in India.[23]

Even without going into a complicated argument about the economics of the matter, it is quite obvious that following the 'green revolution', the political power of large landholders in certain states of India has increased phenomenally. It is the Punjab or the Haryana legislature that today witnesses the most stormy debates on land ceilings or the procurement price of foodgrains. The proportion of agriculturist members of the Congress party in Parliament has also increased significantly, from 18.2 per cent in 1952 to 27.2 per cent in 1962, 36.8 per cent in 1967 and 41 per cent in 1971. Correspondingly, the proportion of agriculturists among all Members of Parliament moved from 22.4 per cent in 1952 to 31.1 per cent in 1967.[24] The Indian capitalist class has always found it difficult to launch a serious attack on powerful landed interests in India. After the 'green revolution', it has become evident that Indian capitalism would have to find room for growth without any major shake-up of the agrarian system.

The final contrast with the earlier phase of Caesarism is that planned development through state capitalism has been virtually

[22] Ashok Mitra, 'Population and Foodgrain Output in India: A Note on Disparate Growth Rates', in Robinson and Kidron, *Economic Development*, pp. 21–8.

[23] See Prabhat Patnaik, 'Current Inflation in India', *Social Scientist*, 30–31 (1975).

[24] From figures compiled by Hung-chao Tai, *Land Reform and Policies: A Comparative Analysis* (Berkeley: University of California Press, 1974), p. 95.

abandoned since 1966. Yet state expenditure has not diminished. Official figures show that the overall expenditure on education and general administration has increased at a much faster rate than the 71 per cent increase in prices between 1960–1 and 1969–70.[25] Even in the private sector, salaries have risen much faster than wages. It is by this method of increasing the share of unproductive labour in both the private and public sectors that employment has been created. Again, by raising the purchasing power of a small number of people, a market has been created for industrial goods.

This phenomenon of 'institutionalized waste' is not new to the Indian economy. It is a continuation of the economic structure under colonialism, and was persisted with under the First and Second Five-Year Plans as well. It is not surprising then that, by taking advantage of this expansion in the unproductive waste sector, there was growth of industrial luxury goods in the 1960s. The trend has continued through the 1960s, as is shown by the fact that whereas the share of the agricultural sector in the aggregate national income declined between 1960–1 and 1971–2 from 51 per cent to 47.8 per cent, that of industry showed virtually no change at all (from 20.1 per cent to 20.8 per cent), whereas the share of trade and commerce went up from 14 per cent to 16 per cent and that of the tertiary sector from 14.9 per cent to 17.8 per cent.[26]

Ever since the scuttling of the Plans, therefore, it is the margin of institutionalized waste that has created the market for industrial goods in India. The viability of this 'enclaved' market was always very precarious: a sudden rise in food prices, for instance, could shatter it. Indeed, the constraint on domestic industrial growth is so severe that in the last few years we have seen the strange spectacle of an industrially underdeveloped and capital-poor country like India exporting steel and heavy engineering products. A new channel for industrial products is now being sought through exports, with active state suppport. In 1960–1, government expenditure on exports was nil; in 1965 it was Rs 198 million and in 1970 Rs 420 million. But the strategy

[25] Reserve Bank of India, *Report on Currency and Finance, 1970–71.*
[26] Central Statistical Organization, Government of India, *Estimates of National Product, Savings and Capital Formation, 1972–73.*

is fraught with the grave danger of substantially increased dependence on foreign technology.

Our comparison between the two phases of Caesarism in post-colonial India thus points to three significant features. First, the internal organization and style of the ruling party has changed. Second, after the 'green revolution', the Indian bourgeoisie now has to seek ways of continued accumulation only after making major concessions to the newly empowered group of large landowners. Third, with the abandonment of planned industrialization, increasing the margins of institutionalized waste has become the pre-eminent instrument for maintaining a home market for industrial manufactures.

Bourgeois Reaction and Indian Politics

Let us recapitulate. Only the first or classical way of capitalist development organically engenders a liberal democracy. The second way of capitalist development tends strongly to go against democracy. The problems of the second way ultimately led in Europe to the rise of fascism. The politics which in India wears the cloak of liberal democracy can be called Caesarism, which has passed through two distinct phases. The question now is: what are the similarities and differences between Caesarism and fascism?

The analysis presented by the Communist International in 1928 pointed out the following general features of fascism:

1. Fascism constructs an economic basis for the organizational unity of large capitalists, rural exploiters and the urban petty bourgeoisie.
2. Fascism rapidly adopts a foreign policy of militarism and imperialist aggression.
3. Taking advantage of the weaknesses of social democracy, fascism mobilizes an organized force of cadres from the urban petty bourgeoisie and the backward sections of the working class.
4. In the stage of seizure of power, fascism adopts populist slogans against capitalism, but soon after it captures power, it comes under the sway of big capital.
5. In place of liberal democracy, fascism establishes a structure of direct authoritarian rule.[27]

[27] Cited in Rajani Palme Dutt, *Fascism and Social Revolution* (Calcutta: National Book Agency, 1977, second Indian edition). There are many debates about this Comintern document on fascism and the strategies of antifascist

We have shown that in the second phase of Caesarism in India, a foundation has been laid for the alliance of monopoly capital, large landowners, the petty bourgeoisie and foreign capital. We have also pointed out that this second Caesarism achieved power by the use of anti-capitalist slogans and has changed the organization and style of functioning of the ruling party in order to deal more effectively with opposition forces. It is true, of course, that the Indian state is not militaristic in the same way that fascist powers in Europe were militaristic. But in the present state of international politics, there are only limited opportunities for the rulers of a country such as India to flex their muscles; those limited opportunities are, however, eagerly seized. Heavily militarized fascist regimes in Europe created, through the rapid expansion of a war economy, domestic markets for industrial manufactures. We have shown that in India under its second Caesarist regime, it is government expediture on unproductive labour that has become the chief instrument for maintaining a domestic market for industrial goods.

The only feature where Caesarism in India is sharply different from fascism in Europe is in the absence of direct authoritarian rule. All of our discussions today about a 'right-wing coup' or 'the rise of fascism' really hinge upon this one question: will electoral democracy survive in India? It should be clear from our above discussion that as far as the present ruling classes in India are concerned, it is not desirable for them, for structural reasons, to abandon electoral democracy. First of all, a complex but flexible political structure is highly suitable for maintaining the internal balance in the ruling class coalition and for creating an economy of institutionalized waste. Second, in the current state of world politics, it is advantageous for a Third-World country seeking various forms of international aid to project a democratic facade. Consequently, when official circles send out repeated warnings about the dangers of a 'right-wing coup' and when left-wing supporters of the government faithfully translate those

---

struggle. Trotskyists in particular reject this analysis as entirely mistaken. It would not be pertinent here to enter into a discussion on the merits of the Trotskyist analysis of fascism. We find ourselves largely in agreement with these general statements made in the 1928 Comintern document on European fascism. We are not making any claims regarding the acceptability of every resolution in that document.

warnings into complex theoretical analyses, one has reasons to suspect that a fictional spectre is being conjured up to hide the reactionary character of the present regime.

It seems obvious that until such time that opposition forces in India can hold out the threat of electorally defeating the ruling party at the centre, there will be no real pressure to completely jettison the structure of electoral democracy. If there are minor fears of losing elections, it is possible for the ruling powers to manipulate the electoral system in order to produce the desired result, as has been demonstrated several times in many parts of India, most recently in West Bengal in 1972. On the other hand, if there is a major electoral challenge, and if electoral democracy is indeed thrown aside, then the progressive forces can hardly meet that crisis solely by electoral means. Only an organized form of the revolutionary unity of the oppressed classes can resist that form of bourgeois reaction. In an underdeveloped, populous Asian country, such unity can only be built around the alliance of the working class and the peasantry. If the working class movement does not consciously seek unity with the peasantry, if it restricts itself merely to battles for increasing the salaries of the urban petty bourgeoisie, then the ruling classes will either use that movement to its own advantage within the present forms of politics, or crush it by unleashing its repressive forces — legal as well as illegal, both from within and from outside the state.

4

Nineteen Seventy-Seven

Economy and Polity: Structural Conditions

In a paper presented at the last session of this Conference[1], I had attempted to delineate what appeared to me the basic structural features of the Indian polity and its mechanisms for maintaining the stability of the system. I had pointed out that India's political economy, as it had emerged after two hundred years of direct colonial rule, was such that no single class in Indian society possessed the strength to rule the country on its own. Although industrial capitalism had grown, it was restricted to sectors of the economy which were dependent either upon the export market or upon the extremely narrow luxury consumption sector at home. Besides, in its ownership pattern, Indian industry already exhibited many of the features of monopoly and stagnation characteristic of capitalist economies at much higher stages of development. The horizons of capitalistic development in industry were severely restricted by the widespread prevalence of pre-capitalist forms of production and exploitation in the agricultural sector. The processes of surplus appropriation in agriculture under colonialism almost inevitably created and fostered semi-feudal relations of production and exploitation. In terms of the whole economy, this created a situation where, in spite of the introduction of commercialization, the agricultural sector remained essentially stagnant. This made it impossible to develop a growing home market on the basis of which domestic industry could break out of its ties of dependence with foreign capital and launch the economy on a path of independent capitalist development. The phase of the nationalist movement brought to the fore, at several critical junctures, this

[1] Partha Chatterjee, 'Stability and Change in the Indian Political System', *Political Science Review*, 16, 1 (January–March 1977), pp. 1–42 [largely incorporating Chapter 3 of this volume].

choice before the indigenous capitalist class: whether to go in for a thoroughgoing campaign to break pre-capitalist production relations in the countryside with a view to leading the economy on a path of self-reliant capitalist development, or whether to compromise with imperialism abroad and the entrenched landed interests at home. Every time the all-India capitalist class, unwilling to take large political risks, chose the latter option.

In the process, India after the transfer of power came to be ruled by a coalition of classes, of which the two most crucial were the big bourgeoisie, on the one hand, and the landed gentry, on the other. The literature on how the political economy of India has grown — or failed to grow — is now fairly sizeable, and the basic dimensions set out with some clarity.[2] It is also fairly well known how, and why, the economy is in a virtually endemic state of crisis, reflected from time to time in food shortages, lack of foreign exchange, inflation, large unsold stocks of industrial goods, excess capacity in basic industries and excess of foreign exchange.

Less studied, I think, are the instrumentalities of the political process by which this precarious balance of ruling class interests is maintained. In the paper mentioned earlier, I had attempted to present an analysis of this process, crucial in which were a ruling party organization; the division of powers between a centre and the states, both in government and in party affairs; a Caesarist leadership; and a populist ideology. We will discuss these features here only inasmuch as they are important in understanding what happened in Indian politics in the period 1975–7.

The organization of the Congress, of course, developed in the course of the movement for the country's independence, and the basic organizational mechanism for maintaining the class alliance

---

[2] A few important readings on this subject are Prabhat Patnaik, 'On the Political Economy of Underdevelopment', *Economic and Political Weekly*, 8, 4–6 (February 1973); Patnaik, 'Imperialism and the Growth of Indian Capitalism', in Roger Owen and Bob Sutcliffe, eds, *Studies in the Theory of Imperialism* (London: Longman, 1972), pp. 210–29; A.K. Bagchi, 'Long-term Constraints on India's Industrial Growth, 1951–68', in E.A.G. Robinson and Michael Kidron, eds, *Economic Development and South Asia* (London: Macmillan, 1970), pp. 170–92; Ranjit Sau, *India's Economic Development: Constraints and Problems* (Madras: Orient Longman, 1974); Ashok Mitra, *Terms of Trade and Class Relations* (London: Frank Cass, 1977).

was evolved in the course of that movement. This took the form of a differentiated structure of the party, organized as it was at the village or union, *taluka* or *thana*, district, provincial and all-India levels. While the committee at each level was subject to the directives of the higher committee, each level also retained some measure of independence. The manipulative possibilities of this arrangement had important implications for the political process. As the Congress broadened its movement, for instance, campaigns on issues involving the demands of the broadest masses were conducted at the lowest levels of the organization; but the necessary political compromises could be made at the higher levels of the structure. The hierarchy of peasant, landlord and commercial interests were thus accommodated within this flexible and differentiated structure of the party.

It is important to note here that the interests of the peasantry, the landed gentry and much of the commercial classes were local or provincial. The one truly all-India ruling class was the indigenous industrial bourgeoisie, and allied to it the upper levels of the professional and salariat middle classes. The influence of the bourgeoisie on the Congress organization was understandably most marked at the all-India level (apart from provincial committees such as those of Bombay or Bengal). Thus, the structured differentiation of areas of relative autonomy within the Congress organization was also consonant with the respective areas of interest that concerned the different sections of the ruling classes.

This differentiated structure of interests was carried on to the sphere of government after the transfer of power. Industry and industrial policy became a subject with which the Union government was concerned; agriculture became a state subject. With large public expenditure going into an effort for the planned development of the economy, the Union government became the focus for various industrial and large commercial interests. There was a perceptible bias towards centralization, but state governments and legislatures were clearly more amenable to pressure and control by the rural gentry.

The populist ideology of the Congress, of course, also evolved from the days of the national movement — a product of the effort to create and foster a broad-based multi-class front against British imperialism. While the class demands of the poorer sections of the people had to be voiced, class conflict could not be allowed to be stressed too far. And all this took place, as we have already mentioned, within the broad political-economic framework of a ruling alliance of the bourgeoisie and the landed gentry. With the inauguration of a parliamentary system based on adult franchise, it was necessary for an acceptable popular image of the Congress to appear to be responsive to the general popular desire for change, and not to appear too closely identified with any of the forces of exploitation in society. This was necessary not only to present an acceptable popular image, but also to pre-empt the issues on which the more organized opposition forces in society — the working class and the lower petty bourgeoisie — could agitate.

It is in this context, of maintaining the rule of a class coalition within a framework of parliamentary democracy, that the role of a Caesarist leadership becomes crucial. Put very briefly, this role consists in a popular leader who can maintain the balance within the ruling class coalition by appearing to stand above any particular interest, and thereby, to present and execute governmental decisions in the interests of the 'people' or the 'nation'. Nehru performed this role in the first several years of the new polity, and then, after a short spell of instability, Indira Gandhi assumed this role after the reorganization of the Congress party in 1969.

The Political Crisis in 1975

There have been some attempts to explain the declaration of Emergency in terms of an economic crisis which defied a solution except through the intervention of an authoritarian state machinery. Such an explanation is not adequate at this level of analysis: it is relevant in delineating the broader context — the more long-term parameters — within which the Indian polity functions, but does not explain why at one particular point of time certain changes in the functioning of the political institutions were thought to be necessary. The evidence about the economic crisis only shows its endemic nature; there is nothing to indicate that the crisis was suddenly aggravated in any major way in the middle of 1975.

It was rather a political crisis which led to the declaration of Emergency. The accentuation of the economic crisis in 1972–4 had led to several agitations against the government, most notably in Gujarat and Bihar. But from all indications it appears that the strength of these movements was distinctly on the wane by April or May 1975.[3] The real crisis was precipitated by the judgement of the Allahabad High Court, for now the opposition was directed not so much against government policies, but against the person of the Caesarist leader. The immediate context of the declaration of Emergency was the attempt to preserve the position of Caesar and to scotch attempts by the opposition to jeopardize this position. If our characterization of the crucial role of a Caesarist leader in the Indian political system is correct, it goes a long way in explaining — a task not quite accomplished by merely labelling the entire political leadership of the Congress as servile or spineless — why such drastic measures were accepted, more or less without major protest, by the Congress party. After all, the most overwhelming vision of the aims of the Emergency was conjured up by that great political theorist D.K. Barooah in the aphorism 'India is Indira, Indira is India!'

The solution to the crisis resembled in many ways the classic examples of Bonapartism.[4] Indeed, it was a Bonapartist solution, relying heavily on centralized executive powers implemented through the bureaucracy and a huge establishment of police and paramilitary personnel. In the process, several essential elements of the earlier institutional structure of politics were given up.

In the first place, the organization of the party was made subordinate to the government, and more particularly the executive, like it had never been before. Secondly, the entire structure of a division of powers between the centre and the states, both in governmental and party affairs, was replaced by a virtually total centralization of all effective powers. Chief Ministers were changed at will, state ministries were shuffled and reshuffled on directives from the Centre, legislatures virtually became defunct, and even disputes in the state party organizations were referred to the Great Leader for arbitration.

As a result of this, an essential part of the institutional mechanism, by which the balance among the constituent parts of the

[3] Ghanshyam Shah, 'Revolution, Reform or Protest? A Study of the Bihar Movement', *Economic and Political Weekly*, 12, 15–17 (9, 16 and 23 April 1977).

[4] It is striking how often there were references and allusions to, and indeed straight reproductions of, Marx's *The Eighteenth Brumaire of Louis Bonaparte* in the opposition literature of the Emergency.

ruling class coalition was earlier maintained, was sacrificed. We will consider the implications of this in a moment.

The new opportunities of centralization were sought to be utilized by the one class which stood to gain most from centralization, namely, the industrial bourgeoisie. Not only did it extend effusive (and servile) support to the policies of the new regime, but it also attempted to provide a new direction to the economic policies of the Emergency. While most of the populist slogans of the 20-point programme merely defaced the walls of government offices, two points which required little effort to implement were a national permit scheme for road transport and the raising of the exemption limit on income tax. In September 1975, T.A. Pai, Minister for Industry and Civil Supplies, announced a plan for a 'national sector', whereby public sector units were to

throw open their shareholding to the public at large and . . . not remain exclusively government-owned. . . . The public sector units should be thrown open to the rough and tumble of market forces; they should neither claim, nor be given, any special privileges . . . the public sector will not in the future be allowed to pre-empt capacity in any particular fields.[5]

In November 1975, major reforms were announced in licensing policy: some fifteen export-oriented engineering industries were allowed automatic expansion of capacity — virtually all of them were marked by low average capacity utilization; blanket exemptions from licensing were granted to twenty-one industries in the medium sector, and unlimited expansion beyond the licensed capacity was allowed to foreign companies and large monopoly houses in thirty other important industries; the procedure for regularizing unauthorized capacity installed by monopoly houses and foreign companies was liberalized.[6]

The whole thrust of the new move was to find a way out for the stagnating industrial sector, mainly through a boost in exports. This required fairly capital-intensive and sophisticated technology, and little additional labour. In any case, a large part of the labour problem had been taken care of by the state of Emergency. There was now a virtual ban on labour agitation; the minimum bonus legislation had been withdrawn. Recent

[5] *Economic and Political Weekly*, 13 September 1975.
[6] *Economic and Political Weekly*, 22 November 1975.

estimates have revealed that the profits as well as the assets of large business went up in the period of the Emergency.[7]

This process of restoring, and indeed reversing, the balance between the big bourgeoisie and the landed interests, which had turned somewhat in favour of the latter in the early 1970s (revealed not only in the adverse terms of trade of industry with agriculture, but also in the significant rise in the proportion of agriculturists even among Members of Parliament), was sought to be pushed even further. The move towards centralization was constitutionally formalized in the 42nd Amendment through a strengthening of the Central executive *vis-à-vis* Parliament, *vis-à-vis* the judiciary and *vis-à-vis* the states. Education was taken out of the State List and put in the Concurrent List. And, most significantly, a move was made (in the proposals of the Swaran Singh Committee) to transfer agriculture from the State List to the Union List. The fact that the proposal had to be dropped only reveals the real political strength of the landed interests in the Indian polity.

The Collapse of the Emergency Regime

This was towards the end of 1976. By then, the difficulties of having to work with a political system lacking an effective mechanism for maintaining the internal balance in the ruling class coalition were becoming clear to its constituents, as was to be revealed so dramatically in March 1977.

In the first place, the vested interests in the agricultural sector had definite reasons to be unhappy with the Emergency regime. The suspension of the earlier system of division of power, and the centralization of effective control, deprived the landed interests of their access to governmental machinery which, as we have noted, was hitherto located in the state governments and the state party organizations. Landed interests in India, except for specially favoured areas such as Punjab or Haryana, are not so organized as to be able to lobby effectively in New Delhi. The attempts to translate the process of centralization into an attack against the position of the landed gentry in the economy

---

[7] Ranjit Sau, 'Indian Political Economy, 1967–77', *Economic and Political Weekly*, 12, 15 (9 April 1977).

undoubtedly brought home to them the dangerous potentialities of a centralized system of authoritarian government. It was, indeed, in a systemic sense that the basic class alliance between the bourgeoisie and the landed gentry was jeopardized by the regime of the Emergency.

Secondly, while the big monopoly houses, and perhaps the industrial bourgeoise as a whole, made the most significant gains from the imposition of authoritarian rule, even for this class the new machinery of popular administration was not entirely satisfactory. For, the centralization of executive power was not based on any rational system of impersonal bureaucratic procedure: it was overwhelmingly, and dangerously, arbitrary. The entire phenomenon of the 'caucus' or 'coterie' surrounding the residence of the Prime Minister and intervening in major and minor decisions of government policy or implementation at national, state and local levels, and even extending into the functioning of public undertakings and nationalized banks (as is now being revealed daily in the proceedings of the Shah Commission) marks the monstrous arbitrariness of this kind of centralization. Normal methods of legislative debate, bureaucratic procedure, lobbying, public discussion, etc. had all been suspended. For organized industry, such arbitrary and irrational modes of bureaucratic behaviour were essentially antithetical to the requirements of large-scale business. True, the regime of the Emergency was beneficial to industry; but the benefits could be, and were, differential, and success or disaster depended very largely on the highly uncertain criterion of remaining in the good books of the 'coterie'.

Not only that, the 'coterie' also included within it and in its close peripheries several industrial and commercial entrepreneurs with no capitalist pedigree but with aggressive ambitions, and arbitrary powers were wielded with complete lack of rationality or scruples in their favour. Latching on to these lumpen elements in the world of business were certain middle-range industrial concerns with ambitions of entering the closed world of the big monopoly houses. All this certainly worked against the long-term, if not the immediate, interests of big business.

Thirdly, the bureaucratic implementation of several schemes of the Emergency, and particularly the much-discussed urban resettlement and family planning programmes, brought home to a very large section of the masses of northern India the truly repressive force of the state machinery. It is particularly important to consider this aspect of Emergency rule, especially in view of the wholly unorganized and spontaneous nature of popular opposition expressed in the March elections in the northern Indian states. Large-scale demolition of houses or *nasbandi* were arbitrary acts; but they were not in any way extraneous to a system of centralized rule which, in the absence of appropriate organizational procedures even for maintaining the rule of the exploiting classes, was specifically characterized by arbitrariness. In such situations, it only requires a fanatical commander such as Dyer at Jallianwalla Bagh, or a pampered and power-hungry infant like our own Sanjay Gandhi, to drop the mask and reveal the true nature of an oppressive state machinery.

Peasant ideology is everywhere characterized by a distancing from the central organs of state power with which peasant life normally has little contact. It is also characterised by an innate sense of peasant democracy, which is quick to react against any tangible evidence of repressive state violence. Unorganized, it has little opportunity to combat the state, except through such sporadic and purely limited acts as the burning of government jeeps or physically attacking government personnel. But given the first chance of registering its protest, it is quick to do so. The elections in March 1977 gave the peasantry of northern India this opportunity, and the results are well-known.

We see, then, that the collapse of the 'Congress system' was fundamentally the result of the failure to preserve the crucial institutional mechanism by which the alliance of the ruling classes functioned. This failure not only alienated the landed gentry from the Emergency system, but even the industrial bourgeoisie had reasons to be unhappy with it and was not, therefore, totally threatened by the spectre of an alternative political leadership coming to power. The crucial act, of course, was provided by the north Indian masses who experienced the indiscriminate repressions of an authoritarian state machinery, so that virtually the entire peasantry and the urban poor turned against the Congress.

5

Charan Singh's Politics

The newspapers are full of stories about the disarray in the Janata Party at the Centre. Up in the cool climes of Shimla, a minister violates prohibitory orders and delivers a fiery speech against his party leaders; the Prime Minister threatens to punish him; this leads another minister to drop hints that he has enough material to nail the Prime Minister's son on charges of corruption; the Prime Minister immediately removes him from his ministry. Now we have statements, counter-statements, resignations, threats of resignation. No one knows who is with whom or who is against whom. And finally, the already muddied waters of the capital's politics have been further agitated by stories about the sex life of a minister's son.

On the other hand, the two Congress parties are in no better shape. In Maharashtra, the coalition ministry of the two Congresses has collapsed; one wing has now joined hands with the Janata Party to form a ministry. There has been a split in the powerful group of Indira Gandhi supporters in Vidharbha. In West Bengal too, factionalism is raising its head in the Congress(I). Stories are circulating about disagreements between Mrs Gandhi and her close associates Devraj Urs and Chenna Reddi over proposals to unite the two Congress parties.

Perhaps never since 1947 has the central political structure in India looked so unstable.

The Crisis of Rule[1]

What is the reason for this instability? Some are saying, 'This was only to be expected. When Indira Gandhi unexpectedly called for elections in early 1977, different·leaders from different parties, united by nothing else but the urge to form an electoral

---

[1] [The following paragraphs summarize two sections that largely reproduce the analysis given in Chapter 4.]

alliance against her, came together to set up the Janata Party. An assembly under a sign does not create a political party. The Janata leaders had neither organizational nor ideological unity. From the very beginning, it was a virtual certainty that as soon as it was sucked into the whirlpool of politics, the alliance would come apart.' Others are trying to bring the Janata leaders to reason, to remind them that their quarrels were only helping Indira Gandhi. If only they would rise above these petty squabbles, these friendly critics seem to be saying, and set their minds on the tasks of government, all would be well.

Although we frequently hear comments like these, even from important political circles, they do not help us in the least to understand the seriousness of the problem or its historical significance. Even in the heyday of its power, the Congress party was riddled with factions, internal rivalries and ideological disputes. Yet it managed to win election after election and to rule the country. How was it able to do this? Why did that structure collapse? Perhaps eighty per cent of the current leaders of the Janata Party were once in the Congress; it is there that they built up their bases of support. When they came to power in 1977, why were they unable to construct an effective structure of rule along the lines of the Congress in the Nehru era?

First, the structure of rule in the Nehru period was characterized by a flexible and differentiated hierarchy of power, in government as well as in the ruling party. Second, at its peak, the form of authority was Caesarist. Third, its ideology was a supra-class populism. Armed with this political apparatus, the ruling classes in India tried to lay the foundations of an industrialized economy. The attempt led to a severe economic crisis in the mid-1960s.

One of the main elements in the subsequent strategy that was adopted in order to get out of the crisis was the so-called 'green revolution'. Backed by huge state support, the strategy succeeded in raising foodgrain production in select regions of northern India. It also increased significantly the political power of large landowners in those regions. This could not but upset the balance of power within the coalition of ruling classes. A very interesting aspect of the many initiatives taken during the period of Emergency by the central executive power was the move to clip the wings of the new rich peasant lobby. That the Emergency regime collapsed because of the combined opposition of practically the entire rural population in northern India, from landlords down to poor peasants, was not in small part due to these moves to curtail the power of the dominant rural classes. This is an important part of the history of the rise to power of the Janata Party.

The Importance of being Charan Singh

Since the emergence of the Janata Party, the rich peasant interests in northern India, now seeking greater political power, are organized principally in the Akali Dal and the Bharatiya Lok Dal. The unquestioned ideological leader of this group is Charan Singh. There is a single political argument that frames Charan Singh's politics. The principal thrust of development in the Nehru years, this argument says, was towards big industry, modern science and technology and the cities. This direction has to be shifted. Now the emphasis must be on the rural economy: the larger part of development funds must be spent there. Not only must there be a ceiling on land ownership, but also a floor, so as to eliminate uneconomic small holdings. Government programmes must provide irrigation, electricity, fertilizers, seeds. With this support, the hardworking and enterprising *kisan* will transform the Indian countryside.

Anyone who knows a thing or two about the conditions in which the Indian economy works, situated as it is within the present structure of the global economy, will see that this is a pipe dream. There is no possibility of sustained development in a country like India along a path exclusively defined by the extension of capitalism in agriculture. Not surprisingly, this is the usual judgement one hears from economists and journalists in India on Charan Singh's proposals. But perhaps the real question is not whether Charan Singh is right or wrong. The more serious question is: is Charan Singh's politics likely to appeal to Indian peasants? If so, what are the probable consequences for the future course of Indian politics?

That it does indeed have an appeal has been shown quite clearly in the past year or so — in the new caste wars. The word has gone around in the north Indian countryside that all this time it was the urban, upper-caste, English-speaking classes that had cornered all of the government's funds. A few crumbs thrown to the Harijans had ensured their support. Now the time has come for the middle castes, the bulwark of the peasant communities, to get their due. They will not accept any more the dominance of the urban classes. Young men from the Jat, Yadav, Ahir, Kurmi and other middle castes have taken to the streets to demand education, employment and more funds for the villages. The new movement has identified two enemies: upper castes on the one side and Harijans on the other. This aggressive politics of the landed middle castes is not confined only to northern India, it has spread to Marathwada, Tamil Nadu, Karnataka and Andhra, all of which have witnessed in recent months a series of brutal killings of Harijans. A 'peasant organization' from Haryana has even put up a demonstration in New Delhi demanding that government land distributed to Harijans should now be given to 'real peasants'. When Charan Singh resigned, there was some talk of a central peasant rally in the capital: many were perturbed by the prospect, since it was clear to all who know the situation in the north Indian countryside that Charan Singh does indeed have the clout to assemble a massive show of force.

The uncertainty over the future of the Janata government has revealed one truth about the political process in India: if the economy is to grow under centralized command in accordance with the needs of big capital, then it is impossible, within the framework of a parliamentary democracy, to give in to the demand of rich peasants for greater political power. Where rapid industrialization is not even a remote possibility, to concede this demand will mean tilting the terms of trade between agriculture and industry even further against the latter. In addition, given the largely local relevance of peasant interests, the tendency will be continuously to take governmental power away from central executive control and devolve it at state and local levels. The owners of large industry and commerce and the all-India professional classes are, not surprisingly, alarmed by this prospect. Of the organized dominant interests, they are the principal opponents of Charan Singh's bid for power. This section of the ruling classes is now looking for a solution somewhat similar to that of the Caesarism of the Congress. In view of the experience of the Emergency, all that these interests will demand is that central executive command be strong, but that it avoid the arbitrariness of the Emergency regime, and that it impose discipline in general and virtually Emergency conditions in the factories in particular. The search is now on for a leader and a political organization that have the ability to reorganize the structure of power along these lines. Needless to say, this provides the greatest opportunity for the return of Indira Gandhi. News-reports indicate that the Soviet Union too will favour a solution of this kind. Even some so-called leftists are saying, 'Well, if the unity of the country is to be preserved and effective government restored, what other option do we have? Don't you see what mess this Janata government has put us in?'

On the other hand, the cry has gone up in some other leftist circles: 'To stop Indira, we must join Charan Singh. He is our ally in the fight to save democracy.'

The Dangers of Charan Singh's Politics

Whenever we are confronted by a formation that is not distinctly capitalist, we have a curious tendency to immediately identify it as feudal. Similarly, when we see an organization demonstrating against authoritarianism, we rush to embrace it because we think it must be deeply in love with democracy. Neither of these responses show that we have any skill with dialectical thinking.

When I say that Charan Singh's politics seeks the aggressive expansion of capitalism in agriculture and that it could pose a serious danger to the prospects of building real democracy and socialism in this country, I do not mean to suggest that feudalism has evaporated from the Indian countryside. Nor do I mean that the principal structural tendency is in the direction of a transition from feudalism to capitalism. Moments of crisis usually contain within them several possibilities of transition. The specific turn that history takes is decided on the battlefield of politics: the outcome depends on the relative effectiveness of the rival social forces in preparing their grounds of support and in creating, through ideology and organization, the possibility for the emergence of an alternative mode of production. Theoretical analysis can only describe an actual, historically given situation and indicate the several tendencies contained in it; it is the task of politics to direct the social forces towards the desired tendency.

What is unfortunate is that at the present moment of severe crisis in the ruling structure, none of the Left forces, and especially none of the communist parties, are succeeding in reaching the people with a credible programme for an alternative mode of productive organization. Nearly all of the parties which call themselves communist are identifying enemies and seeking friends from within the existing structure of organized power. The only concern seems to be the immediate gains and losses of the parties or factions and of their leaders; there is no vision here of pursuing any long-range political objectives.

What is dangerous is that, in the meantime, a clear political message is being sent out to a vast mass of the labouring people of India — the message of Charan Singh's politics. From rich farmers to subsistence peasants, owners of agricultural land are being told: make your demands to the government for grants, for subsidies, for appropriate laws, and the labour that you have put into your own lands from time immemorial will at last be justly rewarded; soon everyone will get rich. In the present state of the economy and of the class structure, this politics poses a grave danger. If this appeal succeeds in finding a stable home in peasant consciousness, it will be impossible at any future time to politically unite owner-peasants, large or small, with the landless. Never has this been done in any country in the world.

If the principles of an alternative structure of agrarian economy are not enunciated in the very near future through the political and economic programmes of the Left, the large bulk of the landowning peasantry will never again be brought around to the cause of socialism. Not only that, peasants could then easily come under the sway of some agrarian populist peddling dreams of *kisan raj*. That is the history of the rise of Mussolini in Italy. A movement of agrarian fascism will of course necessarily end up surrendering itself to big capital or to foreign powers. The ruling class coalition which now finds itself hamstrung within the complexities of parliamentary democracy could then discover an unforeseen opportunity for preserving its class dominance.

That is the danger represented by Charan Singh's politics. It will not do merely to restate the academic truism that no long-term solution to India's crisis will be found by strengthening private property and the means of individual profit. If this is something we believe to be true, we must shape our political programmes accordingly. Our economic struggles must be informed by our desire to establish the political means for an alternative mode of productive organization based on collective labour. We know that without a perspective of capture of political power, no fundamental change can be brought about in the mode of production. Today we should also remind ourselves that without the perspective of an alternative mode of production, the political struggle will be led astray.

6

Some New Elements in India's Parliamentary Democracy

There is enormous disarray and confusion today among those who rule India. When in January this year (1980) the Congress under Indira Gandhi returned to power with a huge majority, many had expected that the political order would regain some sort of stability. The previous five or six years had seen the parliamentary system in India go through severe strains: Jayaprakash's movement in 1974–5, the Emergency, the historic elections of 1977, the falling out among the leaders of the Janata Party, the collapse of the Janata government, the curious ministry headed by Charan Singh, and finally the elections of 1980. During all that time, the Indian ruling classes were searching — without success — for the means of stable political rule. It was not as though their dominance was ever challenged, notwithstanding the uncertainties in the political arena. But they were clearly unable to find an organizational means to balance their mutual relations within a coherent political order.

There is little doubt that the entire administrative apparatus is today on the verge of collapse. Take the institutions of the economy. For many years now, there has been a sense of crisis surrounding the economy, but all governments had somehow tried to muddle through. When Indira Gandhi returned to power earlier this year, many of her supporters thought that steps would now be taken to revive the economy. After all, they said, foodgrains production had been good for several years running, and the mayhem caused in the Janata years was largely the result of political incompetence. Whatever else might be the shortcomings of Indira Gandhi, lack of determined leadership was not one of them.

Yet this year has seen no improvement in the state of the economy. One of the major allegations of the Congress(I) against Charan Singh's government was the latter's failure to tackle inflation. But eight months after the Congress(I) was returned to power, the prices of essential commodities continue to rise. The hike in petroleum prices is one factor in this. Far more important, however, is the control exercised by a small group of traders over the supply of various commodities. Obviously, traders will, when the opportunity presents itself, restrict the supply of commodities in the hope of making larger profits. But how effectively, over which areas, and in which commodities traders will be able to make these speculative profits now depends to a very large extent on political conditions. One must remember that when the prices of mass consumption goods rise, while those who trade in those commodities make quick profits, the interests of industrial manufacturers are usually hurt, because rising prices mean rising costs of raw materials and demands for increased wages.

The most notable feature of the recent spate of rising prices is its direct connection with the process of parliamentary democracy. Many millions of rupees are spent in a general election in India. With the growing spread, intensity and sophistication of election campaigns, the costs too are rising rapidly. There are many ways, all of them outside the sphere of public accounting, of raising the funds to finance election campaigns. A recent method, for instance, is to charge a below-the-counter 'commission' on the many large transactions of state-owned corporations engaged in foreign trade, and on exports and imports carried out through agreements with foreign governments. A single transaction of this kind could bring several million rupees into the coffers of the party in power. Another method is to get the support of traders in agricultural commodities and raw materials. First of all, these are businesses which are still relatively 'unorganized' in terms of modern business practices, which means that they are less amenable to statutory controls and legal regulation. Secondly, these trade networks reach into the interiors of rural society and are therefore tied intimately with the economic life of a large section of peasant producers. The political influence of these traders is, therefore, not limited only to their role as contributors to the election funds of political parties, but arises out of their power over peasant producers in large areas of agricultural production. The local political influence of sugar traders in Uttar Pradesh, cotton traders in Maharashtra, oilseed traders in Gujarat, and tobacco traders in Andhra Pradesh are well known instances. This year saw an election to Parliament, and only a few months later, elections to several state assemblies: the rapid rise in the prices of agricultural commodities can be seen as an inevitable result of these political processes.

But the general sense of administrative breakdown cannot be attributed to the power of local economic interests. In the colonial period, of course, the administration was not limited by parliamentary representation of the subject population; the edifice of imperial rule was premised on the absolute supremacy of executive power. The very last years of British rule saw elected ministries in the provinces: many Congress leaders were first introduced to the business of state administration in the period between 1937 and 1947. It was in those years that many of the conventions regarding the relation between elected ministries and the permanent bureaucracy in India were shaped, within the overall framework of a colonial government. This framework was largely retained in the Nehru period. Many Congress ministers in those days, at the Centre as well as in the states, neither knew nor cared for the intricacies of British-style bureaucratic procedure. Once the overall policies had been determined at the political level, most ministers were content to leave the actual task of daily administration in the hands of the officers. It is fair to say that the general practice among Congress leaders of the Nehru era was to respect the experience and expertise of the permanent civil service, and even to rely upon it to maintain continuity of policy and administrative practice.

But with the rising intensity of party and factional competition, the use of administrative power to further narrow sectional interests became more and more common. As a result, from the central or state secretariat to the district or *taluk* or block, government officers became increasingly entangled in the web of party or factional loyalties. It became common practice for political leaders to exercise their clout by ordering officers to get things done for them and to transfer them if they did not comply. One of the first things that happen these days when a new member is elected to a state assembly is the transfer of administrative and police officers in the constituency. Frequent transfers on this scale clearly mean major problems for the accumulation of experience and expertise in the administration. Following the recent communal riots in Uttar Pradesh, for instance, a former inspector-general of police has written that even ten years ago, an officer appointed to a police station would use the first three months to get acquainted with the area in his jurisdiction. Each police station had a guidebook for this purpose in which every officer-in-charge would add his comments. Now, because of the frequent transfers, officers do not even bother to maintain the guidebooks. Apparently, an officer was seen at the time of the recent riots, accompanied by a team of armed police, asking local people for directions that might lead him to the hideouts of the culprits.

The question of administrative efficiency has varied implications for different constituents of the ruling class coalition. A rationally ordered, non-arbitrary and efficient administrative machinery is required above all for the purposes of a modern industrial economy. If there is laxity or corruption in the bureaucracy, especially at the upper levels and in its central structures, it is industrial capitalists who should be the ones to object first. Small traders, moneylenders or owners of rural property do not bother too much about bureaucratic niceties: in fact, the looser the procedures at the lower rungs of a centralized bureaucracy, the easier it is for these classes to exercise their local dominance.

One of the new features of parliamentary democracy in India in the last decade is the political rise of a rich peasant class following the 'green revolution'. After a subdued spell during the Emergency, this class was particularly prominent in the years of the Janata government. In those years, it attempted to consolidate its local dominance by using its influence over the district administration. One manifestation of this was the proliferation of arms at the local level. A recent estimate shows that there are at present as many as twenty thousand licensed firearms in the district of Moradabad alone. In the 1950s, this figure was less than two thousand. It is also said that for every licensed firearm there are usually three that are unlicensed. This means that in Moradabad alone there are some eighty thousand firearms. By comparison, all of Great Britain has a total of 75,000 licensed arms. There are reasons to suspect that in several districts of Bihar or Punjab, there are even larger quantities of arms in the hands of locally powerful groups. Many observers have been astonished by the extensive use of firearms in the recent communal riots in Uttar Pradesh. If we keep in mind some of the changes in the political process in the north Indian countryside in the last decade and a half, there should be less cause for surprise.

This does not mean, however, that in the central structures of state power in India, the power of rural landowners has increased in relation to that of industrial capitalists. No matter how much the local dominance of landlords or rich peasants, it has not been successfully transformed into an organized force that could stake its claim to state power at the central level. There is a history of the politics of the rich peasant in India, from its rise within the Congress movement in the 1930s, its presence at the local levels of electoral politics in the Nehru era, its visibility even in the central representative bodies in Indira Gandhi's reorganized Congress in the early 1970s, to its bid for central power under the leadership of Charan Singh. The bid failed. The failure signified, first, that the influence of industrial capital in the organized arena of state power is now pre-eminent, and second, that it is virtually impossible to translate the local dominance of the rural rich in the different parts of a country like India into a central force within the ruling coalition.

Nevertheless, the bourgeoisie in India cannot rule except by sharing power with other dominant classes. But in what form? Through which instruments? That has become the principal question of parliamentary democracy in India. There does not appear to be a political leadership with the ability to establish and maintain a new balancing mechanism for sharing power within the ruling classes. Every political party seems to have failed in this task.

We see, consequently, that the political agitations that have broken out in different parts of the country in recent months are eluding the influence of both ruling parties and parties of the opposition. The movement in Assam is the most obvious example. But the agitation against rising prices in Gujarat, the peasant agitation over irrigation waters in Karnataka, and the repeated clashes in Kashmir between the people and the armed forces show the same feature. On top of this, of course, are the endless episodes of communal violence in Uttar Pradesh. What is significant about these events is not only the growing signs of popular agitation, but the failure of every established political party to influence or control them.

When the ruling powers are in such disarray, there is, however, no significant organized political challenge to their rule; which is why the present political crisis could contain many dangerous possibilities. It remains to be seen, for instance, how long the industrial capitalists will endure the breakdown of administration and the lack of political direction. Many influential circles in India had been vocal in the recent past about getting rid of the baggage of parliamentary forms in order to set right the administrative apparatus and the public and private enterprises. Since the death of Sanjay Gandhi, those circles have been somewhat subdued. Perhaps that is the only reason why parliamentary democracy will survive for a while in this country. The largest democracy in the world appears to be hanging from a thread.

7

Indira Gandhi: The Final Year

21 November 1983: Of Monarchs and Democrats[1]

The Queen is in India. Not our Queen, of course. Thanks to the freedom movement and our Constitution, the British monarch no longer reigns in India. But there is nevertheless a special relationship of some kind, and the Queen is in India in connection with the meeting of the heads of governments of the Commonwealth, of which India is a member and the Queen the head.

It has been remarked that the visit of the British monarch has not aroused the same sort of enthusiasm among the people as did her visit to this country twenty-two years ago. Perhaps we have at long last shed our colonial legacy. The reports even say that the royal motorcade driving into Rashtrapati Bhavan had to be diverted, because Rajpath had been taken over by crowds celebrating the *Ekatmata Yajna* organized by the Vishwa Hindu Parishad. Surely such a defiant demonstration of our collective religious will would never have been allowed to interfere with a royal procession in the days of the Raj. We now live in a truly secular country, where the state does not meddle with religion, at least not when it suits its purpose. Perhaps we have also outgrown our juvenile fascination with monarchs and princes. We now live in a democracy where we ourselves elect the leaders of our government.

Or perhaps we have found an even cleverer solution, one which political theorists and constitutional experts have not yet dreamt of. Perhaps, unknown to all, we have quietly built up a system in which we can, to the accompaniment of the full fanfare of a democratic process, elect our own monarchs. Two weeks ago, the AICC(I) session concluded in Bombay with the

[1] *Frontier*, 16, 15 (26 November 1983).

investiture of a Crown Prince, one whom the party expected to be duly elected to the office of our democratic monarchy. The Prime Minister, speaking on the occasion, is reported to have explained with beguiling simplicity: 'I don't come from a royal family but we have acquired the status by our dedicated service to the nation, by sincerity of purpose and hard work.' One party leader after another took up the cue and asserted that it was only in the fitness of things and wholly in accordance with the wishes of the people that Mr Rajiv Gandhi should in due course take up the reins of government from his tired mother. Even Mr Priyaranjan Das Munshi, Congress firebrand and erstwhile rebel against Sanjay Gandhi's authoritarian ways, is said to have confessed his sins and asked to be forgiven: ' . . . like a mother she will forgive her errant son.'

One can ridicule and condemn such abject servility among those who claim to rule this country. But we must also pause to think why, despite the fact that the politics of the ruling party has been reduced to such a pathetic state, it continues to rule and in fact believes that the best way for it to seek another term in power is to project Rajiv Gandhi as the legitimate successor to the Prime Minister. One can argue endlessly about whose 'objective' interests Mrs Gandhi serves by being in power, but what is the sum and substance of her own politics today except to do whatever is necessary to secure, in some form or another, a dynastic succession? Individuals, one hears, play only a limited role in history. But sometimes they play crucial roles. Perhaps it will be individual ambitions and individual weaknesses which will bring about, in the next few months, a situation in this country pregnant with terrible dangers as well as far-reaching possibilities. One can only hope the people will find leaders bold enough to seize those historical opportunities.

In the meantime, Mrs Gandhi will probably envy the quiet graciousness of the British Queen. Being a constitutional monarch, the latter does not need to play at politics to make certain that her family continues to reign. On the other hand, one suspects that at the meeting of Commonwealth heads of governments, Queen Elizabeth too will face stiff competition in the business of regal demeanour. After all, one who thinks she is monarch by virtue of the dedicated services of her family to the nation has much to flaunt.

26 December 1983: Who Wins What?[2]

The results of the by-elections to three Lok Sabha and eleven Assembly seats in Haryana, Rajasthan, Uttar Pradesh, Bihar and West Bengal have come as something of a disappointment to those complacent optimists who had been talking for sometime now of the rapidly eroding electoral support for the Congress(I) all over northern India. The results have shown that, whatever may have been the popular mood a few months ago, the concerted propaganda campaign launched by Mrs Gandhi about the so-called threat to national unity and the imminence of a border war with Pakistan has enabled her, at least for the moment, to hold the opposition at bay. Not only that: by winning the prestige contest at Sonepat where the former Lok Dal and now Janata leader Devi Lal was soundly thrashed, the Congress(I) has come out of this round with a fair bit of advantage.

The results have shown in particular the failure of either of the two opposition combines to emerge as a clear and credible national alternative to the Congress(I). The BJP–Lok Dal combine has had two successes — in the Fazilnagar and Madhogarh Assembly seats, which it has taken away from the Congress(I) and the Janata respectively. But it has lost the Mandawa seat in Rajasthan. The Janata Party has scored one significant victory — in the Bulandshahr (U.P.) Lok Sabha contest — but has lost elsewhere. Maneka Gandhi's party has won the Pilibhit Assembly seat which has for long been her associate Akbar Ahmed's stronghold. The Bettia Lok Sobha seat has gone to the CPI.

The West Bengal results are even more significant because the CPI(M) has lost both seats that had fallen vacant. Admittedly, both Kaliachak (Malda) and Krishnaganj (Nadia) were marginal seats, but the fact remains that despite the pathetic organizational state of the Congress(I) in West Bengal, it has managed to improve its electoral image sufficiently to win those seats. Or perhaps the results are more indicative of a growing popular disenchantment with the Left Front — the inevitable consequence of the complete exhaustion of its narrow programmes of reform, and hence the increasingly strong impression of non-performance on virtually every aspect of government activity.

[2] *Frontier*, 16, 20 (31 December 1983).

Perhaps Mrs Gandhi will now be tempted to call an early election and cash in on the present confusion in the opposition ranks. The Left parties will in all likelihood continue to keep their options open. In recent weeks, every Left leader has uttered the litany about the threat to national unity and the imminent danger of a border war. They have all expressed their praise and support for the supposedly 'progressive' foreign policy of Mrs Gandhi. Mr E.M.S. Namboodiripad is even reported to have said that in the present context of national instability, a certain degree of centralization of power must be conceded; the task of the Left forces is to ensure that this centralization does not lead to authoritarian rule.

So the charade will continue in the next few weeks, each party counting its wins and losses and figuring out how best to respond to Mrs Gandhi's next move. What all this will show once again is the utter inability of the opposition leaders to look beyond the set patterns of electoral arithmetic, to conceive of this otherwise bewildering tactical game of moves and countermoves in the wider and much more real context of the daily struggle of the people for a more decent, more humane and more democratic social order.

9 January 1984: Conclave in Calcutta[3]

The winter's festivities continue this week in Calcutta with an international football tournament and the next round of talks among the all-India opposition parties. The former will be inaugurated by the Prime Minister who is paying her second visit to the city in two weeks, this time on what looks like an exclusively cultural mission. She for one seems bent on pushing to the fullest extent her latest political line on West Bengal: save Bengal's cultural heritage from the marauding Marxists!

Two days later, the West Bengal government will play host to the opposition conclave. The officially announced agenda for the closed-door sessions contains subjects that are both diverse and of varying importance. They cover matters like external debts, lockouts in factories and unemployment on the one hand, and electoral reforms and Congress(I) attempts to topple the

---

[3] *Frontier*, 16, 22 (14 January 1984).

governments in Jammu and Kashmir and Karnataka on the other. It is said that there is no official proposal to discuss the prospects for electoral unity among the opposition parties. Yet there is no doubt that whatever the subjects discussed and resolutions adopted, they will be read not so much for their actual content as for the signs they might disclose about the thinking of each party on the forthcoming general elections — whenever they are held — and about the possibilities of electoral adjustments.

Indeed, the conclave is coming at a particularly crucial time. The recent by-elections have produced very ambiguous results, with no one gaining any decisive advantage. But the signal is clear that if there is a broad oppositional unity, Mrs Gandhi will be put into considerable difficulties in northern India. Already the BJP has issued an appeal to the Janata-led combination for constructive talks on a common programme with a view to setting up a non-communist front. Mrs Gandhi will, of course, desperately try to keep the opposition divided. Already, she has made up her mind to sacrifice her traditional Muslim 'vote bank', play an adroit Hindu-communal line and direct the full firepower of government-sponsored propaganda against the 'anti-national' attitude of Farooq Abdullah and the National Conference. By this, she probably hopes to make the choice more difficult for the Janata group of parties: by coming together with the BJP–Lok Dal alliance, it could risk losing its newly acquired Muslim support. It is strange indeed that at a time when the Congress(I) has raised the bogey of an imminent attack from Pakistan, it is the BJP which is able most strongly to put this down as one more out of Mrs Gandhi's endless stock of vote-catching gimmicks.

But it is the Left which is truly in a quandary. The Soviets have made no secret of their wish that the so-called 'left and progressive forces' should support Mrs Gandhi. The CPI(M)'s central leadership has in recent weeks taken up the cue with great alacrity. But West Bengal is obviously a crucial factor in that party's electoral calculations, and the recent by-election results in Malda and Nadia have upset matters greatly. The Congress(I) in West Bengal has apparently been able to persuade Mrs Gandhi and her son that a sustained campaign against the CPI(M) in the state could earn them considerable electoral dividends. This seems to have unnerved the CPI(M)'s state leadership. Underlying its inept bunglings and indecisiveness' on how to react to the Governor's action on the Vice-Chancellor issue, there is probably a groundswell of opinion within the party which would like, on the eve of the opposition conclave, to bind both its central leadership and a vacillating Chief Minister to a more uncompromisingly anti-Congress(I) position.

21 May 1984: Imperial Strategy[4]

From drift to decisive action. Or is it? The government is claiming that its latest attempts to clean up the Punjab mess are paying off and, slowly but surely, the situation is coming under control. Although terrorist actions by groups such as the Dashmesh Regiment continue to hit the headlines every day and most Punjab cities are under curfew, the police administration claims considerable success from its 'mopping up operations'. A statement by police chief P.S. Bhinder declares that in a series of raids in 359 villages in Amritsar district alone, nearly 250 people with 'terrorist connections' had been arrested and large amounts of arms and ammunition seized. On the other hand, Hindu communal bodies like the Rashtriya Hindu Suraksha Sena have already come into the forefront; they took a leading part in organizing the *bandh* following the murder of Ramesh Chandra, editor of a distinguished Jullundur daily.

In dealing with the Punjab situation, the government of Mrs Gandhi has adopted what looks like a classic imperial strategy. If you do not want a reasonable democratic solution of a political problem, allow the situation to drift, let the disaffection mount. Soon there will be some who will demand quick and extreme solutions. Allow them to put on the pressure, even pamper them for a while. The passions will rise, violence will spread, people — perhaps many people — will get killed. Do not get carried away, stick to your plan. For as soon as the 'extremists' will seem to have gained the upper hand, the moderates will be pushed into a corner. Then, and only then, will you strike a deal.

A classic imperial strategy. And Mrs Gandhi's government is playing it with a degree of insensitivity and ruthlessness which,

[4] *Frontier*, 16, 40 (26 May 1984).

even after a decade and a half of her despotic career, is no less frightening. In a recent interview, she has reportedly stated that a solution of the Punjab problem has been within the realms of possibility for several months now, but every time 'some obstacles came in the way.' And now, after hundreds of deaths, complete disruption of the economic and social life of the people, and a deep entrenchment of feelings of mutual hostility and distrust, the armed forces are going ahead with their 'mopping up operations' and the moderate Akali leaders have been suddenly released from prison. Reports from New Delhi indicate that informal discussions are already under way with the Akali leadership and a 'deal' of some sort may well be in the offing. Perhaps Mrs Gandhi now feels that the wings of the moderates have been sufficiently clipped, so that a deal under these conditions, although its specific terms might easily have been acceptable several months ago, would not give them the credit of a political victory. Unless, of course, some new 'obstacle' comes in the way.

In the meantime, Punjab will live in fear and anguish. And many more will die. That, of course, is of little concern to those who have reduced the business of politics to a sordid game of self-interest and vanity.

19 June 1984: All This for What?[5]

Judging from the fever-pitch excitement now being whipped up by the government media and the all-India press, it would seem that organized public opinion in the towns and cities of India has been swept by a wave of nationalist hysteria. Never has there been such xenophobic fervour and such a frenzy of statolatry in this country except in times of war. All shades of political opinion, from the extreme Right to large sections of the Left, have lined up behind Mrs Gandhi and the Union government and have hailed the military action in Punjab as a bold, decisive and entirely necessary step in fighting 'the grave threat to the unity and security of the country'. The Prime Minister, it would seem, has once again performed one of her famous political tricks, perhaps her most dramatic since the Bangladesh war of 1971.

5 *Frontier*, 16, 44 (23 June 1984).

Everyone appears to be supporting her move — everyone except, of course, the Sikhs.

Not every Sikh in Punjab was a supporter of the extreme communalist politics of the now deceased Bhindranwale. Surely the overwhelming majority was hoping for an end to the violence, bloodshed and complete disruption of normal life in that state. But the few reports from Punjab that have been allowed to pass through the tight net of censorship regulations indicate a quite pervasive mood of sullen anger and bitterness among the Sikhs. The storming of the Golden Temple was not just a military operation. If the objective was simply to flush out 'terrorists', there were other means available. It was meant to be a symbolic act of high political drama, intended above all to impress upon the country as a whole that the government had acted with courage, determination, meticulous planning and bold execution. Yet in choosing this particular form of action, the Union government has inevitably alienated the Sikhs as a community. The Sikhs feel they have been accused as a community of being criminals and enemies of the nation, of harbouring secessionist sentiments and deserving punishment and humiliation. Every day now, responsible members of the community, not even remotely supporters of Bhindranwale, are coming out in public to express their sorrow and dismay at what has happened and to protest against the military action. Virtually the entire moderate Akali leadership is in prison, detained indefinitely under the National Security Act.

Most 'disturbing' perhaps are the signs of unrest among Sikh soldiers in the army. There have been mutinies in at least eight army camps in various parts of the country, the most serious being in Ramgarh in Bihar where the officially confirmed figure of desertions is over 500. Numerous mutineers have been killed in encounters with loyal troops; most seem to have been arrested and will doubtless be proceeded against according to normal military procedures.

All this for what? The Prime Minister has achieved her political objective. She had already decided that she would not make any political settlement on the issue of Centre–State relations in Punjab which would give the moderate Akali Dal leadership any electoral leverage. This was the primary reason why the abnormal situation there had dragged on for such a long time; for, the moderates, unable to clinch the issue, kept losing ground in the face of pressure from the extremist wing as well as the mounting threat from Hindu communal organizations. Now, having herself brought the situation to such a pass, the Prime Minister has acted 'decisively'. She has obviously decided that it was not worth her while trying to woo back the traditional minority vote. She needed something dramatic to swing the crucial Hindu vote in northern India. The Punjab situation gave her this chance, and she has seized it with her customary alacrity and ruthlessness.

16 July 1984: Stepping Up Repression[6]

The inevitable is happening. Having immersed itself in the quagmire of armed counter-insurgency operations in Punjab, the Union government is now taking increasingly repressive measures on a national scale. It has used the most blatantly undemocratic means to dismiss the government of Farooq Abdullah in Jammu and Kashmir, and has sought to justify this outrageous step in terms of the need to fight subversive and anti-national activities. And now it has come out with an ordinance empowering the Union government to declare any part of India a 'terrorist-affected' area and to set up special courts to try 'crimes against the country's security and integrity'. The powers given to the Union government under this ordinance are drastic, and fall little short of declaring an Emergency by other means. The offences which can be construed as anti-national and terrorist crimes include waging war against the state, abetting mutiny, promoting enmity between classes, assertion of imputations prejudicial to national integrity, and serious offences like murder, dacoity and hijacking.

The so-called White Paper is a classic document of official deception. It puts the whole blame for what happened in Punjab not, as one might have expected, on the extreme communalist section led by Jarnail Singh Bhindranwale or even on external sources, real or mythical, supporting 'separatist elements'. Rather, it lays the blame squarely on the Akali Dal as a whole for launching a movement which it could not

[6] *Frontier*, 16, 48 (21 July 1984).

control, and which provided a 'respectable cover for subversive and anti-national forces' as well as for the involvement of 'criminals, smugglers, antisocial elements and Naxalites'. The document alleges that it was the Akali Dal leadership which 'lacked the will to arrive at a settlement on the basis of any reasonable framework offered by government'. It refused to dissociate itself from the separatism of the extremist groups and ultimately allowed the initiative to pass out of its hands. The Union government, the White Paper asserts, had no alternative in the end but to take armed action. As the most damning sentence in the whole document puts it: 'The government have affirmed, in the only way open to them, the imperatives of national integrity against all forms of separatism.'

The White Paper, of course, is completely silent on the role of the Congress(I) leadership itself in systematically setting up Bhindranwale as a counter to the Akali Dal leadership in Punjab. It does not mention why Bhindranwale, at the time of his rise to prominence, was repeatedly given political protection despite several criminal cases being brought against him. It does not say that it was the Union government, and not the Akali Dal, which went back on its word on the eve of the Haryana elections in 1983 when it suddenly became apprehensive that a settlement with the Akalis might mean a loss of Hindu votes for the Congress(I) in Haryana. It does not mention the provocative role of Hindu communal bodies in Punjab and Haryana in aggravating the situation early this year. It does not mention Union Home Minister P.C. Sethi's infelicitous dithering on the eve of the final round of talks with the Akali Dal. The document, in other words, has nothing to say about the narrow, shortsighted and sectarian political calculations which guided the Union leadership into postponing a political settlement on the main issues concerning Centre–State relations which lay at the heart of the Akali demands. It was this, and not the intransigence of the extremists or the lack of will of the moderates, which finally brought about a situation in which the government could show that it had no alternative but to unleash armed violence on a massive scale.

Now repression will spread all over the country. What the forces of opposition will do to meet this challenge remains to be seen.

27 August 1984: A Decisive Moment[7]

The All-India Protest Day on 25 August has passed off peacefully. There was much greater response in the southern states and in West Bengal than in the rest of the country. In Andhra Pradesh, the deposed Chief Minister, Mr N.T. Rama Rao, despite his precarious health, began in Vijaywada a campaign to mobilize public resentment against the outrageous way in which he was ousted from office, and to demand his reinstatement. The crowds he is drawing are a fair indication of the massive and spontaneous feelings of the people of that state against the undemocratic actions of the Governor and the autocratic powers in New Delhi. The Governor, Mr Ram Lal, has apparently brought to a close a series of incidents at once disgraceful and farcical by announcing his resignation. Yet, at the moment of writing, there are no signs that the basic wrong will be undone by giving Mr Rama Rao a fair chance to prove his majority and come back to an office from which he was removed.

All this has, of course, suddenly galvanized the opposition into united action against Congress(I) misrule. After their speeches in Parliament and a deputation to the President failed to produce significant results, there was no course left but to launch a sustained countrywide agitation. The programmes taken so far have been cautious and limited. The Protest Day envisaged bandhs only in West Bengal, Kerala and Karnataka, while the leftist trade unions were asked to carry out industrial action wherever feasible. The opposition leaders do not appear to have too many ideas about how to sustain the agitation if Mrs Gandhi remains obdurate and chooses to bide her time. This time they do not have a Jayaprakash Narayan to lead them, and the leaders of the rightist and centrist opposition are not made of the kind of stuff that can pass through a prolonged, possibly bloody, period of struggle against a centralized, autocratic and thoroughly ruthless regime. All they are hoping for is to ride into power on the crest of a popular electoral wave; they cannot be expected to relish the prospects of a long spell of political turmoil. Already Mr Chandra Shekhar is reported to have expressed his anxiety that countrywide agitations might provoke Mrs Gandhi to declare an Emergency.

[7] *Frontier*, 17, 2 (1 September 1984).

Mrs Gandhi is obviously counting on the limited staying power of the opposition. She is reported to have decided to shift the elections from November 1984 to January 1985. By then, she hopes, the opposition will have run out of steam and the challenge withered away. Perhaps her new-found protégé Bhaskar Rao will find enough time and opportunity to buy up the requisite MLAs to prove his majority in the Andhra Assembly. If that fails, President's Rule could be declared in the state. Other issues might come up in the meantime, including foreign adventures in the southern seas. If her prospects do not improve by early-1985, she could make a move for drastic constitutional amendments or even an Emergency. The present opposition leadership does not seem prepared for such ordeals.

For the first time in many years, a historic opportunity has arisen in which the Left might be called upon to perform the role of leading a sustained phase of popular struggle on an issue that is national in scale. At such moments, the question is not so much the real limits, sectoral or regional, of organized strength. The question is that of the will and the ability to step into the breach, to lead the popular democratic cause through a phase where repression becomes harsh and the established leadership is found wanting. Mrs Gandhi's reluctance to abdicate power, even in the face of popular disapproval, may provide the Left with just such an opportunity to project itself as a truly national alternative. Will the Left be found wanting?

The signs are not entirely hopeful. Only two days before the All-India Protest Day, Mr E.M.S. Namboodiripad is reported to have made a statement that there is little chance of an electoral adjustment of the Left with parties like the BJP or even the Janata. He also added that the Left still supported the 'progressive' foreign policy of Mrs Gandhi. The timing of the statement is as significant as its content; for it indicates fear, a reluctance to seize the moment, and needless to say, an ingrained slavishness to the modes of parliamentary politics.

15 October 1984: Riots and Politics[8]

There have been a series of incidents in recent weeks involving violent Hindu–Muslim clashes. The distinctive feature of these

[8] *Frontier*, 17, 9 (20 October 1984).

incidents is that they have not been restricted to any one part of the country. Relations between the two communities in the cities of Hyderabad have been tense for several months, and things have flared up at least half-a-dozen times in the course of this year. In Maharashtra, after the terrible killings in Bombay and Bhiwandi a few months ago, we now have reports of riots in Malegaon — once again, a powerloom town. Communal violence also broke out at more or less the same time in Belgaum in Karnataka, Pulampur in Gujarat and Azamgarh in Uttar Pradesh. It has been suggested that the trouble has been caused by the fact that this year Muharram and Dusserah have coincided, and this sort of conjunction of Hindu and Muslim festivals always creates the possibility of conflict. This seems too facile an explanation. The coincidence of public festivals might mean additional problems for the civil administration in towns and districts, but there is no reason why it should necessarily cause antagonism and bitterness among ordinary people.

Much more plausible is the explanation that, this being election year, politicians of all grades and descriptions are seeking the opportunity of getting into the act, and any kind of public event is being drawn into the vortex of politics. Not necessarily is there a countrywide conspiracy or organization behind the series of communal disturbances in recent weeks. Local issues and local forces are enough to precipitate an incident that will make the news. The riots in Bombay and Bhiwandi a few months ago, and the more recent ones in Hyderabad, have shown quite clearly that a handful of well-organized and well-financed troublemakers can create havoc in densely-populated urban areas. There is not much doubt that much of what has happened in Malegaon or Belgaum or Azamgarh is the handiwork of such forces out to make quick political capital.

But that is not all. Two other things need to be remembered. First, the willing participation, or at least connivance, of the administration. Both in Bombay and in Hyderabad, the clear connivance of the police as well as the political leadership holding office at the time was responsible for the way in which rioters had a field day. If indeed it is true that many of these incidents are the handiwork of small groups of troublemakers, it is hardly likely that they would have either the courage or the ability to cause such large-scale destruction and killing if the administration was prompt and decisive in taking action. Moreover, the Congress(I) itself, in its bid to stave off the opposition in northern and western India, has created the clear impression that it will stop at nothing to win the so-called 'organized Hindu vote'.

The other important fact is that there is at the moment a general sense of political uncertainty in the country. The popular mood is restive; people feel that something ought to be done about their growing hardships. Yet the political scene does not offer any decisive hope of a national leadership willing or able to provide a credible alternative. That the people desire a change has been indicated over and over again. When this popular mood finds a worthwhile political cause, it can show, as it has done in Andhra, amazing determination and powers of resistance. Without such a cause and without genuine political leadership, such periods of uncertainty can create situations in which even small-time troublemakers can have a field day.

29 October 1984: Jockeying for Position[9]

Mr Charan Singh sprang a major surprise last week by declaring the formation of a new party. It will be called the Dalit Mazdoor Kisan Party (DMKP). With the growing profusion of splits and mergers among political parties, even their names are getting more and more cumbersome. The new party is the result of the coming together of the erstwhile Lok Dal, Mr Bahuguna's DSP, Mr Ratubhai Advani's Rashtriya Congress, and a significant section of Janata dissidents including Mr Devi Lal and, hopefully, Mr Karpoori Thakur. The new party, needless to add, will be headed by Charan Singh himself.

The impact of this latest move by the irrepressible old war-horse from Jatland will be felt most severely by the Janata Party, and by Chandra Shekhar in particular. For several days before Charan Singh's announcement, talks had been conducted with the intention of a merger between the Lok Dal and the Janata Party. It was even reported that a broad agreement on organizational unification had been reached: Charan Singh was to become president and Chandra Shekhar working president, and a joint parliamentary board was to be set up. But obviously, Charan

9 *Frontier*, 17, 11 (3 November 1984).

Singh thought there were possibilities of a better bargain. Now he has virtually pulled the rug from under Chandra Shekhar's feet. With Devi Lal and Karpoori Thakur gone, and Satyendra Narayan Sinha already joining the Congress(I), the Janata Party will now be left with Karnataka as its only secure base. It is hardly surprising therefore that it has accused Charan Singh of the 'politics of piracy'.

Already, DMKP leaders have begun to air their expectations about how strongly the new party will perform in north India. Charan Singh is clearly a considerable force in Uttar Pradesh, but now with the addition of H.N. Bahuguna, backward caste leaders like Karpoori Thakur and the expected campaign support of Syed Mir Kasim and Farooq Abdullah, DMKP leaders are exuberant.

But everyone realizes that the chances of a decisive opposition victory lie crucially in its ability to prevent the splitting of anti-Congress(I) votes. Hence, the fielding of unanimous opposition candidates all over the country is something everyone agrees is a primary requirement. The trouble is that each party is also interested in getting as much as possible for itself out of a unanimous agreement. And this is pushing back the prospects of unanimity. It is not true, as Mrs Gandhi so frequently alleges, that the opposition has only a one-point programme — that of removing her from power. If it did, the opposition would have been united long ago.

With the brief flush of enthusiasm over Mr Rama Rao's ouster and reinstatement quickly receding into the distant past, Indian politics is now fully engaged in the electoral market place. It is certain that in the coming weeks there will be many more moves and countermoves, small and big bargains, splits and realignments, all with the objective of maximizing one's chances of a seat in Parliament. It will be incorrect to accuse, as Congress(I) leaders are sure to do, only the opposition leaders of such unprincipled politics. The ruling party itself is no haven of selfless servants of the people. The recent expulsions of F.M. Khan and J.R. Dhote are only a surface indication of the equally unscrupulous jockeying for position that is engaging the leaders of that party at the moment. The only difference, probably, is the cringing sycophancy which gives to Congress(I) politics the doubtful appearance of the passionate fervour of devotees at a shrine.

5 November 1984: Troubled Times[10]

The last week was one of the most momentous in the recent history of this accursed country — grim, harrowing and full of dark portents. Despite the cycle of violence into which Punjab had been drawn since early this year, and the dramatic escalation in its scale and intensity since the storming of the Golden Temple in Amritsar by the army and its continued operations in the countryside, the manner in which Mrs Indira Gandhi was assassinated was, and still remains, incredible. That there could be such an appalling failure of security and intelligence is a measure of the incompetence of the most vaunted and well-funded section of the administrative machinery.

And then, while people were still in a state of shock and disbelief at the outrageous act by two of the Prime Minister's bodyguards and perhaps a minuscule group of conspirators, still unidentified, who believed that this could be a solution to any of the country's problems, it was plunged into the worst communal holocaust since Partition. The full details of the carnage are still to come in, but what has already appeared in the press is horrible enough. From West Bengal to Haryana, across the whole stretch of central and northern India, virtually every town and city, particularly the capital, was in the grip of a mad orgy of murder, loot and arson. Although reports are still incomplete, the death toll is already being put at over 1000, and no one has yet attempted to estimate the losses of property. The overwhelming majority of those killed, maimed or plundered were completely innocent of any complicity in the act for which their assailants claimed they were taking revenge; it can hardly be believed that anyone other than a tiny minority even sympathized with Mrs Gandhi's murderers. It is far more likely, as is usually the case on such occasions, that groups of hoodlums at many places took advantage of a situation of uncertainty and panic; helped by the Hindu backlash, either on their own initiative or at the behest of others, they took the 'law' into their own hands.

At the time of writing, the situation appears to be slowly coming under some semblance of control. The army, incidentally, has been deployed over a wide area for peacekeeping

[10] *Frontier*, 17, 12 (10 November 1984).

purposes, further boosting its image as our saviour, and numerous towns and cities are still under curfew. Whether there was a large-scale conspiracy and organization behind the disturbances over such a wide area will probably not be known for a long time, although the suddenness with which the pretext for the trouble appeared would seem to militate against the possibility of any prior planning. What is true is that the administration at most places was slow on the uptake, tardy in keeping pace with developments and hesitant about what to do. Here again the administrative lapses are a pointer to the political reality of a governing machine packed with sycophants and most obedient servants, always waiting for orders from the impervious top, neither able nor willing to act according to any interests other than the wishes of their masters.

Indira Gandhi, who of late made a series of political miscalculations on Sikkim, Kashmir, Punjab and Andhra Pradesh, has now been succeeded in office by her son Rajiv. For at least the last two years, this was known to be her personal mission — to install her son as Prime Minister. Given the extraordinary circumstances in which the succession has taken place, criticisms about the perpetuation of a dynastic rule have been somewhat muted. However, some opposition leaders have complained about the procedural impropriety of the way in which the President took it for granted that Mr Rajiv Gandhi's election as leader of the Congress(I) Parliamentary Party was virtually assured, and could be formalized as soon as things were a little more normal.

But the procedural point, although it is worth making, is not really the most serious malady which the succession signifies. Senior leaders of the Congress(I) realized immediately after Mrs Gandhi's death that their best chance of survival lay in installing her son as quickly and with as little acrimony as possible. For, the ruling party of India is not really a political party in the usual sense, and has not been so for at least a decade. It is a party whose organization, procedures, ideology, electoral support — in short, its very existence — has flowed from a single source, that of its supreme leader. In her absence, the only way the party can hold together is with the survival of a symbolic presence, a representation. And who better to perform this role than one who in his person and name is a living memory of that singular source of power and authority.

In all likelihood, the Congress(I) will now go in for parliamentary polls as soon as possible, in order to cash in on the post-assassination sentiments of shock and grief among the people whose memory of the terror of the Emergency and the killings of thousands — victims of state violence — in the past few years, has faded. The feelings of shock will undoubtedly be stoked in order to persuade the people of the dangers to the integrity of the country and the need to consolidate a strong centralized power. It is even possible that some elements of the opposition, who have until now cried themselves hoarse about the undemocratic implications of dynastic rule, will now be brought around to support Mr Rajiv Gandhi in this so-called 'hour of crisis'. The question is, how long will this appeal remain credible. The new Prime Minister's political acumen and ideological preferences are still very largely unknown factors. But even his most optimistic supporter will be hard put to it to deny that he will face a daunting task to simply hold his party together, with no resources to go on except the memory of the departed leader.

The most critical question today is the nature of the wound the polity has suffered as a result of the events of last week. Will it be allowed to fester and further breed deep-rooted feelings of hatred among the people? Such are the questions which must engage the immediate attention of politically conscious people today. And let us not forget for a moment that members of the hunted Sikh community form a large contingent of the armed forces. Punjab is the crucial factor. What happens there may determine what happens to India. Things are falling apart. Talk of the 'healing touch' after what has occurred in large areas of the country sounds like mockery. Not even the solemnity of the funeral procession in the presence of world leaders can compensate for the lapse into barbarism.

19 November 1984: Election Prospects[11]

The expected has happened, perhaps sooner than expected. Even before the endless ceremonies of a state mourning had been gone through, this time with the full ritual grandeur of a royal

[11] *Frontier*, 17, 14 (24 November 1984)

funeral in some ancient Hindu monarchy (recreated for television in a secular democracy), Congress members were eagerly talking about the great wave of sympathy that was rising in electoral waters all over the country. In death as in life, Indira Gandhi had acted as their saviour, miraculously transforming what looked like a precarious electoral prospect into one in which the ruling party had only to romp home to a new term in office. Barely three days after the mourning formalities were completed, the new Prime Minister announced that parliamentary elections would be held on 24 and 27 December, allowing only for the statutory minimum period of notice. No Congress member can complain that his new leader has failed, at least on this instance, to seize a political opportunity at its most favourable point.

The Congress(I)'s campaign strategy will be simple and straightforward. Indira Gandhi, it will tell the electorate, alone stood for that supreme political value — the unity and integrity of India. Relentlessly, to the last day of her life, she warned her countrymen of the grave danger to that unity, of the dark forces of regional separatism and communal divisiveness that were threatening to tear the nation apart. Support a strong central government, she had said, so that the unity of the country could be properly defended. And who was more willing or able to hold a strong Centre than the Congress(I)? Many had doubted her words then, claiming they were merely a clever ploy to justify her policy of concentration of power and her desire to perpetuate an authoritarian and possibly dynastic rule. Now, the Congress(I) campaigners will remind the voters, Indira Gandhi had paid the ultimate price to prove that she was right.

The Congress(I) will hope that in the face of a saturation campaign of glorification of the assassinated leader, coupled with patriotic fervour and a subtle undertone of Hindu chauvinism, the more unpleasant questions about the actual record of Congress(I) misrule will not be asked. Will the strategy succeed? It all depends on the effectiveness of the opposition campaign, for there are a great many unpleasant questions which can and should be asked. The so-called threat to the unity of the country, which has now acquired the dreadful forms of communal hatred and political assassination, is integrally and inseparably tied with the history of authoritarianism, mindless opportunism, corruption, and the extravagant use of state violence which were the hallmarks of Congress rule in the last decade and a half. It is no secret that the seeds of communal extremism of the Bhindranwale kind were sown with the active connivance of the Congress(I), in the years when its sole political objective was to discredit and disunite its electoral opponents in Punjab. Its pretensions to a democratic political process were shown to be a complete sham as recently as four months ago — in the series of government topplings in Sikkim, Kashmir and Andhra. Despite the much-vaunted achievements in high technology and the hosting of international sporting events, its economic policies have led, in the last few years and perhaps more decisively than ever before, to a rapid sharpening of income differences between a top crust of luxury consumers and a huge substratum of the poor and dispossessed, reeling under the impact of ever-increasing inflation. About the administrative competence or moral integrity of the present leaders of the ruling gentry, the less said the better — the cases of A.R. Antulay and Ramrao Adik have temporarily receded from the front pages of national dailies, but they cannot be forgotten, for they were by no means exceptional cases. And as to cohesiveness and mutual trust within the party itself, the cracks have only just been papered over by organizing a lightning succession to the highest office and presenting Congress members with a *fait accompli*; the cracks will reappear as soon as tickets are distributed for the coming elections.

Despite the presumed wave in favour of the Congress(I) in the northern states, the talk of a landslide Congress victory is not wholly credible. In the last Lok Sabha, the Congress(I) had won a huge majority of seats from the south — 42 out of 42 in Andhra, 27 out of 28 in Karnataka. It may now lose most of those seats. In Maharashtra, Gujarat, Rajasthan, Haryana, Uttar Pradesh, Madhya Pradesh and Bihar, most seats were won by narrow pluralities, and only because the opposition votes were more or less evenly split between two contending candidates. A reasonable degree of opposition unity can still make things extremely difficult for the Congress(I), even assuming that a certain wind of sympathy will blow in its favour in the northern states. But perhaps the petty ambitions, greed, shortsightedness and unprincipled opportunism that has characterized so much of opposition politics in recent years will prevail. That is surely what the computer boys at 1, Akbar Road are counting on. If they are proved right, they will then embark on their cherished project of giving a new look to India's economy and polity. For the vast majority of the people of this country, that can only be a change for the worse.

8

The Writing on the Wall

There is much talk these days about a national crisis. The year 1984 had opened for us with a smug dismissal of George Orwell's apocalyptic predictions. Little did we know then that the year would have in store some of the most harrowing experiences in our country's recent history. As 1984 comes to a close, a feeling of anxiety and uncertainty has gripped every segment of political opinion in India.

The crisis this time is not immediately an economic one, although there are crucial economic questions which are tied to it at a more basic level. Viewed from the standpoint of the ruling classes, particularly that of big capital, 1984 has been a relatively comfortable year; and with the new emphasis on high technology, import liberalization and relaxation of controls having taken a quite definite shape, Indian industrialists were looking forward to a period of relatively rapid expansion and accumulation. This is why the present crisis has emerged even more sharply in its purely political form.

Essentially, it is a very deep crisis in the political organization of the Indian ruling class. Never since 1947 has the structure of political rule in India faced such terrible possibilities of rupture and disintegration. In fact, one might even argue that never since the 1930s, when the Congress acquired its fully developed form as an organization of national power, have the Indian ruling classes been brought face to face with such a crisis of organized political leadership. It is not simply a question of the absence of national leaders — personalities possessing the requisite authority to speak on behalf of 'the nation', whether in the ruling Congress party or in the opposition. This absence is symptomatic of a much more fundamental problem of political organization. It is there that the crisis truly lies.

How has this situation come about? Recall the 'bright' days of the post-colonial state in India. The Nehru era saw this state in full blossom — not because of what it was able to achieve in improving the conditions in which the Indian people live and work (the so-called 'progressive' aspects of Nehru's politics, over which our present generation of 'progressive' intellectuals wax so eloquent), but because it represented the fullest development yet of what this state was meant to be as a viable machinery of power exercised by the ruling classes. It was an elaborate system of balances, structured hierarchically as well as over geographical regions, providing for a reasonable degree of autonomy at each level. This process of balancing between the different sectional interests within the ruling class alliance was sustained by a federally structured party organization, led and managed by local, regional and national leaders enjoying considerable popular support on their own, and each having a recognized area of legitimate operation. Above it all was the charismatic personality of Nehru himself, standing above all sectional interests, his power not despotic but rather that of a supreme arbiter and guide. A Caesarist leadership and an interventionist state, but within a complex political organization which ensured the rule of a not necessarily harmonious alliance of dominant classes in a system of electoral democracy.

This 'golden' age could not survive the repeated crises of the 1960s. After the many uncertainties of the mid-1960s, caused by the massive food crisis, devaluation, the two wars with China and Pakistan and the shock of the Congress defeats in several states in 1967, the polity was reorganized on a new basis after the split in the ruling party. Indira Gandhi's Congress was never the same as Nehru's Congress, and the longer she exercised power the more different it became. The basic accent was now on the centralizing of executive power, and with it, the centralizing of the balancing mechanism. Thus, the representational function of the ruling party, which was earlier diffused and layered across different levels and regions, was now concentrated in the fountainhead of all representation — the person of the Prime Minister who, beyond all political divides, loyalties, interest groups, etc., supposedly stood in a direct relationship with the nation. The consequences for the polity were: concentration of executive power in the central cabinet and bureaucracy; the devaluation of Parliament and the legislative organs; the virtual elimination of internal democracy and federalism within the Congress party;

and hence, the vast accumulation of arbitrary power in the hands of a small leadership, which took upon itself the ultimate responsibility of maintaining the delicate balances between the different power groups, regional interests, sectional lobbies and so on that make up, in concrete terms, the ruling class alliance.

To be sure, this centralizing tendency, and an increasing reliance on state violence to meet oppositional moves, was itself a response to growing unrest, and to agitational movements by the oppressed classes as well as by disaffected sections from within the ruling alliance. As is usual for such politics, concentration itself aggravates divisive tendencies, and these in turn are met by still more centralization.

The Emergency and After

The difficulties of this system as a viable representative machinery for the exercise of power became clear during the Emergency period. If nothing else, the Emergency showed the inherent difficulties of an undemocratic and centralized system in maintaining the balance between different sections of the bourgeoisie and the powerful landed interests divided up regionally and locally. It also showed how massive the information gap could become between the governing authority and the state of popular opinion.

Mrs Gandhi's return to power in 1980 did not alter these tendencies. The Indian ruling classes, it seemed, had no option but to go along with Indira Gandhi's political organization; no other viable organization of class rule seemed available after the rapid break-up of the Janata alliance.

The critical dangers of the system have now been revealed. In fact, the signs were appearing in the last two or three years. In the sphere of the economy, a shift in direction was asked for and accomplished. Thus, the opening up of the Indian economy, relaxation of controls, import of high technology, and greater access to foreign funds for investment have all now become established policy in the sphere of industrial development. But the nexus between government decision-making and corporate funding of powerful political groups, at their current levels of operation, had dangerous possibilities of arbitrariness and manipulation for narrow political interests. The Swraj Paul–Escorts affair has sent shock waves through Indian big industry, and such tremendous concentration of arbitrary power in the hands of a political leadership can never be conducive to the maintenance of a stable climate which the big bourgeoisie desire.

Even more than this, Assam, Punjab and Andhra showed that the ruling Congress(I) leadership in Mrs Gandhi's last year no longer had the political acumen to manage the polity even as a machinery of class rule. The problem was not the sudden 'emergence' of regional and sectarian tendencies. Such tendencies are inherent in India's multinational polity. The point of an effective ruling machinery is precisely to manage the contrary tendencies within a viable state order. It is not that there were no linguistic or religious movements in India in the 1950s or 1960s — some of these movements, such as in Andhra, Maharashtra, Telengana, or even Punjab — were no less massive than the recent movements in Assam and Punjab. The problem is that the present ruling party fundamentally lacks the means to contain, defuse and finally appropriate these movements within itself. This is the state to which Mrs Gandhi's politics has reduced every organ of legitimate class rule in India. She reduced the ruling party to a shambles, and left behind a bureaucracy ridden by corruption and factional loyalties. The country's economic institutions have been rendered subservient and impotent, and finally, after Operation Blue Star, even the army is suffering from an unprecedented crisis in morale. It is a terrible historical irony that Indira Gandhi, who always spoke of the need for a strong state under firm and determined central leadership, finally failed the Indian ruling classes on whose behalf she was meant to rule.

Fundamental Crisis

This is the most significant dimension of the present crisis. It is a fundamental crisis of the state. There are few alternatives which are open. Perhaps many are hoping that Rajiv Gandhi will win a substantial majority in the forthcoming elections and renew the ruling organization under a legitimate and viable leadership. But the signs are not hopeful, not only because the election prospects themselves remain uncertain, but because the political acumen of the new leadership — its appalling inexperience, a distressing narrowness of political vision and the apprehensions of 'coterie rule' — is highly suspect. It is now well known that the fiasco of N.T. Rama Rao's abortive ouster, the farcical attempt to set up Santa Singh as the representative voice of the Sikh people, and the widespread dissatisfaction with the distribution of tickets for the Lok Sabha elections — only partially mitigated after Kamalapati Tripathi's threatened revolt — were all results of the inept political acts of the coterie. The present campaign of false-hood, vilification, barely concealed Hindu communalism and obtuse hostility against the opposition being carried out by Rajiv Gandhi himself will not raise hopes that the new leadership will be able the reorganize a legitimate and popular basis for the exercise of class rule. Besides, the situation within the ruling party itself is such that there is no guarantee that even a sizeable majority in Parliament will ensure a stable Congress government at the Centre.

No Viable Organization

That then is the writing on the wall. The ruling classes in India no longer have a viable political organization of class rule. And they have very few options left. This is why the indecision and immobility on the part of the Left becomes still more significant. True enough, there is no realistic basis today to claim that the Left in India can itself step into the breach and immediately take up the mantle of a national alternative, although there are many instances in history where even more dramatic transformations have occurred. But the Left must face this fundamental crisis of the state, and work out in its campaigns and programmes the outlines of an alternative. This cannot be done if slogans such as national unity, secularism, divisive tendencies, etc. are adopted by the Left on the same basis and in the same terms as those laid down by the ruling classes. For, today these are precisely the slogans which offer the Left the opportunity to launch a fun-damental critique of the Indian Constitution and the Indian state order as it exists now. Unfortunately, the electoral Left is shying away from this task. Instead, we hear 'progressive' intellectuals shamelessly pleading for support to Rajiv Gandhi in order to 'protect the unity, integrity and progressive development' of the country. Or else, we see the two communist parties criticizing the failures of the Congress(I) and speculating on the relative merits of possible opposition candidates for the Prime Minister's office, but stopping short of analysing the consequences of a prolonged period of governmental instability at the Centre.

There can be no doubt that the foremost electoral task today is to defeat the Congress(I). But the crucial political task is to educate the people that an unstable structure of central power is proof that the ruling classes are unable to rule India, and that instead of this being a cause for fear and anxiety, it offers wholly new opportunities for popular mobilization and radical transformation.

9

Rajiv's Regime: The Rise

25 February 1985: Wanted Another Mandate[1]

It is the final wiping of the slate. After this, everything will begin afresh. Or that at least is what the new rulers of the country have sought to convey to the electorate. The Assembly elections on 2 and 5 March 1985 in eleven states and the Union Territory of Pondicherry must put the final stamp of popular approval on the new project before the nation: to do away with the corrupt and inefficient system of old and bring in a fresh, clean, dynamic and forward-looking system of administration. And the indications are that, except in Andhra Pradesh and Karnataka, Rajiv Gandhi's Congress(I) will coast through to comfortable margins of victory. This is despite the fact that traditionally the Congress has done worse at Assembly elections than in elections to the Lok Sabha, and despite the possibility that the very expectation of easy victory will mean a low turnout and a drop in the winning margins.

Once again it is Rajiv Gandhi's election. The new government has done remarkably well in its first two months in giving the impression of undertaking wholesale changes in policy without actually doing anything. Every now and then, one has heard announcements — from the Prime Minister himself or from some of those reputed to be among his close advisers — that there will be a completely new policy on taxes, industry, foreign trade, education, administrative recruitment and numerous other areas; but except for vague professions of intent, nothing tangible has emerged so far. Even Punjab and Assam, which were said to have been top priorities in the new government's agenda of problems that needed immediate solution, remain in exactly the same state as they were before the Lok Sabha elections. On some

[1] *Frontier*, 17, 28 (2 March 1985).

of these issues, Rajiv Gandhi's position seems to be that the best way to solve these problems is to deny altogether that they exist. On the Delhi riots, for instance, he has gone on record as saying that commissions of inquiry or prosecutions would only reopen old wounds, which would not be in the interests of the security of the Sikhs, and that therefore, it was best to treat the riots as a thing of the past. And so the perpetrators of one of the worst communal holocausts in independent India have been given a clean chit by a Prime Minister whose main promise is 'clean' government.

The cleansing operations have, of course, been carried out with much fanfare in the Congress(I) stables. Drastic changes were made in the lists of nominations to the various Assembly constituencies. Between 25 and 50 per cent of sitting Congress MLAs in different states, including a large number of ministers, were dropped from the lists because of charges of corruption, casteism or inefficiency. As a result, practically every established power group or faction within the Congress(I) has been hurt. In many cases, the disaffected power lobbies have put up rebel candidates. There are, of course, many snags in this so-called cleaning-up operation; detailed studies of the lists have revealed many names with not-so-saintly reputations that have somehow passed through the sieve, and what is more, a very large number who are close relatives of people who are supposed to have been axed. But the intentions behind the operations are clear: Rajiv Gandhi would like to have a party of his own, but more than that, he would like to keep alive for as long as possible the impression that he is changing things. It is of course a dangerous game in the uncertain world of electoral politics to keep raising popular expectations to such high levels without actually having concrete ideas on how to achieve them; but he has so far ridden the crest of a wave, and surely wishes to stay there as long as possible.

His task has been made easier by the pathetic condition of the opposition. Except for Andhra Pradesh, where N.T. Rama Rao and his Telugu Desam are aiming to repeat their 1983 and 1984 victories, and Karnataka, where despite the breakdown of the alliance between the Janata and the BJP, Ramakrishna Hegde will at least be fighting hard to retain his government, the opposition in every other state is yet to recover from a state of shock.

The real test will begin after the polls — when the rulers try to match up to the claims they have themselves made about their intentions and capabilities. The Indian electorate, they will remember, does not deny a serious claimant to power a fair chance; but it is cruel to those who let it down.

13 May 1985: The Century and After[2]

Public celebrations to mark the centenary of the birth of the Indian National Congress began in New Delhi last week under the auspices of the Congress(I), with the full complement of official media coverage. Yet neither among Congress members nor among the general public was there any noticeable enthusiasm. The immediate political objective was to firmly instal Rajiv Gandhi as unquestioned leader of the party. To go by appearances, this objective was achieved, to the accompaniment of the usual panoply of obsequious display and sycophantic verbiage. More than ever before in its hundred-year history, the Congress today looks like a dynastic institution; and every time its glorious heritage is recalled, the obligatory names are Motilal, Jawaharlal and Indira — and now Rajiv to take us into the twenty-first century.

Given the state of activity in the party in recent weeks, marked as it has been by abject surrender to the dictates of the ruling caucus around the Prime Minister, no one was expecting any political controversy at the AICC session immediately preceding the public celebrations. Yet it did show up, perhaps not quite a controversy, but at least an inkling of certain underlying tensions, with ideological as well as organizational overtones. The economic resolutions adopted by the AICC reaffirmed 'unequivocally its commitment to socialism'; socialism was the goal 'because in India's social and economic conditions, no other way was conceivable for solving the problems of the people'. This statement, it transpired, was a major departure from the original draft proposed by V.P. Singh, the Union Finance Minister. The drafting committee for the AICC's economic resolution apparently became the forum for a significant discussion on the policies of the present government. Apart from emphasizing the continued

2 *Frontier*, 17, 39 (18 May 1985).

relevance of Jawaharlal's socialistic orientation, the committee insisted on several other changes to V.P. Singh's draft, including complete deletion of any reference to the introduction of modern technology, and inclusion of a paragraph expressing concern at 'the unwarranted upward trend in the prices of some commodities'. As Congress resolutions go, there was nothing particularly striking in these statements; but such has been the tone of the recent pronouncements of the Prime Minister and his economic pundits in residence, that the note of discord sounded in the AICC could hardly be missed.

There is emerging, it would seem, a considerable hiatus between the economic dreams of the present rulers and the political compulsions of ruling the country. Rajiv Gandhi and his cronies speak of bringing in modern technology, giving greater incentives to the private corporate sector, inviting foreign investors, and removing the inefficiencies of the public sector as the solution to the poverty and stagnation of the country. Whether this is naive ideology or an astonishingly narrow class interest, one cannot tell; perhaps it is a bit of both. It is this brand of thinking that was reflected in the recent budget proposals.

But the political compulsions of ruling within a framework of electoral democracy impose an entirely different set of constraints on economic policy. The implications of the budget for the common man have become apparent in a dramatically short time, with a whopping 2.3 per cent price rise in five weeks. Taken together with the recent by-election reverses, it is hardly surprising that many Congress members have become worried about how they will keep their constituents quiet. The message from the AICC to the new leadership is clear: tread cautiously.

For the moment at least, Rajiv Gandhi seems to have read the message. At the public sessions, he dutifully mouthed all the obligatory slogans about socialism, the public sector and anti-poverty programmes. This has worried his supporters in the business world, who have seen in this an unexpected and entirely undesirable buckling under pressure. Of course, the framers of India's economic programme for the twenty-first century have hardly given up; after all, they have only just begun. But the signs are clear that their plans will not go through without a considerable political struggle, even within the ruling power bloc.

For a hundred years, the Congress has served its historical

role as the principal political organization of the Indian ruling classes. As such, it has also reflected on its surface the many contradictions among those classes. No matter how impatient the party's new leader may be with the slow and contentious process of political bargaining which has characterized the way the organization has functioned over these years, he is unlikely to succeed in keeping together a viable coalition of ruling class interests if he chooses to bypass the organization altogether. And senior Congress members are trying to explain to their inexperienced prince the lesson of one hundred years of politics; without a viable ruling class coalition, you cannot beat back the challenge of those you have to rule!

20 May 1985: Another Black Act[3]

The Union government has seemingly exhausted its political resources in trying to produce a settlement in Punjab. The brief spell of attempts at negotiation was shattered in early May by the series of bomb explosions in various north Indian towns. Now the government seems to have decided once again to 'get tough'. Among the many measures being adopted is a new piece of legislation giving it sweeping powers to deal with 'terrorism'.

The Terrorist and Disruptive Activities (Prevention) Bill was tabled in Parliament on 18 May 1985, and at the time of writing it has yet to be debated and passed. But the provisions are clear enough. The Bill gives a detailed definition of what constitute 'terrorist acts' and 'disruptive activities', provides a maximum punishment of death for such offences, and empowers the government to set up 'designated courts' for the speedy trial of such cases.

A 'terrorist act' is now defined as involving the use of bombs or other explosives, inflammable substances, firearms or other lethal weapons, poisons, noxious gases or other chemicals, in order to cause death or injury to persons or destruction of property or disruption of essential services, the intention being to overawe the government or to strike terror in the people or to adversely affect the harmony among different sections of the people. Whoever commits a 'terrorist act' will now be punishable

[3] *Frontier*, 17, 40 (25 May 1985).

by death. Even if such an act does not kill, the offender will be imprisoned for a minimum of five years, extendable to life.

These provisions are, of course, for explicitly violent acts of terrorism. But even more wide-ranging are the powers claimed by the government to contain 'disruptive activities'. Such activities are defined to include 'any action taken, whether by act or by speech or song or ballad or verse or words or by any book, pamphlet, paper, writing, record, tape, video cassette, drawing, painting, representation or in any manner whatsoever which questions, disrupts or is intended to disrupt, whether directly or indirectly, the sovereignty and territorial integrity of India or which is intended to bring about or support any claim, whether directly or indirectly, for the cession of any part of India or the secession of any part of India from the Union'.

Further, any act which 'advocates, advises, suggests, incites, predicts, prophesies, pronounces or otherwise expresses, in such a manner as to incite, advise, suggest or prompt' the killing of any public servant will be deemed a disruptive activity. The minimum period of imprisonment for such an offence will be three years, and the maximum, for life.

These provisions are ostensibly intended to deal with inflammatory and secessionist propaganda. But the terms are so broad that virtually any kind of oppositional agitation can be brought under its sway (note the very redundancy of the items listed as offences). Besides, the Bill gives the Union government immense administrative powers to deal with 'terrorist and disruptive activities'. These include censorship, entry into any place suspected of harbouring terrorists, prohibiting meetings and processions, demolition of buildings, preventing circulation of reports likely to promote hatred between different classes of people, and the right to compel any person to comply with any scheme for the prevention of terrorist acts.

Once again, therefore, the government is claiming extraordinary powers to deal with internal political instability. No one will dispute the need to take active security measures to protect state dignitaries, or disagree that the outrageous tactics of bomb attacks on unsuspecting people in buses, trains and public places need to be foiled. It is also quite clear that as far as Punjab is concerned, the so-called moderate Akalis have shown a pathetic political ineptitude in dealing with threats from the 'extremist' sections. Yet there can be no gainsaying the fact that it is the Union government which, through its actions over the last few years, is primarily responsible for creating the appalling mess which is Punjab today. And now it is claiming extraordinary powers to deal with 'terrorist and disruptive activities'.

It is one more proof, if proof is needed, of the utter incompetence of the law enforcement agencies of the state, including the police and the intelligence services, to do their job within the normal ambit of the law. The greater their failure, the more they clamour for extraordinary powers. The latest legislation to deal with 'terrorism' is tantamount to giving the administration the powers to act as in times of Emergency, without actually declaring it. And who are being entrusted with these extraordinary powers in the belief that they will use them with discretion? A bureaucracy which has distinguished itself by selling official secrets for bottles of whiskey, and a police which only the other day went on a rampage in Ahmedabad because the newspapers had complained about them.

The pretext for claiming greater and more arbitrary executive powers has been carefully prepared. Now the claim has been made. And more is being promised in the form of an Anti-Sedition Bill in the next session of Parliament.

3 June 1985: No Peace in Sight[4]

Amidst massive security arrangements and the full blast of media publicity, the country has been made to await with much anxiety the course of events during what the press is referring to in a perfectly matter-of-fact way as 'genocide week'. The first of June was the day when 'Operation Blue Star' was launched, and this is the first anniversary of those fateful days when the Golden Temple in Amritsar was stormed by the Indian armed forces. After the series of bomb blasts in several north Indian towns a few weeks ago, which effectively scuttled for the time being the various inchoate moves towards a negotiated solution to the Punjab crisis, it was widely apprehended that there would be more trouble in the first week of June. Security arrangements were made on a quite unprecedented scale. All road, rail and air

[4] *Frontier*, 17, 42 (8 June 1985).

traffic proceeding to and from the north of Delhi have been subjected to meticulous security checks. The border with Pakistan has been sealed off, ostensibly to block the smuggling of arms and personnel across the border. Police and intelligence forces in most north Indian cities are on full alert. Thousands of people suspected of having 'terrorist' connections have been arrested. And in Punjab itself, the armed forces have been deployed on a massive scale. Until the time of writing, however, no major incident has been reported from anywhere in the country.

In the meantime, the prospects of any solution to the immediate problem in Punjab seem as elusive as ever. It appears that the possibility of a settlement with the Longowal group in the Akali Dal has been given up: not only because of the factionally inspired impediments put up by the Tohra and Badal groups, but also in recognition of the plain fact that Harcharan Singh Longowal does not possess the credibility and moral authority to make a settlement which would be acceptable to the various sections of organized opinion among the Sikh people. There is no doubt that those who are described as 'extremists' enjoy considerable prestige and popular support. This section has now found a new symbol of public identity in the person of Baba Joginder Singh, father of the deceased Bhindranwale. There are speculations that the government is looking for a suitable opportunity to strike a deal with at least a sizeable section of the 'extremists' through Joginder Singh. If this is so, it would not be surprising if the venerable Baba feels it necessary to start by making a lot of defiant noises.

In objective terms, the government is counting on the fact that the most important organized interests which are said to be behind the recent spate of agitations in Punjab, would certainly prefer a solution which gives them more power within the framework of the Indian Union. Once again, objectively, this would demand a more broad-based and democratic devolution of power at the regional and local levels of government. The difficulty is that in the course of the last decade and a half, the Indian ruling classes and their political leaders have continuously undermined those very political institutions which could have made such a solution possible. Pushed into a crisis by its own political incompetence, the government must now rely on the armed forces to suppress the people while the bureaucrats fumble their way in search of a negotiated solution. No one has the moral authority to make a settlement stick. No one can claim that he has control over his own supporters. Even the government is not sure how the Congress(I) politicians in Punjab, or in neighbouring Haryana, Himachal Pradesh, Jammu and Kashmir or Western UP, will take to a negotiated settlement with the Akalis. And so the stalemate continues, broken periodically by sudden bursts of insane violence and the no-less-disagreeable ordeal of a peace enforced by armed strength.

17 June 1985: Gujarat Still in Flames[5]

It is already being called the longest 'riot' since independence, having continued for over four months. Is it a riot? A series of riots? A civil war? Or is it society breaking apart, a war of all against all? The labels do not matter any more, and as political observers and social analysts spout one new 'theory' after another on the Gujarat phenomenon, each explanation seems as true or as unenlightening as the next.

In terms of the immediate political situation, it is evident that all semblance of legitimate authority in the form of a civil administration has virtually evaporated from the towns and cities of Gujarat. If the eruptions of violence seem to die down from time to time, it is either out of sheer exhaustion or because of the heavy deployment of armed troops in the troubled areas. And soon after, the violence explodes somewhere else. The immediate issue which sparked off the trouble was the question of reserved seats in educational institutions for 'backward castes' in addition to the statutory quotas for 'scheduled castes and tribes'. The Madhavsingh Solanki government was thought to be 'pampering' the backward castes, particularly the Kshatriyas, for electoral reasons. The upper castes got together under the banner of the anti-reservation campaign, ostensibly to fight for equality and merit. As always, the first target of the agitation was the government and its law-enforcement agencies. The police retaliated with unseemly arbitrariness and complete disregard for the processes of law. The floodgates were

5 *Frontier*, 17, 44 (22 June 1985).

opened, Every interest seemed to require its own instruments of armed protection. Criminals had a field day, offering their services for the technical organization of civil violence. Targets proliferated, offence and defence blurred into a medley of organized armed clashes between upper castes and backward castes, backward castes and scheduled castes, Hindus and Muslims, until no one knew any more the precise lines of alliance and antagonism.

The 'causes' of the continuing violence are now a subject of much discussion. The very proliferation of 'theories' on the subject is an indication that, in a quite fundamental sense, the processes of change now under way in India's economy and society are eluding the comprehension of policymakers as well as their critics. It is certain that the spread of capitalism in agriculture in the last two decades, the eviction from the land of large sections of the rural poor, the growing economic and political aspirations of the regional and local bourgeoisie spawned by this process, the rapid and seemingly irreversible obsolescence of the traditional sectors of Indian big industry, the rapid spread of an underpaid and unorganized 'informal' industrial sector, the increasing insecurity of the literati and urban middle classes — all of these have something to do with what is happening today in Punjab or Assam or Gujarat. The question is not simply one of the intrinsic theoretical or ethical merits of the case for 'reservations for the uplift of the socially disprivileged castes'. The more crucial problem is the inability of the political process either to constrain the new forces and antagonisms within a framework of legitimacy and order, or to channelize them into an organized struggle for revolutionary change. Thus, both the defence of privilege and the demands for an end to privilege remain sectional, fragmented, open to manipulation and, in an atmosphere of pervasive violence, to criminalization.

The irony is that the greater the proliferation of sectionally organized and criminally inspired violence, the stronger the claims of the government for extraordinary powers to maintain 'law and order', and the feebler the will and the ability of the parliamentary opposition to resist those claims. We have seen this happen in the case of the Anti-Terrorist Act as a sequel to the Punjab events.

30 July 1985: The Punjab Pact[6]

What is the accord? It is perhaps the first-ever formal 'accord' signed between a Prime Minister of India and thè leaders of an opposition agitation. What does that indicate? The gravity of the Punjab problem? Its unprecedented nature? A new style of leadership which Rajiv Gandhi wishes to foster? Or perhaps, sheer thoughtlessness about the implications of such a precedent for the future governance of such a large and variegated political entity as India?

What are the terms of the accord? Eleven points were agreed upon, of which three — the territorial claims of Punjab to Chandigarh and of Haryana to the Hindi-speaking areas of Punjab, the dispute over the sharing of the Ravi–Beas waters between Punjab, Haryana and Rajasthan, and the Akali Dal demand for revision of Centre–State relations — have been on the agenda for several years now. Of the others, those relating to an enquiry into the November 1984 riots, rehabilitation of army deserters, the disposal of cases in special courts in Punjab, and compensation for property damaged in agitations and armed action, arose in the course of events following upon the army action in Punjab in June 1984. The government has conceded the demand for a judicial enquiry into the riots in Delhi as well as in Bokaro and Kanpur. The cases under the Armed Forces Special Powers Act will be withdrawn. Only those charged with waging war and hijacking will be tried at special courts; all other cases will be transferred to ordinary courts. People whose property has been damaged 'in agitation or any action after 1 August 1982' will be compensated. Deserters will not be taken back into the army, but will be provided 'gainful employment'.

Of the more long-standing demands, the agreement on the disputes over territory and river waters had been available for a long time. The obvious argument can be made that if the fundamental points had been sorted out as late as early-1984, the tragedy of Punjab could well have been avoided. What prevented such an agreement? Disunity and indecision among the Akalis, the unwillingness of the Congress(I) to concede a 'victory' to the Akali Dal, and the fear of loss of Hindu support

[6] *Frontier*, 17, 50 (3 August 1985).

in Haryana, western UP and Rajasthan. Have these calculations changed now, after a bloody army action, a Prime Minister assassinated, and the worst communal carnage in post-independence India? That is what the publicists would have us believe. But the proof is still to come. Three months ago they were saying that an agreement with the Akalis was impossible because they had no credible leaders. Now, suddenly, Sant Longowal has emerged as the universally accepted leader of the Sikhs. The transformation is hardly credible. It is still to be seen to what extent the Sant can carry, not just the faction-ridden band of *jathedars,* but the Sikh masses among whom a sense of injury and injustice has deepened far more in the last year or so than disputes over river waters. On the other side of the fence, it is obvious that all is not well with the 'Hindu vote bank' in Haryana and Rajasthan. For the time being, New Delhi has been able to muzzle the anxieties of Congress(I) leaders in those states, but the opposition can hardly be expected to let such a juicy agitational opportunity slip by. How local Congress members react to such an agitation needs to be watched. In other words, Rajiv Gandhi and his chief adviser on this matter — Arjun Singh, Governor of Punjab — have sought to use the accord with Sant Longowal to signal a dramatic change of scene, but it is not at all clear that the underlying political and organizational conditions have changed all that much.

Even more interesting is the question of Centre–State relations and the Anandpur Sahib resolution. During the December 1984 elections, Mr Gandhi had flogged the resolution for its 'anti-national and secessionist' overtones and castigated every opposition party for not having opposed it. Now, apparently, he is satisfied by the assurance of Sant Longowal that the resolution is 'within the framework of the Indian Constitution', and has agreed to refer it to the Sarkaria Commission. Most observers, including opposition leaders, have chosen to ignore this doublespeak. But this is perhaps the most crucial issue of the Indian polity which the Punjab events have brought to the surface — not the specific reference to the Sarkaria Commission, but the general problem of centralization of powers at the top of the structure, and the contrary tendency of the rise of 'regional power blocs'. Indira Gandhi had managed one sort of accommodation with the Tamil Nadu power bloc. Her son, after last year's fiascos over the attempted ouster of Mr Rama Rao, is attempting much the same sort of thing in Andhra. But Punjab is much closer to the centres of power, the emotional pitch of the dispute is much higher, and the people there have recently had much more direct exposure to 'great' political happenings. It is hardly likely that a power-sharing formula between a few Akali factions and the Congress(I) will resolve the fundamental tensions that are emerging in India's politics.

26 August 1985: The Gift Turns Sour[7]

The Punjab agony continues. Sant Harcharan Singh Longowal, once vilified by the Congress(I) for his inability to face up to the extremist threat, and in recent weeks hailed by the national press for his courage in taking the most decisive step so far in bringing peace to Punjab, has now been removed from the scene. Despite the proclamations of the Prime Minister, the future remains as uncertain as ever in that hapless part of the country.

Did the Sant's death have something to do with the sudden announcement of the decision to go in for immediate elections, despite the warnings of every opposition party including the Akali Dal itself? Was not an attempt on his life a virtual certainty? Looking back on events relating to Punjab in the last few weeks, the answer is a very definite 'yes'. And a review of these developments also brings out the utterly cynical calculations which lay behind the decisions taken by the rulers in New Delhi. The 'accord' was meant to signify their readiness to end a period of confrontation by coming to some arrangement of sharing power with the agitating groups in Punjab. After many explorations and experiments, they finally settled on Sant Longowal as the most acceptable partner with whom to strike this agreement. Immediately, there began an orchestrated media campaign celebrating the Prime Minister's youthful dynamism ('a government that works faster' is the latest slogan) and wisdom in seizing the right opportunity to bring peace to Punjab. The accord had been universally acclaimed in that state, and the 'extremists' were

[7] *Frontier*, 18, 2 (31 August 1985).

completely isolated — or so at least the media would have had us believe.

However, G.S. Tohra and Prakash Singh Badal, both of whom are far more adept at manipulative power-sharing politics than the late Sant Longowal, scrupulously dissociated themselves from the Sant as soon as the accord was announced. Underlying the mood of euphoria, the political realities in Punjab were far more complicated. This became clear from the unwillingness of every major political party in Punjab, except the Congress(I), to go in for elections. A competitive campaign for votes at this stage would only reopen the wounds, they said. The electorate could not but be split along communal lines, and with the tempo rising, the slogans would get more and more extreme on either side of the communal divide. Besides, the terrorist groups would surely try their best to scuttle the elections, by whatever means available.

New Delhi read these warnings as signs of the electoral weakness and organizational disarray of the opposition groups. The going was good, the rulers thought, for a quick Congress(I) victory in Punjab; or failing that, even a coalition with the Longowal group. Hasty calculations were made about how the Hindu vote or the Mazhabi Sikh vote would break, and how much abstention there was likely to be among Sikh voters because of extremist propaganda to boycott the elections. And then, in an amazing act of thoughtlessness, the Union government announced that elections would be held by 22 September 1985. Within three days, the Sant was dead.

What happens in Punjab now? The Prime Minister has reiterated that elections must be held; not to do so would be to surrender to the terrorists. The opposition parties — including a leaderless Akali Dal — are still, at the time of writing, pleading with New Delhi to postpone the elections. The terrorists have flexed their muscles once; everyone seems to be apprehending more trouble. The sense of relief has evaporated rapidly. It is true, perhaps, that terrorist acts of this sort enjoy very little active support among the people. But the wounds in Punjab are deep and still festering. It is significant that extremist groups are reported to have openly celebrated Sant Longowal's death in several cities in Punjab. Now the nation awaits with trepidation the next round of trouble.

30 September 1985: New Phase in Punjab[8]

The Akali Dal (Longowal group) has won an unprecedented victory in the Punjab elections. Taking as many as 29 seats away from the Congress(I), it has come out victorious in 73 of the 100 seats it contested, winning a clear majority in a house of 117. It has also won 7 of the 13 Lok Sabha seats from the state. An Akali ministry under the leadership of Surjit Singh Barnala has also been sworn in. Never in the history of Punjab has the Akali Dal formed a ministry on its own. In fact, a common saying in Punjab was that it never could, given the very small majority of Sikhs in the religious break-up of the state's population. It is ironical that the most bitterly communalist phase of Punjab's history since independence should end with such a sweeping victory for the Akali Dal, and that the victory should be greeted with such a widespread sense of relief.

Once again, the meticulous electoral arithmetic based on religion, caste, patronage, etc. has been thrown by the wayside in a massive swing of votes away from the Congress(I) and in favour of the Akali Dal. The Dal itself could hardly go into these elections with anything like its normal organizational preparedness. The Union government, by unilaterally declaring elections with only the minimum statutory period of notice, did not give any of the political parties — particularly the Akali Dal — time to recover and reorganize after nearly two years of extremely abnormal political conditions. On top of that, the tragic assassination of Sant Longowal, who until the day of his death was urging a postponement of elections, threw the party into still greater trouble. Mr Barnala appeared as the successor to the Sant, but his influence over such important faction leaders as Mr Badal and Mr Tohra seemed questionable. Yet, despite these organizational shortcomings (reflected in the fact that the Dal was finally able to put up candidates in only 100 of the 115 seats for which elections were held this time), it has won a victory which no political analyst of Punjab would have thought possible before the series of incidents that began with 'Operation Blue Star'.

News-reports indicate a much sharper polarization of votes along communal lines than ever before. The fundamental strategy

8 *Frontier*, 18, 7 (5 October 1985).

of the Congress in previous elections in Punjab had been to split the Sikh vote, especially by winning over the large scheduled-caste Mazhabi Sikh electorate. This time, it appears, the Mazhabi vote has uniformly gone in favour of the Akali Dal — such has been the emotional impact of the events following the storming of the Golden Temple, including the assassination of Sant Longowal. In some pockets, even Hindus have voted for the Dal as the best guarantee of peace in the state.

The popular verdict has proved, not what the bourgeois press is now claiming — that extreme communalist politics has no place in our present political system — but rather that extreme and violent communalism is allowed to raise its head when it becomes an instrument in the squabbles among the dominant class interests, and that the people are allowed to say 'no' to it only after a power-sharing arrangement has been worked out at the top. Organized terrorism of the kind practised in Punjab or Delhi, or financed and masterminded by extremist groups operating from abroad, does not require and never had a large popular support. This is indicated by the defeat in two constituencies of the widow of Beant Singh, one of those who killed Mrs Gandhi and was lionized by extremists and even moderates. As such, a popularly elected ministry in Punjab is no guarantee that such groups will cease to operate. Whether they will still have the support of powerful people in key positions is, of course, another matter.

The commercial and state media, in their usual fawning manner, have also showered praise on the Prime Minister for his 'wisdom' in sticking to his decision to hold the elections in Punjab, despite the pleadings of virtually every opposition party including the Akali Dal. The fact that the elections have gone through without much trouble is proof, they say, of Rajiv Gandhi's foresight and perspicacity. They have, of course, conveniently forgotten the fact that the run-up to these elections saw the killing of one of the foremost political leaders of Punjab, Sant Harcharan Singh Longowal, without whose cooperation there would have been no 'accord' and no election. Also not mentioned is the unprecedented, massive mobilization of security forces at the time of the elections.

Finally, what indeed will happen to the 'Punjab problem?' The Union government is said to be operating in terms of the so-called 'Tamil Nadu model', of allowing regionally dominant class forces to come to power in the state while working out a political alliance at the Centre. But in many ways, the Punjab case is quite different. For one thing, the dominant agrarian interests in Punjab are much more intimately linked with the all-India foodgrains economy. There has also been a massive accumulation of wealth in the hands of small and medium entrepreneurs in Punjab who are seeking to enter the world of all-India commerce. These forces cannot easily be accommodated within the present structure of the Indian economy without jeopardizing established monopoly interests. It is by no means certain, therefore, that the more basic dimensions of the 'Punjab problem' have been resolved in any significant way.

23 December 1985: The No-win Choice[9]

By-elections, it is said, usually turn out badly for the ruling party. People with even minor grievances go out and vote against the government, knowing fully well that the result can only shake things up a little; no major convulsion will be caused. That at least is how Congress(I) spokesmen are trying to explain the results of the latest by-polls. But even their supporters appear to be sceptical.

For, the signs of waning public support are clear. Of the Lok Sabha seats outside Assam, the Congress(I) has lost three important contests: Kishanganj in Bihar to the Janata (a seat the Congress(I) had held previously), Bolpur to the CPI(M), and Kendrapara also to the Janata. It has held four other seats — Churu in Rajasthan, Bijnaur in U.P., Banka in Bihar, and South Delhi — but all with considerably reduced majorities. Of the Assembly by-polls, the significant results are from Jullundur in Punjab where the BJP has won two urban and presumably predominantly Hindu seats, and from West Bengal where the CPI(M) has retained the Nanur seat in Birbhum despite much organizational embarrassment over the Banamali Das affair. Besides, the CPI(M) almost managed to snatch away the Aurangabad seat in Murshidabad, a traditionally Congress seat.

These signs emanating from various parts of the country do not, therefore, look good for the Congress(I). They cannot be

[9] *Frontier*, 18, 19 (28 December 1985).

explained away merely in terms of mid-term electoral impatience. First of all, it is only a year since the party under the new leadership of Rajiv Gandhi was swept into power under extraordinary circumstances. Those elections held a year ago were by no means normal, run-of-the-mill elections; and the new government, over the last year, has used every available opportunity to drive it into our heads that it is bent on making a clean break with the past. There has indeed been a conscious effort to bring in a change of style. Even so, the latest results show, if not a rejection, at least evidence that voters in different parts of the country have not been particularly impressed by the new style. It is now being said quite openly in Congress(I) circles that the new Prime Minister's clean-cut, modern-management style of functioning is not proving to be an effective vote-catching strategy among the larger electorate. And if a member of the Nehru family is not going to be a vote-catcher for the Congress, why have him at the top anyway?

These rumblings of discontent and dissension within the Congress(I) have grown louder with the decisive defeat of the party in Assam. Disproving every prediction, the newly formed Asom Gana Parishad, organizational successor to the movement which in the last six years has so often made Assam front-page news in the national dailies, has won an absolute majority. At the time of writing, it is set to form only the second non-Congress government in Assam since independence. The AGP virtually swept the Assamese vote, and was able to win a majority of seats despite the fact that it did not even contest in some 15 per cent of seats. On the other hand, the Congress(I) lost its traditional support among the minority and tribal populations of the state. The Bengali-speaking and Muslim voters flocked to support the newly constituted United Minorities Front, while the Plains Tribal Council has won more seats this time than ever before. The result is that the Congress(I) has ended up with a paltry 25 seats in a house of 125.

As far as election results go, the Assam results are decisive, for the AGP will have the chance to make its own government and to carry out its own programmes. As far as those programmes go, however, the portents are dire. The last several years saw a campaign against Bengali-speaking and predominantly Muslim 'immigrants' whom the movement leaders designated as 'foreigners'. That movement directed itself against the Union government and the Congress(I), principally because the Congress(I) in Assam was thought to be protecting minority interests for electoral purposes. Indira Gandhi had no qualms about using such divisive ploys for electoral gains: the outcome was the Nellie massacre and the farcical elections of 1983. Rajiv Gandhi, zealously setting out to 'solve' one after the other the 'problems' left behind by his mother, signed an 'accord' on Assam in the same way that he had on Punjab, and at one stroke signed away any viable electoral strategy for the Congress(I). For, the accord began to be flaunted by the protagonists of the Assam movement as their historic victory, whereas the minorities, made ever more insecure, felt they had been betrayed by the Congress(I). The polarization of votes was virtually complete: the Congress(I) became the loser on both sides.

Having won the elections, the AGP leaders are now trying to assuage the minorities by declaring that those who are 'genuine' Indian nationals have nothing to fear. Of their broader socio-economic programmes, nothing is known because nothing has been thought of. The AGP, after all, is an organization born out of a one-point movement. How far the new leadership will be able to control its hordes of overenthusiastic and chauvinistic supporters is anybody's guess. There is no doubt that the minorities in Assam will now carefully watch every move of the new government. The decisive electoral result has thus heightened the tension and anxieties in Assam, not resolved them.

At the all-India plane, Assam becomes the eighth state with a non-Congress government, not counting Tamil Nadu where the ruling party is an electoral ally of the Congress(I). Already, the discrepancy between the massive Congress(I) majority in Parliament and its lack of support in the states is becoming stark. More fundamentally, the strategy of the new leadership under Mr Gandhi seems to be to contain regional forces by allowing them a measure of power at the state level: not in the old way by absorbing them within the Congress, but by retaining their autonomous identity. Bureaucratically, the strategy might seem viable, because as long as the real powers rest with the central executive, it matters little if regional parties run the government in some of the states. The problem lies at the level of the ruling political party, for this strategy appears to have spelt doom for the state-level Congress leadership everywhere. And without nurturing support at this level, where will the central leadership find the popular support to sustain its new bureaucratic endeavours?

17 February 1986: Mosque or Temple?[10]

It seems like a throwback to the days of the Raj. A local dispute involving the conflicting claims of the 'Hindoo' and 'Moslem' communities; the judicial wing of the state called upon to pronounce its judgement by looking at the 'historical and other' evidence on the matter; a decision of the court which leads to open clashes 'between the two communities'. That is what we have witnessed in the last few weeks following an order of the district and sessions judge of Faizabad in Uttar Pradesh, directing the government to 'open forthwith' the gates of a place of worship in Ayodhya which for at least four hundred years has been known as the Babari mosque, but which some local Hindus claim was the site of a 2000-year-old temple which was converted into a mosque in Mughal times. The order was 'greeted with massive victory celebrations' by Hindu organizations in different U.P. towns, while Muslim organizations have launched a 'country-wide agitation' to demand the restoration of the Babari mosque. The tension is still building up, but already there has been a serious communal clash in Old Delhi and several minor incidents in different places in the country.

The history of the dispute itself reads like a history of Indian communalism in miniature. For more than three centuries, the particular premises in Ayodhya town had been a mosque, said to have been established by the first Mughal emperor. But stories had survived of its once having been a temple, built by none other than Emperor Vikramaditya, on the site of the birthplace of Rama. The recent spate of conflicts had its roots in the middle of the last century, when there was a series of Hindu–Muslim clashes all over northern India. That was a period of large-scale change, turmoil and realignment of power relations in the wake of the spread and consolidation of British rule in that region. It was then that wealthy and powerful

[10] *Frontier*, 18, 27 (22 February 1986).

Hindus in the area demanded that the status of the site as a place of worship of Rama be recognized. Sometime in the late 19th century, British administrators permitted both Hindus and Muslims to use the place for religious purposes in separate parts of the building. The latest phase of the dispute dates back to 1949, when a Hindu group forcibly entered the premises, installed idols of Rama and Sita, and declared it the Rama Janmabhumi temple. The matter went to court and had been lying there for the last thirty-six years, with numerous claims being made not only on the matter of the specific religious status of the building, but also on which particular group or individuals had rights of ownership over it. Now, on 31 January 1986, the district court has passed an order: not on the whole series of disputes before it, but simply clarifying a 1950 directive, to say that the premises should be unlocked to allow devotees to perform puja. This has been read as a sign of 'victory' by organizations such as the Vishwa Hindu Parishad and the RSS, and correspondingly by Muslim organizations as yet another violation of minority rights.

The matter is no longer something to do with the local history of a small town in U.P. It has been drawn into the vortex of communalist politics in India today. All-India Muslim bodies such as the Majlis-e-Mushawarat have launched campaigns throughout the country to mobilize Muslim opinion on the issue. The communal situation in India today is very delicately poised, and this has to do with the general feeling of crisis and uncertainty that has crept into political life given the continued intractability of the Punjab problem, the demise of familiar leaders and parties, and the sudden talk of rapid change without anyone being sure of where exactly we are heading. In a situation like this, minor matters can become major irritants, and there is no dearth of people and organizations who will do their utmost to exploit any available issue to make their voices heard. Besides, religion is good business, especially when associated with no less a personage than Lord Rama and the place of his birth. Behind the talk of ancient tradition and spirituality, there are hard-headed, money-minded people who are already fighting over the possible spoils of a Rama Janmabhumi temple made suddenly famous by being 'liberated' from the hands of the Muslims. And the ruling political order, having chosen to

function within exactly the same legal and administrative framework as the British colonial state, can only pronounce upon
the comparative merits of 'Hindu' and 'Muslim' claims, and
then send out the police to maintain 'law and order'.

10 March 1986: Walling Off Women?[11]

While the opposition to the proposed Muslim Women (Protection of Rights on Divorce) Bill has gained in strength over the
last two or three weeks, the government still seems bent upon
pushing it through Parliament in the current session. The reasons
which suddenly prompted the Prime Minister and his advisers
to decide to conciliate Muslim fundamentalist opinion were
unconvincing from the very beginning, even from a purely pragmatic standpoint. Now opinion against the move is mounting,
and is being voiced openly even within the Congress Parliamentary Party: the men who rule are now having to use the whip to
silence the dissenters, and to persuade the doubters that the
Prime Minister's political prestige is involved in the matter, for
which reason they must vote in favour of the Bill. Why the Prime
Minister should have allowed himself to get caught in a jam
entirely of his own making is of course a question that is being
politely avoided.

If one attempts to unravel the reasoning behind the government's move, the point to begin is the Supreme Court judgement
last year on the Shah Bano case. The Court had ruled that when
a Muslim woman is divorced, the responsibility of the husband
to provide maintenance was not restricted only to the so-called
iddat period of three months, and that the *mehr* promised at the
time of the wedding was not an adequate compensation for
divorce. It further ruled that if there was a conflict between
sections 125 and 127 of the Criminal Procedure Code and the
relevant sections of the Muslim Personal Law, the former must
prevail. This judgement was hailed in progressive circles as an
extremely bold move to defend the rights of Muslim women,
who normally do not have the means to demand even the min-
imal rights given to them under the *shari'a* but are burdened with
all the deprivation enjoined upon them by a harsh medieval

[11] *Frontier*, 18, 30 (15 March 1986).

religious code. Not surprisingly, the judgement led to protests from various conservative Muslim bodies. This was inevitable; but at least the signs were clear that the debate within the Muslim intelligentsia in India on matters of religious reform had reached a qualitatively new stage.

It is here that the thoughtlessness of Rajiv Gandhi's advisers altered the situation completely. With the economy not behaving in the way they had ordered, the Punjab problem — once believed to have been 'solved' — suddenly bouncing back with unexpected severity, and a series of by-election upsets, the ruling clique in New Delhi suddenly discovered that the people were no longer loving their rule the way they had a year ago. The advisers rummaged through their computer printouts, went into a huddle, and came up with the brilliant suggestion that the one electoral group which needed immediate conciliation was the Muslims. They seemed to be agitated by the Shah Bano judgement. Do something to please them, and that would ensure the support of a crucial minority group!

Thus came the Muslim Divorce Bill. It was drafted, the Prime Minister said, after consultation with 'Muslim opinion'. This could only have been the most conservative opinion going. The tactic was to get the Bill through Parliament as quickly as possible, without allowing much time for a debate to develop on the issue. But the opposition in Parliament succeeded in stalling the introduction of the Bill by a vital two days. In that time, a memorandum was submitted to the Prime Minister with an impressive list of signatures of Muslim intellectuals, including several who are not only known to be supporters of the Congress(I) but are closely associated with the present government. This gave the lie to the Prime Minister's claim that Muslim opinion had been consulted. Several women's organizations, including those of Muslim women, also protested against the Bill. Finally, the government's credibility was damaged beyond repair when Arif Mohammed Khan, Minister of State for Energy in the Union government, resigned from Rajiv Gandhi's ministry.

Reports indicate that there is considerable resistance to the Bill even within the solid phalanx of Congress(I) Members of Parliament. Much of this opposition, of course, comes not from any progressive appreciation of the role of the state in matters of religion. The new regime had played its Hindu-communal card with unconcealed glee in the days following the assassination of Indira Gandhi; and a large bulk of its supporters, firmly wedded to the dominant ideology of the 'cow belt', are now rejoicing at the so-called 'liberation' of the Ram Janmabhumi temple in Ayodhya. These are the people whom Rajiv Gandhi's aides are now finding it difficult to keep in line. On the other hand, the Congress has historically drawn towards it the support of much of the progressive opinion among Muslims. This section the government has now chosen to ignore. As a result, the regime finds itself in a mess.

5 May 1986: Right on Target[12]

Until a few days ago, it would have seemed to an outside observer that the terrorist groups in Punjab were on their last legs. Their actions were becoming indiscriminate and desperate. They were finding it far more difficult than before to get cover, and their reckless killings were turning them away from the very people they were supposed to be fighting for. The Akali Dal government under Surjit Singh Barnala seemed to be in control. Nevertheless, the situation seemed favourable enough for New Delhi to take decisive and firm 'police action' against the terrorist groups with the full support of the Barnala government.

Then, on 29 April 1986, came a 'declaration' from the so-called Panthic Committee that 'Khalistan' had been established in Punjab, and that a 'parallel government' was operating from the Golden Temple in Amritsar. It also made the extravagant declaration that ultimately Delhi would be the capital of Khalistan, and that the *Kesari* flag would fly on top of the Red Fort.

It was a farcical claim, and the government need not have taken it with greater seriousness than the many so-called 'governments in exile' which dissident Sikh groups have been running in Britain and Canada for several years now. But almost on cue, security measures were stepped up around the Golden Temple complex. Mr Barnala was in Delhi holding consultations with the central leadership. Twenty-four hours later, men of the CRP and the Punjab Police, along with a group of commandos, entered the Golden Temple, supposedly

---

[12] *Frontier*, 18, 38 (10 May 1986).

to round up the members of the 'parallel government'. Surprisingly, the police found not a single political activist of note.

There are strong indications that New Delhi, now represented in Chandigarh by the redoubtable Mr Siddhartha Shankar Ray and the new police chief Mr Ribeiro, was waiting for an opportunity to enter the Golden Temple complex which, despite the many splits and counter-splits in the ranks of the 'extremists' (many of them undoubtedly engineered by the government), was still functioning as the political headquarters of the rebels. Whether the 'Khalistan declaration' itself was part of the preparations for such a move is still a matter of speculation.

The police action in the temple has turned the situation against the Barnala government. Now he has been made to appear a complete stooge of Delhi, ordering the police into the precincts of the temple for no reason at all. It also appears that, while Mr Barnala discussed in general terms the subject of stronger steps against terrorism with his cabinet colleagues on the eve of the police action of April 30, he did not take specific clearance for the move.

The reaction set in within a few hours of the incident. There were four resignations from the Akali Dal ministry, and Mr P.S. Badal and Mr G.S. Tohra publicly dissociated themselves from Mr Barnala. Now as many as twenty-nine MLAs of the Akali Dal have reportedly signed a statement criticizing the police action. Even more significant are reports of widespread popular reaction among Sikhs, who are seeing the police action as a pointless desecration of the temple. Suddenly, Mr Barnala now seems friendless and isolated. His political predicament is not being helped by the declarations of support for him from the opposition groups in the Punjab Assembly. If the Barnala government has to survive with the help of the Congress(I), it will only strengthen the claim of his critics that he is a puppet acting at the behest of New Delhi.

19 May 1986: Retooling Democracy[13]

When the Congress(I) under Rajiv Gandhi won the elections barely a year and a half ago with the largest ever majority in the

[13] *Frontier*, 18, 40 (24 May 1986).

Lok Sabha, he had promised to give the country a clean, efficient and open government. Many at the time had greeted the announcement as a welcome change from the secretive and thoroughly despotic style of rule practised in his mother's time. They also thought that the fact that the government enjoyed such an unassailable majority in Parliament would help in bringing about this change. Rid of the constant anxiety about retaining support in the House, the new government, it was thought, could well afford to permit free flow of information and a certain degree of internal criticism. Parliamentary illusions die hard.

Nothing of the sort has happened. It took very little time for the euphoria to vanish. With that, it has become clear that the massive parliamentary majority, artificially propped up by the Anti-Defection Act, is devoid of all substance. Now the government seems jittery about any discussions in Parliament, not so much because of what the opposition would say, but because it is unsure of what its own party members might do. The recent Muslim Divorce Bill was rammed through the House after care was taken to gag potential critics in the Treasury benches — something one would have thought entirely unnecessary for a party which has more than three-fourths of the seats in the Lok Sabha.

And now it seems the government is keen to avoid Parliament as far as possible. It is resorting more and more to that familiar technique already perfected in many Congress(I)-ruled states: namely, rule by ordinance. But last week's ordinance on commissions of enquiry must go down as one of the crowning achievements of fraud and duplicity in the field of democratic government.

Barely two days after the closing of the budget session of Parliament, the government has announced that it will not be bound to place before Parliament, and hence before the people, the report of any commission of enquiry if it feels that its publication will jeopardize 'the national interest'. It is, of course, the executive branch of government which has been given the power to assess whether something in the report would harm the national interest, and therefore, whether it should be kept away from the prying eyes of the elected representatives of the people.

The fact that this latest edict of secret governance deals with commissions of enquiry makes the assault on even our so-called democracy doubly blatant. And the unscrupulousness and cynicism of the present bunch of rulers is made even clearer because the immediate pretext for the ordinance is also known. It appears that the report of the Thakkar Commission of Enquiry to probe into the assassination of Indira Gandhi has already been submitted, while that of the Ranganath Mishra Commission on communal killings in Delhi immediately following the assassination is on its way. Both events have been of monumental significance in the recent history of the country. And the second commission in question was set up after persistent demands from civil rights groups and opposition parties. In fact, the provision for setting up commissions of enquiry is justified by the need for an authoritative and impartial probe into the conduct of government officials and police functionaries, so that the people are satisfied that those who rule them do so in a fair and legitimate way. To say that commissions may be set up (at the cost of the public exchequer) to enquire into incidents in which the actions or motives of government personnel have been called to question, but that their findings may not be made public if the government so decides, is fraud of the worst kind imaginable.

There is rampant speculation about the exact reasons why those who are in power have felt it necessary to keep the findings of the Thakkar Commission a secret. Were important people implicated in the conspiracy to murder Mrs Gandhi? Whom are the rulers trying to protect?

9 June 1986: Tinkering Again[14]

New Delhi seems to be tying itself up in knots tackling that intractable problem of Punjab. In a mystifying move last week, the Haryana Chief Minister, Bhajan Lal, was asked to quit; and Bansi Lal, Union Defence Minister, sent to Chandigarh to head the Congress(I) government in Haryana. Bhajan Lal, faced with an angry popular mood skilfully fomented by the wily opposition leader Devi Lal, had made no secret of his lack of enthusiasm about the implementation of the Punjab accord. Now, New Delhi has seen it fit to send in the indestructible Bansi Lal to ram the unpopular accord down the throats of unwilling Haryana politicians.

14 *Frontier*, 18, 43 (14 June 1986).

The decision appeared to have taken most people by surprise. Bhajan Lal, it is reported, was prepared to answer the summons from New Delhi by organizing a large-scale resignation of Congress(I) MLAs were he asked to resign. In the end, he did nothing of the sort. Whether he was persuaded to desist from open revolt by promises of further personal advancement or by threats of dire consequences is not known. He accepted the decision of the High Command with apparent equanimity, and handed over his charge to Bansi Lal. The new Chief Minister immediately pronounced that the people of Haryana should be prepared to accept the unpalatable fact of the transfer of Chandigarh to Punjab, because it was 'in the overall national interest'. However, he immediately added that while Punjab would have formal jurisdiction over Chandigarh, the city would continue to serve as Haryana's capital for another five years or until such time as a new capital is built for Haryana. The argument was odd, because that has been precisely the ground on which Chandigarh has served as a dual capital for the last twenty years — ever since Indira Gandhi's agreement with Sant Fateh Singh on the terms of the Punjab–Haryana partition. So what is new in Bansi Lal's sincere resolve to implement the Punjab accord? One wonders whether Mrs Gandhi's trusted hatchet man was celebrating his return to Chandigarh by pulling yet another fast one 'in the national interest'.

There is another line of speculation which suggests that this sudden move has little to do with the transfer of Chandigarh, or the impending decision of the Venkatramaiah Commission on demarcating the Hindi-speaking regions of Punjab which should go to Haryana. Rather, the calculations range over a slightly longer time-frame to cover the Haryana Assembly elections early next year. Bhajan Lal, it is said, would have been unable to ensure a Congress(I) victory, because in an atmosphere of general resentment in Haryana over the events in Punjab, he would have had no means of finding any support from the formidable Jat lobby which has virtually ruled that state ever since its creation. Hence, the decision to send Haryana's most celebrated Jat politician Bansi Lal to Chandigarh, to try and recoup the Congress(I)'s electoral chances in his home base.

Whichever be the real reason behind the latest change of *subedars* in India's new imperial system, it is intimately connected with the continued intractability of the so-called Punjab problem. The Punjab accord has not been the magic solution it was claimed to be. Instead, it has led to further complications: a series of boundary commissions and political instability in Haryana being the most important of them. A vigorous attempt to tackle the 'extremists' in Punjab by massive use of state violence has not yielded any significant results. Despite the much-publicized appointment of Siddhartha Ray as the new Governor and the blank cheque give to the new police chief Ribeiro, all that has been accomplished is widespread state terror, a predictable rise in 'encounter deaths', and overflowing prisons. The spate of terrorist killings has not diminished, and a daily average of fifteen to twenty civilian deaths has become a routine affair. Insecurity, fear and a sense of hopelessness have struck deep roots in Punjab, and mutual distrust and antipathy between communities has reached a quite unprecedented level. Even the Punjab Chief Minister, Mr Barnala, has been forced to recognize the magnitude of the problem of migration of non-Sikh residents out of Punjab. In the midst of such a massive churning of the social set-up, with no apparent purpose except the spreading of hatred and mistrust among the people, the tinkering of the rulers in New Delhi with Governors, Chief Ministers and police chiefs cannot but seem somewhat puerile.

15 September 1986: Valley of Intrigues[15]

The political situation in Jammu and Kashmir continues to hang in a limbo with President's Rule being imposed on the state. Constitutionally, this is a slightly different procedure from Governor's Rule, a provision that exists only for Kashmir and which is how Mr Jagmohan, the present Governor, had been exercising his highly personalized rule over the valley. But there was no constitutional provision for extending Governor's Rule any further, and the rumour was rife that there would be some moves towards installing a popular government. Obviously, these moves have not yielded any results yet, or at least not results that would be satisfactory to the rulers in Delhi. Hence, central administration will continue in Jammu

15 *Frontier*, 19, 5 (20 September 1986).

and Kashmir under the more familiar procedures of President's Rule.

What has caused much greater sensation in Kashmir, however, is the story of an impending rapprochement between Farooq Abdullah and Rajiv Gandhi. Dr Abdullah has been, of course, in the frontline of the anti-Congress(I) forces in Kashmir ever since he was unceremoniously removed from power nearly three years ago, by the Congress(I) in league with G.M. Shah. But suddenly in the last few months, there seemed to appear signs that the leadership in New Delhi was searching for other alternatives, the experiment with the unpopular Shah government having failed miserably. And the strongest alternative was a coming to terms with Dr Abdullah. There was indeed a series of meetings between the Prime Minister and Dr Abdullah, in which the former is said to have suggested a coalition government between the Abdullah-led National Conference and the Congress(I). This suggestion Dr Abdullah rejected. But the efforts did not cease, and the ebullient successor to Sheikh Abdullah was appointed official leader of the Indian delegation to the Haj in Mecca. This Dr Abdullah accepted. Ever since his return from Mecca a few days ago, speculations have gained ground that new terms are being discussed.

The effects of these rumours in Kashmir cannot have gladdened Dr Abdullah's heart. There is said to be a 'whisper campaign' warning of a sell-out to Delhi. There are growing murmurs of discontent within the National Conference. Dr Abdullah's popularity in recent years has been no less due to his opposition to the Congress(I) and the halo of martyrdom at having been unfairly ousted from power by the machinations of New Delhi, than to his claim to be the real successor to Sheikh Abdullah's political legacy. Any hint of compromise on that position is bound to cost him dearly.

On the other hand, given the constraints imposed by New Delhi, and especially now in view of the continued instability in neighbouring Punjab and all the hullabaloo about security on the Pakistan borders, Dr Abdullah seems to have little alternative but to come to some kind of understanding with the central power. He is said to be insisting on fresh elections before the installation of any ministry in Jammu and Kashmir. He has also made strong public assertions rejecting any suggestion of a 'political sell-out'.

But he has also warned of the dangers posed by Muslim fundamentalist forces operating in the valley. There is no doubt that speculations on Dr Abdullah's secret confabulations with Mr Gandhi are grist to the propaganda mill of these fundamentalist forces.

New Delhi, as always, is viewing all this from the only standpoint it knows — the immediate costs and benefits. It had to do something in a hurry because Governor's Rule could not be extended any further. It tried the option of installing a coalition ministry with Farooq Abdullah. But this would have been political suicide for the latter. Delhi was then left with the only option of imposing President's Rule and delaying a long-term solution. At this moment, it cannot accept the risks of fresh elections in Jammu and Kashmir. But without it, any agreement with Dr Abdullah will cut at the roots of his political support in the valley. What will emerge victorious from all this are precisely those forces which the Prime Minister daily warns his countrymen against — those of religious fundamentalism and disruption.

3 November 1986: The Regional Dimension[16]

The 'accords' continue. As more and more power concentrates in the hands of the central executive, and particularly the office of the Prime Minister, the principal method to contain the opposing force of what is called 'regionalism' has become one where the chief executive personally negotiates a settlement with the regional leader by offering him a legitimate share of provincial power. This was done with the late Mr Longowal in Punjab, with Mr Prafulla Mahanta in Assam, and with Mr Laldenga in Mizoram. The same method has now been followed with Dr Farooq Abdullah in Jammu and Kashmir. It seems a somewhat new phenomenon in Indian politics. As a matter of fact, however, it is a rather old technique, received from the days when Hindustan was a sprawling empire, where provincial rebels who could not be put down by force were simply incorporated into the imperial structure of government by recognizing them as regional satraps. Indian democracy is, in more senses than one, a system of imperial rule.

16 *Frontier*, 19, 12 (8 November 1986).

What is called regionalism is not a recent product. There was a massive spell of regional movements in the 1950s and 1960s, which basically demanded the redrawing of the administrative boundaries of the states according to a linguistic principle. In the main, this demand was conceded. Thus we had the formation, after intense mass movements, of the states of Andhra, Gujarat, Maharashtra, Punjab and Haryana. In all these cases, the movements were at first directed against the ruling group in Delhi. In each case, however, once the main demand was conceded, the bulk of popular support was reintegrated into the ruling Congress party. This was accomplished not by an 'accord' with the rebel leaders, but rather by accommodating the principal content of the regional demand within the overall constitutional framework of federal rule. Thus, the very existence of a distinct regional political movement was made redundant, and the locally dominant forces found it far more profitable to insert themselves into the countrywide structure of the ruling Congress party. The relatively flexible and decentralized structure of the party itself made this possible in the 1950s and 1960s.

Both the framework of the Congress party and the process of governmental rule have changed fundamentally in the last two decades. The ruling party is now openly recognized as more or less the personal staff of its supreme leader — the Prime Minister. And the governmental structure has its centre in the Prime Minister's office, a few chosen advisers, and the topmost levels of the Union bureaucracy. The regional movements today have few specific demands. Whatever the nature of their leadership and whatever the particular issues on which they express themselves (and these vary from straightforward separatism as with the Khalistanis, to protection of Assamese identity with the AGP, to the restoration of Telugu honour in the case of Mr Rama Rao, to what is it now with the AIADMK?), the basis on which they draw their political support is a vague sense of disaffection with a system of government where the centre of power lies at a great distance from the people, and which seems to threaten their immediate and familiar cultural identities. All regional movements in recent years have been built around the question of cultural identity, and all have posed their demands in relation to the central power structure located in New Delhi.

Rajiv Gandhi, it is true, inherited these problems; he did not create them. He has proceeded to solve them by giving the regionalist leadership a legitimate share of governmental power. Thus far, the formula seems to have worked in Assam; Mizoram is too recent to enable one to make a judgement. It has clearly failed in Punjab. The government of Mr Barnala has been caught in the unenviable position of being regarded by the extremists as a stooge of New Delhi and by New Delhi as being soft on the extremists. Given the harrowing experience of daily violence on the people perpetrated both by terrorists and government forces, it cannot be said that the central framework of governmental rule has been validated in any way in the popular mind of Punjab.

It could well be argued that a similar scenario will unfold in the Kashmir valley. Farooq Abdullah was a champion of the popular opinion in Kashmir as long as he was seen as an implacable opponent of New Delhi. Now that he has taken, after much prevarication, the final step of entering into a coalition government with the Congress(I) without seeking a popular mandate at a general election, he is more likely than not to lose that basis of popular support. Perhaps there will be splits in the National Conference. The greater cause for apprehension is the definite possibility of the rise of communal tensions. The politics of ethnic loyalties is fertile ground for the play of reactionary politicians of all sorts, whether they operate from the citadels of power in New Delhi or whether they roam around the streets and bazaars in small provincial towns.

17 November 1986: Managing Congress[17]

Not so long ago, it was being said that the new Prime Minister would dismantle the decrepit structure of arbitrary authority built up in the days of his mother and bring in a whole new era of dynamic, democratic politics. Soon afterwards, we heard complaints that the Prime Minister was being manipulated by a small coterie of his friends: it was they who were running the show. Before, it was said that the new regime was youthful and forward-looking, not tied down by custom or protocol. Now we hear that this government acts first, thinks later. People have apparently had a lot of difficulty in deciding what

[17] *Frontier*, 19, 14 (22 November 1986).

Rajiv Gandhi's regime is all about. Who runs it? To what ends?

Speculations of this sort took a new turn last week when Kamalapati Tripathi announced his resignation from the post of working president of the Congress(I), and the general secretaries of the AICC were removed. What was the Prime Minister up to this time? The Tripathi resignation was not surprising in itself. After his abortive rebellion earlier this year, when his letter to the Prime Minister complaining bitterly about the goings-on in the Congress was released to the press, Mr Tripathi was more or less serving time, pending settlement of his post-retirement benefits. These matters have apparently been sorted out now to the satisfaction of all concerned, and Mr Tripathi has bid good-bye, wishing the Prime Minister well and pledging to support him come what may.

It is the removal of the general secretaries that has given the impression that the Prime Minister, who is also the President of the Congress(I) party, now intends to clear the deck and refurbish the party in his own image. This was on the agenda for some time. Rajiv Gandhi after all began his political career, brief though it may have been, not in the government but in the Congress party. It was believed that in association with Arun Nehru, Rajiv Gandhi was particularly keen to infuse fresh blood into the party, beginning from below. There was apparently a grand plan to induct dynamic, young, forward-looking and competent young men and women at the district level Congress organizations. These people would be politically and ideologically committed to the new regime, and through them an organizational base would be built which could replace the old and corrupt system of support based on the discredited power-brokers.

The plan has been under way for some time, and there have been more organization-building activities in the Youth Congress, the Congress Seva Dal and the various district Congress levels than at any time in the recent past. Most of these have been run like management training programmes. The other part of this grand plan was to hold organizational elections in the Congress throughout the country, and use this democratic machinery to wipe out the regime of the power-brokers of the past. That is where the plan faltered. The old guards proved far too wily and well-entrenched, and Kamalapati Tripathi's sudden outburst about bogus membership in the party electoral list was only one example of the enormous difficulties of replacing the Congress structure from the top.

Now Rajiv Gandhi seems to have changed tracks. He has openly broken with his former friend and comrade, Arun Nehru. Neither Arun Singh nor Arjun Singh figure any more among his closest political advisers. He has come to terms with the opposition in Jammu and Kashmir by clinching an agreement with Farooq Abdullah, to the intense displeasure of the Kashmir Congress(I). An agreement with Sharad Pawar of Congress(S) is in the offing in Maharashtra: what his reward will be is still not clear, although the larger plan of a wholesale merger of the Congress(S) with the Congress(I) may not come through. Perhaps another agreement with Jagannath Mishra is on the cards, and this may mean a change of government in Bihar. Possibly, what all this means is that Mr Gandhi has decided that to take on the much despised power-brokers as a body would prove too much for him, and that it is better to come to an arrangement with those among them who could be relied upon to keep their own regions in order. In the meantime, it is goodbye to organizational elections within the Congress. The leader must first have enough time to make up his own mind: party democracy can wait. Perhaps by then we will have a sufficient number of PCC resolutions urging Mrs Sonia Gandhi to become Congress President!

1 December 1986: Gorbachev's Visit[18]

Despite an unprecedented media blitz calculated to produce the impression of a 'historic' occasion, Mikhail Gorbachev's visit to New Delhi contained virtually no surprises. Nothing new or significant transpired in the course of three days of protocol-signing and press conferences. There were, of course, a few ceremonial firsts, like a special red carpet at Rashtrapati Bhavan and the use of the Ashoka Hall in that building for a joint press conference by Mr Gorbachev and Mr Gandhi. These privileges, the country was told, had never before been extended to any visiting dignitary, not even to the Queen of

18 *Frontier*, 19, 16 (6 December 1986).

England. We were left to draw our own conclusions from that regarding the 'historic' nature of the visit.

That word was repeated endlessly on radio and television, as official hacks worked overtime waffling away on the everlasting friendship between India and the Soviet Union. For five days, Doordarshan was virtually taken over by the huge Soviet delegation, and there was no escaping the inevitable scenes of dignitaries sitting down to a banquet or the interminable translations of interminable speeches from Russian into English and vice versa. The press was around, but kept at a distance by the heavy security arrangements. Still, they dutifully reported what Mrs Gorbachev wore and what she bought.

Amidst all this fanfare, stage-managed to the very end, what is it that has materialized? Very little, it would seem. The official high point was the so-called Delhi Declaration which Mr Gorbachev described as a 'unique and extraordinary document'. In it, the Soviet and Indian governments have jointly called for a ban on the use or threat of use of nuclear weapons. Apart from this specific declaration, the rest of the document is an exercise in redundancy and hyperbole. It is understandable that after the failure at Reykjavik, Mr Gorbachev should wish to push ahead with his propaganda advantage in the 'peace war' with President Reagan. It was only to be expected, therefore, that he would enlist Indian support in some new and dramatic peace offensive. Yet the document produced has succeeded in recording nothing more concrete than homilies like 'human life must be recognized as supreme', 'understanding and trust must replace fear and suspicion', 'conditions must be guaranteed for the individual's harmonious development', and so on. This by itself is telling evidence of the immense gulf that separates the genuine desire of the people of the world for nuclear disarmament and peace, and the strategic calculations of the nuclear powers themselves.

On the economic front, there has been an agreement for a Rs 23,000 million credit by the Soviet Union for projects such as the construction of the Tehri hydroelectric complex, the modernization of the Bokaro steel plant, the opening of new coal mines in Jharia, and the exploration of oil and natural gas sources in West Bengal. Nothing concrete has been achieved on the trade front, which has been sagging of late, except a pious wish to increase trade between the two countries by two-and-a-half times in the next five years. How this is to be done is still not clear, and Mr Gandhi was cautious enough to say in his press conference that this would have to be left for 'experts' to decide. He has learnt that the compulsions of regional dominance and world politics make it imperative for his government to depend on Soviet political and military support, but that is no reason to restrict one's options in the matter of trade and economic relations. Mr Gorbachev also made a proposal for an international space research centre in India for the training of astronauts and the launching of spacecraft. Mr Gandhi did not seem overly enthusiastic.

The visit underlined once again the fact that, in the international context in which the Indian ruling classes hold and exercise their power in this country, the strategic relation to the Soviet Union is more or less invariant. This was shown earlier in the brief period of Janata rule, when professedly anti-Soviet politicians, after suddenly coming to power in the 1977 elections, found themselves having to sign agreements with Moscow. Rajiv Gandhi too was said to have pro-Western sympathies, and the European and American press made much of this in the first few months of his regime. Now they know better.

Even the parliamentary Left in India, having now been fully appropriated into the structure of ruling power, has fitted into this scheme of things. In the last few years, there has been little difference between the CPI and the CPI(M) in their arguments on the Soviet Union. This fact, it seems, has been recognized by the Soviets as well, because this time Mr Gorbachev officially met separate delegations from the two parties. Another 'historic' first, but only confirming what has been well known for a long time.

15 December 1986: Congress Culture[19]

'There is now only one Congress,' Sharad Pawar declared in Aurangabad last week. Gone are the days when one had to search for the correct letter in the alphabet to insert in parentheses, in order to describe a particular fragment of the Congress party. Most of the tiny splinters had vanished anyway, readmitted

---

[19] *Frontier*, 19, 18 (20 December 1986).

into the Congress(I) by Indira Gandhi in a sudden spell of generosity and forgiveness in the last year of her life. A few organizations had died with the death of their leaders who gave them their distinctive names. The Congress(S) was, of course, the major opposition group which still claimed to be the real Congress. Its early stalwarts were either dead or back in the Congress(I). Younger firebrands like A.K. Anthony and P.R. Das Munshi had undergone the elaborate ritual of repentance, and having shed their image as rebels with a cause, had been readmitted into the ruling party. Sharad Pawar remained the only leader of any consequence in the Congress(S), and with most people having forgotten what the (S) originally stood for, had often lent his own name to describe the organization.

Now that his prolonged efforts to establish a formal rapport with Rajiv Gandhi have finally succeeded, Mr Pawar feels that it is he who deserves the credit for having reunited the Congress. This is a historic moment, he thinks. Not only is there a crisis in the country which requires all Congress members to come together, but the fact that there is really only a single 'Congress culture and ethos', born out of the long history of the party, makes the erstwhile divisions in the ranks of Congress members wholly artificial. There were no real ideological grounds for these divisions. Now, says Mr Pawar, when 'the leader of the nation and the Congress(I) party', Rajiv Gandhi, is bringing in 'a new spirit of reconciliation' (meaning presumably that he is not as tough on party dissidents as his mother was), there is no point in wasting one's time sitting in the opposition. In other words, now is the time to seize the opportunity and get a share of real power.

The Congress(I)–Congress(S) merger had been on the cards for some time now. And as expected, the merger has not been entirely smooth, because a few notable leaders like T. Unnikrishnan of Kerala and Sarat Chandra Sinha of Assam have refused to accept it. But, of course, as an organization of any electoral consequence, the Congress(S) existed only in Maharashtra where it was by far the largest opposition party in the Assembly. Mr Pawar's prize, it is being said, is the chief ministership, although the person concerned is still being very coy about this. It is also said that the industrialists of Maharashtra, who have always regarded Mr Pawar as a reliable and effective political representative, have quietly persuaded him to take this decisive step. There may be many subtle implications in this well-known tie-up between Mr Pawar and the Bombay businessmen. He may be expected to deliver the goods either as Chief Minister of Maharashtra, or perhaps at an even higher level — may be as a check to the unpredictable and troublesome V.P. Singh: who knows?

All this may also be part of Rajiv Gandhi's grand plan for building a new ruling party. He has systematically weeded out from his organization the closest associates of Indira Gandhi. And in one sudden swoop last month, he dismissed both the working president Kamalapati Tripathi and the entire secretariat of the party. Mr Gandhi has thus far given no inkling as to what he intends to do after this; and at the moment at least, the ruling party exists and functions (so far as it is required to function) without an executive body. All that is apparent is that the Prime Minister is seeking to build bridges with people who have independent sources of electoral support in the regions — Dr Abdullah in Kashmir and now Mr Pawar in Maharashtra. This is a style quite different from that of his mother. Whether it develops into a clear and consistent policy is still to be seen. After all, whatever may be Rajiv Gandhi's qualities, clarity and consistency do not figure in that list.

10

The Politics of Appropriation

It is as old as the history of bourgeois politics in this country — of bourgeois politics seeking to forge the solid edifice of a bourgeois state. As the contours begin to take shape and each little part is brought to bear a definite relation to the whole, the cracks are neatly papered over; all the signs of friction, of hindrance and resistance, carefully erased from public view. And for those particularly stubborn marks of dissension which refuse to go away — well, they are simply made part of the structure itself, as if they were meant to be there all along. Thus the myth is built up of the bourgeois state as the great reconciler of differences, so representative that it is virtually one with the nation itself.

That is the story of the appropriation of opposition politics in India. It can be seen in the ways in which the state has, from time to time, sought to usurp the politics based on the economic demands of various exploited classes: by the creation of high-wage islands within the working class; the fixing of procurement prices for agricultural products; the poverty-eradication programmes; and a variety of special schemes for backward or scheduled castes, and for the tribes. But nowhere is this process more dramatic than in the state's handling of the 'national question' in India, for that is where every expression of opposition involves, whether implicitly or explicitly, the questioning of the very territorial basis of the state and of how power is distributed over that territory.

For reasons of space, we will not go too far back into history, although there is a lot there that is relevant to the present discussion. Let it suffice to say that the Congress-led national movement only met the question halfway. The antagonism between colonialism and the 'Indian nation' was ideologically posed in the pre-Gandhian era of bourgeois politics in India, without however discovering any practical means by which to politically organize the masses for the struggle to create a national state. Those means were developed in the period since 1919–20. One of the basic organizational innovations was the formation of the provincial Congress committees based on more or less homogeneous linguistic units, ignoring the existing administrative demarcation of provinces by the colonial state in India. These provincial committees were the main organizing foci of the mass movements of the Congress. It was at this level that the democratic demands of the people, voiced through the various movements at the localities and districts, were organized and coordinated — in the language of the people and in conformity with regional economic and cultural specificities. It was also at this level that the all-India leaders of the Congress sought to assert their control over the organization of the national movement throughout the country.

Two Tendencies

The provincial level of the Congress was, one might say, the site where two tendencies in the Indian national movement met. One was the tendency of opening the movement towards the democratic aspirations of the masses against the domination exercised by alien rule. As with all bourgeois-democratic movements of nationality, this tendency accompanied or followed the development of certain cultural forms, which could become the standard for emulation by all classes and strata within the linguistic community. In the Indian case, this tendency found its true home in the large linguistic communities formed by the modern Indian languages, and these were in the main the domain of the provincial organization of the Congress. The other tendency was towards the consolidation, through this process of popular struggle against colonial rule, of the interests of the all-India bourgeoisie, including within it the big bourgeoisie as well as the top strata of the professional middle classes. In political terms, this tendency always preferred the relative centralization of governmental powers and the containment of democratic mass movements within limits that conformed with these all-India interests.

This inherent conflict between the two historical tendencies was not resolved in the period of the national movement. The history of the post-colonial state in India shows that the conflict has still not been resolved within the framework of the Indian

Constitution. In the colonial period, the democratic content of the movements of the nationalities found relatively free expression precisely in the periods of the mass movements launched by the Congress. Then, when these mass movements were sought to be contained, we notice the assertion of the organizational dominance of an all-India Congress leadership, and the emergence of many regionally-based factional groupings within the Congress.

Centralization

After the formation of the independent Indian state, the conflict between the two tendencies came to a head in the 1950s. The Constitution sought to strike a compromise between the two tendencies by laying down a federal structure of government, without however recognizing the existence of 'nationalities'. This diplomatic silence on the part of the Constitution-makers did not pass muster, because strong demands began to be voiced from different parts of India for the reorganization of states on a linguistic basis. Implicitly, these demands only represented the normal bourgeois-democratic aspirations of nationality. In the Indian case, the specific demand was that the federating units of the Indian Union should in fact be the linguistic nationalities. This was, as we have said before, the implicit assumption of the Congress organization at least since 1919–20. Now, however, important sections within the all-India state leadership, including Jawaharlal Nehru himself, began to raise doubts about the desirability of such a reorganizaton of states. They argued that to recognize the linguistic principle would mean sowing the seeds of destruction of the political unity of India. Their argument, in fact, implied the belief that India could only be effectively ruled in the administrative style of centralized empires, by concentrating power in the capital and dividing up the basis for democratic solidarity in the provinces.

In this particular period, the centralizing tendency had to retreat in the face of massive popular movements in Andhra, Maharashtra–Gujarat and Punjab–Haryana. The States Reorganization Commission accepted with qualifications the linguistic principle for demarcating states. But the problems were not necessarily resolved, because the principle of the matter was never clinched. The Indian state always took the position that there was only one nation — India — and its territorial sovereignty was unitary and inviolate. All matters of formation and demarcation of states (or Union Territories) were a matter of 'practicality': no firm principle was ever laid down or accepted. On certain occasions, demands for the redrawing of state boundaries were conceded; on others, they were denied. The ground was laid, therefore, for the play of pressure politics of the most unprincipled sort. It became evident that if you could put enough pressure on the government, your demand stood a good chance of being conceded. Quite obviously, this also created room for the manipulative politics of the central state power itself: it could employ the carrot-and-stick policy, both to contain democratic movements of the nationalities and to appropriate their results. The most dramatic example of this has been the handling of the nationalities question in the north-eastern regions of India, the latest episode in that story being the 'accord' with Mr Laldenga in Mizoram.

The Communist Stand

The communist movement had for a long time theoretically accepted the principle of linguistic nationalities in India. In the early 1940s, this principle was sought to be twisted in the so-called Adhikari thesis to justify the demand for Pakistan, but this was soon regarded as a mistake. After 1947, the communist movement theoretically identified the Indian state as multinational in character, although it was not very forthright on the question of 'the right of secession' (for entirely valid reasons, one might argue, because except for the case of the north-eastern region, this was not yet a serious political issue).

But with the incorporation of the bulk of the communist movement into the exclusive form of parliamentary politics, the theoretical principle on the question of the Indian nationalities has now been totally abandoned in favour of the criterion of 'practicality'. In the 1950s, communists were in the forefront of the movement for a separate state of Andhra Pradesh. They supported the division of Bombay into Maharashtra and Gujarat, and of Punjab into Punjab and Haryana. They virtually led the movement against B.C. Roy's proposal in 1954 to merge West

Bengal and Bihar into a single state. All this was in accordance with the principle that the component units of the Indian Union were linguistic nationalities which had a right to separate political existence within the federation. Today we read reports of an incredible statement from Benoy Chowdhury, one of the senior-most CPI(M) leaders, accusing the Congress of having started the process of disintegration of the country by creating states on a linguistic basis!

What is it that has happened in the last decade or so to bring about this remarkable transformation in communist politics? We need not recount here what the CPI and the CPI(M) have or have not said on the recent controversies over Punjab, Assam, Mizoram or the so-called Gorkhaland movement. Any questions on these matters will, we know, be answered essentially by an appeal to 'practicality'. There will be one set of criteria used to assert the 'democratic' content of moderate Akali politics in Punjab and the 'anti-national' character of the demand for Khalistan; and quite a different set of criteria to condemn as 'chauvinistic' the politics of the AGP in Assam. And no one among the CPI(M) leaders is more forthright in his adherence to 'practicality' than Jyoti Basu, self-proclaimed propagator of 'commonsense' Marxism in India. Helped by his deep-seated contempt for 'theoretical' debate, it is Mr Basu who has now supplied us with a ground rule for understanding the CPI(M)'s new politics. We must, he says, give up the whole line of thinking on the nationalities question based on the right of self-determination of nations, because Lenin's arguments on this matter are inapplicable to Indian conditions.

What, we may well ask, are these specific variations in socio-historical conditions in the Indian case that make Lenin's arguments inapplicable? Mr Basu has not given us the benefit of a detailed presentation of his thinking on the subject: he, after all, is a 'practical' man who has little time for the luxuries of theoretical rumination. But let us, for the sake of argument, construct a case for Mr Basu.

No Oppressor Nationality

He would, we presume, point out above all the absence of an oppressor nationality in India, which would make the political question of the self-determination of nationalities wholly ir-relevant. Where, he would ask, is the alien national body from which the so-called Indian nationalities must seek their separa-tion? With the ending of British rule and the founding of an independent Indian state, this matter has been settled.

Has it? The answer would depend on what we make of the story of Indian independence and the place of the nationalities within the new Indian state. The CPI(M) argues, and we still do not know of any change in this position, that the dominant power in the state structure is held by the Indian big bourgeoisie which rules in alliance with the owners of large landed property. The big bourgeoisie, it further argues, is incapable of completing the bourgeois-democratic revolution in India because, first, it is de-pendent on foreign capital; second, it is politically incapable of abolishing pre-capitalist forms of exploitation in the countryside; and third, because it necessarily impedes the development of small capital which exists in the local and regional markets. It would follow from this that the organized interest which would most strongly favour the centralization of governmental power in the Indian state structure is the Indian big bourgeoisie.

Now this big bourgeoisie also has an 'all-India' character, inas-much as it cannot be identified as belonging exclusively, or even predominantly, to any particular ethnic community. Its members hail from different parts of India and its 'home market' is spread all across the country. It exploits the mass of the Indian people, but its oppression cannot be identified as that of an oppressor nationality. Does this mean then that the Indian big bourgeoisie has succeeded in unifying the people into the bourgeois-demo-cratic framework of a single nation? That cannot be the case, for then we would have to regard the bourgeois-democratic revolu-tion in India as something that has been largely completed.

What, then, is the specific socio-historical form which enables the Indian big bourgeoisie to rule through an independent 'nation–state' without actually completing the historical task of forming a single bourgeois-democratic nation?

The All-India Sector

It was Lenin who in 1914 had cited with approval Kautsky's proposition that 'the multinational state represents backwardness'.[1] It is in fact the historical backwardness of Indian capitalism which gives the present Indian state its multinational character. Yet it is not the same kind of multinational state as Czarist Russia was in its last years, for here we do not have capitalist development based on the cultural unification of an oppressor nationality — Russia — imposing its oppression on other subjugated nationalities. But we must be careful here. Indian Marxists have generally agreed on the origins of the big bourgeoisie in this country, in its role as subordinate collaborators of British colonial capital, however much they may differ on the characterization of its subsequent role in the later phase of the national movement and in the post-colonial era. It was colonial capital and the British colonial state which created an 'all-India' market for the operation of big capital, whether commercial, financial or industrial. It was this 'all-India' market which the Indian big bourgeoisie subsequently took over and consolidated.

This market is spread all over India, but it does not incorporate the whole demographic mass of the country. It only skims off a thin top layer of consumers from all the regions, and constitutes itself as an 'all-India' market. This layer, thin as it is in comparison with the whole population, nevertheless includes not only the bourgeoisie, but also most of the middle classes, the richer landed classes and even a section of the relatively better-paid working class. The big bourgeoisie does indeed seek to build homogeneous cultural patterns within this market — in the print medium, principally by the adoption of the English language as the practical language for 'all-India' communication; but more effectively in the audiovisual media (radio, cinema, and now television), through the propagation of a peculiarly neutral, aseptic and non-literary brand of Hindi, purged of all the richness of idiom and nuance of a vital cultural tradition. The cultural homogeneity which big capital in India has imposed on this 'all-India' market through its management of the consumer media, is now being consolidated by the state through its new policies on education and the management of television programming.

But the important feature of this 'all-India' market is that it

[1] V.I. Lenin, 'The Right of Nations to Self-determination', in Lenin, *Selected Works*, vol. 1 (Moscow: Progress Publishers, 1970), pp. 597–647. The reference to Kautsky is on p. 599.

does not even attempt to include within it the whole of the Indian people. Consumerism in India, which is the 'growth sector' on which Indian monopoly capital banks for continuing its process of accumulation, is a phenomenon restricted only to something like the top 10 or 15 per cent of the total population of the country. The rest are outside the pale of the 'all-India' market, and can *never* be incorporated into it unless the full historical process of a bourgeois-democratic revolution can be completed. Perhaps the big bourgeoisie does not even need to include, in its effective market, this vast mass of people with little income to spend on industrial commodities. For, even with 15 per cent of the population, this 'all-India' market is already larger in demographic size than the home markets of most European capitalist countries. We thus have the makings of a nation within the nation: a privileged minority of consumers economically and culturally integrated into a capitalist home market, and increasingly separated from the majority of the people of the country.

It is in that vast peripheral mass that the sense of oppression takes on the form of the cultural aspirations of oppressed nationalities. This is most unambiguous in the case of communities which contain no significant stratum that is incorporated into the 'all-India' sector — in particular, various tribal communities in the north-eastern and central parts of India. But even for the rest of the population, the signs of cultural oppression are evident in the aspirations for political identity of linguistic communities all over the country. These are not only marks of the necessary incompleteness of the bourgeois-democratic revolution carried out under the auspices of the all-India big bourgeoisie, but also of the historical necessity of extending and deepening the bases of democratic politics in this country.

Relevance of Lenin

The fact that there is no identifiable oppressor nationality in India does not mean that nationalities in this country are not oppressed. They *are* oppressed by what has come to be called the 'all-India' sector of capitalism. The difficulty is that the movements of the nationalities cannot direct their struggle against an easily identifiable target. That, in fact, is the greatest strategic strength of the Indian big bourgeoisie — its oppression

cannot be identified as one carried out by an oppressor nationality. This is why we have so much ambiguity and confusion
in the movements of the nationalities, with the Nepali-speaking
people of Darjeeling being led to believe that it is the Bengalis
as a whole who oppress them, or the Sikh peasants of Punjab
that it is the Hindus. The closest the nationalities ever get
to their real target is when they vaguely point to 'Delhi' as
the source of their oppression, but that too is a misconception.
Only a consistent bourgeois-democratic programme, recognizing the reality of the oppression of the nationalities and
aimed against the economic domination and cultural privileges
of the 'all-India' agglomeration, can harness the general democratic content of these popular aspirations towards a historically
progressive movement.

This, therefore, is the question: whether the bourgeois-democratic revolution in India will be allowed to ossify in its present
form, of an all-India monopoly bourgeoisie ruling over a 'sovereign' India which excludes the vast mass of the peoples of India
from any participation in sovereignty; or whether the battle for
a truly federal democracy will be carried on, by locating its bases
in the democratic aspirations of the nationalities. As long as
Marxists agree that this is a matter of principle and not of 'practicality', Lenin's discussion on the right of self-determination of
nations will remain vitally relevant.

It is by succumbing to considerations of 'practicality' that
the parliamentary communists in India have allowed their politics to be appropriated by the Indian state. They have been
trapped in the bourgeois game of practicality, as the CPI(M)
has now been trapped in relation to the demands of the Nepali-
speaking people of the hill areas of Darjeeling. For a long time,
and for entirely principled reasons, the CPI(M) had supported
the political and cultural demands of these people, whose very
status as Indian citizens is not clearly recognized by the Indian
state. Whether the CPI(M) had done enough to fulfil those
demands is another matter. Now, when a rival leadership —
clearly instigated or at least tacitly supported by the ruling powers
in Delhi — threatens to take the wind out of the CPI(M)'s
sails, and the West Bengal Congress and the all-India press
accuse the communists of having sown the seeds of separatism
by supporting the Nepali demands all this time, the CPI(M)

responds by prevaricating on its principled stand. The 'practical' constraints of running a government and winning elections force it to backtrack. Tomorrow, if there is a movement to protect minority rights in Assam, and the ruling party in Delhi chooses to manipulate it to its electoral advantage (as it undoubtedly will), the CPI(M) would be hard put to declare its support for the minorities in Assam without inviting the charge of supporting 'separatism'. That is how bourgeois politics entraps and appropriates the politics of the opposition.

It was Lenin who strongly asserted that the party of the proletariat must not in any event succumb to the bourgeois demand for 'practicality' on the national question. He said that the proletariat would refuse to give a categorical 'yes' or 'no' answer to the question of secession by any nation. The proletariat, he said, will support the right to self-determination without giving any guarantees or privileges to any nation.[2] Now, in India, we are witnessing the remarkable spectacle of the CPI(M), which claims to be the party of the proletariat, asking the ruling party in New Delhi for a categorical answer to the question: 'Does or does not the Government of India regard the GNLF as a secessionist movement?' One can hardly imagine a more farcical example of a communist party trying to be more nationalistic than the nationalists themselves.

[2] Ibid., especially pp. 608–13.

11

Rajiv's Regime: The Fall

11 May 1987: Hour of Trial[1]

A cloud of uncertainty still hangs over New Delhi. Everybody, whether in government or in the opposition, seems jittery; and every day seems to hold the possibility of some dramatic event. It is a measure of the utter exhaustion of the strength of our political system that, with an unprecedented majority in Parliament, Rajiv Gandhi's government should still consider so seriously the danger of being toppled by some sort of parliamentary coup.

As soon as the Fairfax affair was pushed away from the glare of controversy by the appointment of a commission of inquiry, and the nasty questions about the purchase of military equipment from a Swedish company led to the ouster of V.P. Singh from the Union Cabinet, Congress MPs seemed to rally round the present leadership in a way not seen before at any time during the two-and-a-half years the government has been in power. Their calculations were clear and wholly cynical. They had been elected to Parliament on the expectation that they would be there for at least five years before they were required to face the electorate again. Factional rivalries within the ruling party over sharing the fruits of power were permissible, as long as there was no question about remaining in power. But if the future of the government itself was in jeopardy, Congress members would instinctively declare their faith in their leaders. Indeed, the lower the credibility of the government, the less the chances of Congress members being re-elected in any mid-term election, and hence the greater their loyalty to the incumbent regime. It was this chain of political reasoning that was in evidence in New Delhi immediately after V.P. Singh's resignation.

[1] *Frontier*, 19, 39 (16 May 1987).

But doubts about the inner strength of the regime persisted. A lot of hue and cry was raised about the combination of external and internal forces trying to destabilize the country. The argument was specious in the extreme. It seemed to say that whatever be the sins of the government, and of the law-breakers who were flourishing under the protection of the government, any criticism of their activities would threaten the stability of the regime and hence add support to the efforts of the 'destabilizers'. Similar noises had of course been made before in Indian politics, most notably during the time of Indira Gandhi. What was curious this time was the reason why, with an unchallengeable majority in Parliament, the government should feel it necessary to woo the support of opposition groups, particularly the Left parties.

The uncertainties continued, with growing speculation — assiduously cultivated from within ruling party circles — that the President was contemplating dismissal of the government. Constitutionally, this is absurd, and virtually everybody has said so. And yet, doubts about the future actions of Giani Zail Singh have not been removed. The Union Cabinet last week took the unprecedented step of writing collectively to the President, telling him that he had no right to demand information about the working of the government (the immediate issue being the Bofors deal), and that the Cabinet would only give him as much information as it deemed necessary. Now there are rumours (it is remarkable how much of the 'news' emanating from Delhi these days consists of a listing of the rumours circulating in the capital) that the President might resign, or do something equally dramatic, before nominations for the next Presidential elections are made at the end of this month (i.e. May 1987). For this reason, Parliament, it is said, will be kept in session until that time.

The other side of this picture is the uncertainty surrounding V.P. Singh. The expression of loyalty in Rajiv's leadership has been matched by widespread condemnation by Congress MPs of the 'treacherous' role of V.P. Singh. But the top leadership has been undecided about how strongly they should move against this maverick U.P. politician, for his ouster has made him a hero in much of northern India. The indecision is compounded by the impending elections to the Haryana Assembly in June. That, by all counts, will prove a crucial test to the present regime.

And yet, no matter how low the public credibility of Rajiv

Gandhi's government, it is difficult to foresee how any change can be brought about from within the Congress party. There is no focus that has emerged for an alternative leadership. The attempt to perpetuate the Nehru dynasty has eroded every shred of democratic vitality in the Congress. Nothing is more telling than the present occupation of the Prime Minister and his advisers (whoever they are), which consists of running from one fire-fighting job to another. Only sheer political ineptitude can reduce a government with such a huge majority in Parliament to such a state in a matter of two-and-a-half years.

30 June 1987: Democracy, Indian Style[2]

After much drama and suspense, the nominees for the next Presidential elections have been finally announced. It will be, for all practical purposes, a straight contest between the Congress(I) candidate, Mr Venkataraman, and the joint opposition choice, Mr Krishna Iyer. A third candidate, Mr Mithilesh Kumar, has managed to get himself proposed by ten independent MLAs from Bihar, which is an achievement in itself; but he is unlikely to have any effect on the final outcome of the presidential race.

Mr Venkataraman had been the most likely choice as Congress(I) candidate for a long time. He is the Vice-President of the country; also, he is from the south, which satisfies the unwritten Congress convention that while Prime Ministers must come from Uttar Pradesh (preferably from Allahabad), Presidents should alternate between the north and south of the country. He would have been an automatic choice had not Mr Gandhi become unnerved by the real or imaginary pranks played by Mr Zail Singh. There was talk of the President dismissing the government, and of running for a second term, if need be as an opposition candidate. Coming on top of the successive electoral defeats and the growing din about the Bofors scandal, Mr Gandhi for a while seemed uncertain about the intentions of Mr Zail Singh, and even about the prospects of victory of the Congress(I) candidate. He was the one who broached the possibility of a 'unanimous' candidate, and even went through the whole gamut of talks with individual

[2] *Frontier*, 19, 46 (4 July 1987).

opposition parties on this matter. In the end, nothing came of it and Mr Venkataraman's name was announced as the Congress(I) candidate.

The drama, as always, was far more intense in the opposition camp. A three-member committee, consisting of Mr N.T. Rama Rao, Mr Chandra Sekhar and Mr E.M.S. Namboodiripad, had been set up to suggest names of possible candidates. Mr Namboodiripad was keen on Mr Krishna Iyer, who had served on his first ministry in Kerala, later went on to become a judge of the Supreme Court, and after retirement has devoted himself energetically to various civil rights causes. Other names, such as those of Mr P.N. Bhagwati, Mr Ramakrishna Hegde and Mr V.M. Tarkunde were also mentioned. The real drama began with the suggestion that Mr Zail Singh might be agreeable to being sponsored by the opposition. Mr Namboodiripad suddenly threw a fit, walked out of the opposition meeting and issued a press statement dissociating himself from such machinations. The issue was settled by Mr Zail Singh himself, who let it be known that he would not be a party 'to a losing game'. Apparently, the President was waiting for a signal that a sizeable section of Congress MPs would come out openly in his support. This was obviously not forthcoming; and those in the opposition who were waiting to seize this opportunity to split the Congress(I) and bring down Rajiv Gandhi along with it, were bitterly disappointed. Mr Namboodiripad finally won the day.

There is still much acrimony over whether the Left, and the CPI(M) in particular, was up to a devious game to save Mr Gandhi. The 'inside story', if there is any, may not be known for some time. The plain fact, however, is that Congress MPs, once having been elected, are unwilling to go for a mid-term poll. It must be clear as daylight to most members of the ruling party that with their present leader, despite his immaculate dynastic credentials, they have little certainty of winning the next general elections due in 1989. Yet, while they must be looking for a change in leadership, they will desperately seek a way of doing this without splitting the party — a way that has not been found as yet. In such circumstances, it was unlikely that a large number of Congress legislators would have come out openly to support Zail Singh as a rebel candidate. The shrewd politician from Punjab, who has been through the rough and tumble of Congress politics in Indira Gandhi's time, knew that this was not the best way to secure his future. He withdrew from the race, and saved Mr Namboodiripad from having to defend his action against the rest of the opposition. He may also have provided Rajiv Gandhi a temporary reprieve, because given the party strengths, Mr Venkataraman should now win comfortably. But Mr Gandhi's fate does not depend on the President. It depends on the fickle and entirely mercenary loyalties of his partymen, whom he has treated for so long with utter contempt.

13 July 1987: Fever Pitch[3]

As legislators all over the country prepare to elect a new President for the republic, all of northern India remains a seething cauldron of hatred, distrust, insecurity and panic. The Punjab terrorists struck again — with the mindless killing of bus passengers in Punjab, and then in Haryana where a new government has just come into power on a platform that was sharply critical of the Congress handling of the Punjab situation. The political objectives of those who can hold up and shoot down in cold blood an entire busload of helpless travellers are as clear as they ever were: to spread terror and panic, provoke a communal backlash, precipitate conditions for what would virtually be a civil war, and thus ingrain in the popular mind the belief that the only hope for peace is to concede to the demands of the extremists. It is a maddening strategy, absurd in its simplicity and naïveté, and one which any political regime with solid foundations of legitimate authority would have defeated with ease. And yet, such is the ineptitude and brittleness of our present rulers in Delhi that even this absurd campaign of terrorism seems to be succeeding. About ten weeks ago, when the Barnala government in Punjab was dismissed and President's Rule clamped down, the Prime Minister had admitted that things were 'back to square one'. He did not mention that, in politics, there is never an exact return to the same position; historical processes are not reversible. Superficially, things were back to the days of Operation Blue Star. The Union government had swept aside the complications of parliamentary politics in Punjab,

3 *Frontier*, 19, 48 (18 July 1987).

and was concentrating on the security aspects of trapping down and eliminating the terrorists. The men in charge included a Governor who boasted of his 'success' in dealing with 'Naxalites' in West Bengal, and a police chief whose exploits had earned him an award for the 'Most Notable Indian of the Year'. And yet, the crucial difference now is that a whole phase of political experiment with popular government, initially supported by a massive expression of goodwill from people of all communities in Punjab, has now been swept into the dustbin. Failure to tackle the law-and-order situation at this juncture — and failure seems inevitable — cannot be redeemed by another spell of popular government. The political options have been closed off.

This is why the mood in northern India seems to get more and more desperate every day. Helplessness breeds panic. It also breeds extreme political reactions, like urging the government to stop at nothing in taking 'strong measures' against the terrorists. It also induces people to take it upon themselves to protect their lives and property, since the government cannot be trusted to do this adequately. That is precisely the condition which precipitates civil strife. The Punjab terrorists wish to provoke riots between Hindus and Sikhs in Delhi and Haryana. Yet a crisis of authority could well give rise to Hindu–Muslim riots elsewhere in northern India, where tensions and suspicions have reached a quite unprecedented level in recent months. While Punjab has gone from bad to worse, the present crisis of political authority could lead to far more dangerous and destructive events, of which Meerut is probably only a curtain-raiser.

Our rulers in the meantime have just returned from a 'good-will mission' to Moscow, sufficiently fortified to get down to the task of demonstrating their political loyalties in the forthcoming Presidential election.

14 September 1987: Left Right Left[4]

While it may be all right for Kanu Sanyal of the Communist Organization of India (Marxist–Leninist) to issue a call to 'opposition parties of every hue' to join in ousting the corrupt government of Rajiv Gandhi and not to shirk from using 'extra-parliamentary

[4] *Frontier*, 20, 5 (19 September 1987).

means' to achieve this end, the parliamentary Left has other things to worry about. Its main problem at the moment is V.P. Singh. E.M.S. Namboodiripad has urged Mr Singh to 'make up his mind', which is the surest indication that the Left parties, with the CPI(M) in the forefront, are finding it increasingly difficult to make up *their* minds.

The situation has arisen time and time again in the history of the Indian Left. Whenever the principal party organization of the ruling classes in India has found itself in a quandary — weak, internally divided, often leaderless — the Left has suddenly woken up to the fact that the situation called for its intervention. And every time, its attempted intervention has taken the form of picking out a set of so-called 'progressive and left-oriented' Congress members — sometimes a single leader — and latching on to them in a bid to provide a 'leftist thrust' to the policies of the Indian state. The results have not been a success, judging by the present strength of the Left even in terms of parliamentary seats.

The present problem arises because the Left is yet to decide whether V.P. Singh is indeed a 'progressive and left-minded' Congress leader. Following the revelations about improprieties and kickbacks in various arms deals, V.P. Singh has emerged as the leading figure in the campaign against Rajiv Gandhi in northern India, and is being looked upon as the most credible alternative leader around whom disgruntled Congress members can rally. Whether an alternative leadership will mean alternative policies is of course a moot question. Congress leaders have had little qualms about advertising their commitment to whatever policies seem to suit the mood of the day; yet, regardless of the slogans emblazoned under the tricolour, the state runs the same way as ever. V.P. Singh, it may be presumed, will be no exception. At the present moment, he has refused to commit himself to anything other than his one-point campaign against the corruption of the Rajiv Gandhi government. This is precisely what is to be expected, since that is the issue which has thrown him to the top of the popularity chart in the Hindi belt; and he is unlikely to do anything that might confuse the picture. His aim at the moment is to build the largest possible coalition of those opposed to Rajiv Gandhi, and to present himself to those Congress members who are still sitting on the fence as the most likely leader of a viable alternative government.

The parliamentary Left's dilemma stems from the fact that it does not know whether a change will necessarily further its own electoral interests. While V.P. Singh keeps repeating his disingenuous platitude that the people must focus on issues and not on heroes, the Left unfortunately is able to present neither. Ever since its conclave politics was aborted three years ago, the CPI(M) and its allies in the Left have continuously talked of the building of a left and democratic front on a national scale, but have failed to come up with a credible set of programmes on which such a campaign might be launched. Their own strength is localized in a few regional pockets; and while they rejoice at the fact that nearly half the states in India today are ruled by non-Congress governments, they have yet to come up with the sorts of issues around which the growing resentment of the people all over the country can be mobilized, in the direction of an assault upon the existing structures of state power. A popular rejection of the Congress only seems to mean the installation of a few more Rama Raos and Devi Lals in various state capitals. Like it or not, therefore, the only political choice before the parliamentary Left is to decide on whether, and how far, it will follow the popular hero of the day. That is precisely the problem which V.P. Singh has posed to the Left.

And so the Left finds itself in a quandary. Its call to all Congress members to take 'a bold stand' and to demand a new government still stands. It invites V.P. Singh to address a seminar organized by its student wing. At the same time, it disapproves of Mr Singh's unwillingness to discard the BJP, or his eagerness in accepting the title of 'Raj Rishi' awarded him by the venerable Brahmins of Banaras. It is a waiting game on all sides; nobody is willing to commit too much.

1 December 1987: Pushing for Peace?[5]

The Union Minister of Defence, K.C. Pant, has rejected the suggestion from certain opposition parties that the Indian government open negotiations with the LTTE for an end to the hostilities in Sri Lanka. He has said that the government is determined to implement the Indo-Sri Lanka accord, which

---

5 *Frontier*, 20, 16 (5 December 1987).

presumably means that the Indian 'peacekeeping' forces will continue their present operations in Sri Lanka until the LTTE has been completely crushed. At the same time, however, with Indian casualties from sniper attacks continuing to mount in the Jaffna peninsula, the government has also offered a set of 'incentives' to the Tamil Tigers — including free food and shelter, a monthly stipend, educational facilities and employment — in exchange for the immediate surrender of their arms. In short, then, Rajiv Gandhi's government is now fully engaged in fighting a protracted civil war on foreign soil, in a way which the Sinhalese hardliners could not have imagined in their wildest dreams when they had first protested against Mr Jayawardene's signing the accord. They have realized once again, but this time with pleasure, that their President is a wily customer indeed.

The military situation has not changed very much in the last two weeks, and is unlikely to shift decisively either way. Having mobilized an overwhelmingly superior force, some 30,000 Indian troops are now in the unenviable situation of an army of occupation facing a hostile civilian population. The stories coming out of Jaffna have all the classic marks: professionally trained foreign soldiers losing their way in unfamiliar territory, urban guerrillas suddenly encircling an Indian unit and shooting from all sides, little boys moving around with automatic weapons, house-to-house searches by the occupying troops who are afraid that even women and children might shoot them in the back. How long will all this continue? Quite simply, if the melancholy history of similar campaigns in different parts of the world in the last two decades is any indication, it can continue indefinitely, with rising body counts and burning hatred on both sides. There has never been a purely military solution to such campaigns before, and one cannot see how there will be one this time.

It is clear now that the Rajiv–Jayawardene accord did not resolve any of the fundamental conflicts which lay at the bottom of the ethnic problem in Sri Lanka. It only opened a new chapter in the political alignments and armed hostilities based on those conflicts. When Indian troops first went into Sri Lanka, they were ostensibly going there to protect the Tamils from the official Sinhalese forces. But clearly the Tamil guerrillas, and the LTTE in particular, were unwilling to take Rajiv Gandhi's word that once they had surrendered their arms and the Indian forces were out, they would not be at the mercy of the Sinhalese hardliners. It was at this point that the Indian government, bullied by an irate Sri Lanka President, decided to adopt a tough line and landed its own troops in this unprecedented mess.

The hardliners in Jayawardene's party are unlikely to relinquish this opportunity of getting the Indians to finish, once and for all, the military resistance of the Tamils. Already the Sri Lanka press is clamouring about 'secret deals' between the absconding LTTE chief Mr Prabhakaran and the Indian government. The campaign against the guerrillas, it says, must not be halted. 'If India did not play the role of godfather to the terrorists, Indian jawans need not die in the sands of Jaffna.' And rounding off this macabre and yet perfectly logical argument, it has concluded: 'Nations which aspire to the status of great powers and have taken upon difficult tasks have to implement them in the manner of great nations.' One can hardly fail to hear in this, echoes of the Saigon press exhorting Johnson or Nixon to send more troops to fight the 'Viet Cong'.

21 March 1988: At Odds[6]

Even bad dreams unfold in phases. Last week, Punjab moved into yet another phase of its continuing nightmare. The 59th Constitutional Amendment Bill has now empowered the Union government to declare an Emergency in Punjab on grounds of internal disturbances. The Bill also allows the Centre to continue President's Rule in Punjab beyond 11 May 1988, when the present sanction of Parliament to the Siddhartha Shankar Ray–Ribeiro dyarchy is due to expire. Despite the vociferous protests of virtually the entire opposition, the ruling party used its whip to push through the Bill in both houses, only condescending to make a minor change in the wording of the Bill specifying that its provisions would apply only to Punjab. In sum, the Amendment has restored to the Constitution the criterion of 'internal disturbances' as a ground for the imposition of Emergency. This was precisely the reason Indira Gandhi cited when she declared her Emergency in 1975; and one of the few lasting achievements of the short-lived Janata government was to have this phrase

[6] *Frontier*, 20, 32 (26 March 1988).

struck off the Constitution when it passed the 45th Amendment in 1978. Now her son has proceeded to restore all of those legal conditions for authoritarian rule.

It was significant that the Constitutional Amendment Bill was passed in Parliament on the very day the opposition parties had called for a *Bharat bandh* demanding the resignation of Rajiv Gandhi. If AIR and Doordarshan are to be believed, the general strike on 15 March 1988 was a complete flop. A more careful reading of the news, however, suggests a quite different interpretation of the mood of the people. In West Bengal, Kerala and Karnataka, where the opposition parties are quite firmly in the saddle, the *bandh* was more or less total. In Andhra, the Telugu Desam has already lost control, largely because of its own failings: whatever else might be its qualities, Mr Rama Rao's government can have little credibility in the matter of civil liberties or in the campaign against corruption. Tamil Nadu is under President's Rule, and the quite massive repression and arrests on the day of the *bandh* in that state were more closely connected with the continuing battle over MGR's legacy than with questions of all-India politics. In Bihar and Orissa, on the other hand, the positive response to the opposition call was significant. Not so, however, in the crucial northern belt of U.P. and Haryana, where the unresolved tangle of alliance politics which plagues the opposition today was painfully apparent. Neither the BJP nor the Bahuguna-led Lok Dal was particularly keen to join the call to demand Rajiv Gandhi's resignation. And V.P. Singh, who still retains a position of crucial importance in U.P. politics despite his relatively low profile in recent weeks, is apparently determined to bide his time until the forthcoming by-election in Allahabad. If there is a groundswell of antipathy to Rajiv Gandhi's follies in northern India, the *Bharat bandh* did not show it because there was no one to channelize the popular disapproval into the forms of organized protest.

The experience of the *bandh* should suggest a quite obvious course of action to the Prime Minister's political advisers, whoever they may be. Keep the seeds of divisive movements alive, for they provide the best pretext for claiming greater executive powers and continuity of leadership. Prepare the institutional grounds for assuming extraordinary powers should the occasion arise. Keep the opposition divided by selective rewards and punishments. And when it is time for the next general elections, who can say that a change of regime will mean a better government! It is the same strategy which Indira Gandhi followed when she was in power; and her son can only be thankful to the opposition parties that they have not required him to learn anything new.

31 May 1988: The Foreign Hand[7]

With the Lok Sabha by-elections round the corner and the option of an early dissolution of Parliament not entirely ruled out, it is time for New Delhi to step up the hue and cry about the ubiquitous 'foreign hand'. Over the last month or so, official 'leaks' have virtually flooded the media with stories of how Pakistan is arming itself with the latest weapons developed in U.S. defence laboratories. The most sensational report was the one culled from an American daily, suggesting that Pakistan had managed to develop and test a missile capable of carrying nuclear warheads that could reach New Delhi or Bombay. The report suggested that the missile had been developed with Chinese assistance, but the whole matter was confused by the speculation that the missile closely resembled a well-known Soviet short-range missile: it was suggested that the Pakistanis had somehow managed to procure some of these Soviet missiles and develop them for their own use with Chinese help. The Indian government has officially denied any knowledge of such a nuclear delivery system possessed by Pakistan, but of course the point of the whole matter is not to make an official allegation, but rather to allow the seeds of suspicion and fear to be sown in the mind of the electorate.

There is much at stake. It is clear that the by-elections two weeks from now will not see the end of the controversy about defence purchases, their propriety and the manner in which these deals are struck. It is also clear that, besides mucking up the trail of hush-hush deals and below-the-counter payments, one of the strongest arguments on the government side, will be the age-old appeal to protect and strengthen the country's defence forces. The greater the atmosphere of threat and insecurity, the stronger the government's case that all this talk of

[7] *Frontier*, 20, 42 (4 June 1988).

irregular defence purchases is merely the ploy of subversive forces to weaken the country's security programme.

The other area in which the Pakistani hand has been rediscovered is that of 'internal destablization'. Once again, we have had a series of official disclosures — incontrovertible evidence, we are told, that Pakistan has been both the brain and the brawn behind the Khalistani insurgency in Punjab. Supposedly, these are discoveries made after interrogating arrested Khalistani terrorists. It seems that from 1985, Sikh terrorists have been recruited from Canada, Britain and the United States, brought to Pakistan, 'indoctrinated in the Khalistan ideology', trained in the techniques of terrorist violence and subversion, supplied with arms, and sent across the border into India. The 'evidence' trotted out repeatedly speaks of something that can hardly cause any surprise — that Sikh terrorists have procured and stocked arms in various places in Pakistan, and that these have been smuggled across the border into India. Most insurgent movements today seek out safe places across the country's borders in order to acquire arms, regroup forces, train cadres, and so on. The Tamil insurgents did this for years on end on Indian soil. If the Indian government has officially denied having actively helped in arming and training these groups, it cannot but accept the fact that it was unable to prevent them from using Indian territory as their base until it became politically necessary — after the Rajiv–Jayawardene accord — for the Indian government to move in against the Tamil insurgents. Surely, something very similar has been going on in Pakistan; and it does not need much 'evidence' in the form of garbled reports of 'interrogation' sessions to prove that Khalistani activists have been using the borders as a crucial element in their strategy of insurgency.

The problem surely does not lie in the very existence of borders, although that would seem to be the last resort in the Indian government's argument about its failure to resolve the Punjab situation. Now we are being told that it was Pakistan (what, we may ask, is this entity called 'Pakistan' — its government, some of its officials, certain elements in its population?) which forced upon a reluctant group of disgruntled Sikhs the very 'ideology of Khalistan', coaxed and badgered them into making the 'Khalistan declaration' in exchange for arms and training. As if, without the proximity of Pakistan, the Punjab problem would simply vanish. It is the last ploy of an incompetent and discredited state apparatus to explain away its failure to resolve, through a political process, the conflicting demands within the body politic. Every step in the long and bloody history of Punjab has been a move from one depth of short-sightedness and incompetence to another.

20 June 1988: The By-Elections[8]

From the very beginning, there was something prefigurative about the Allahabad by-election, like the trailer of a new film yet to be released. First, it was Mr V.P. Singh who threw down a challenge to Amitabh Bachchan, declaring that he would fight the superstar and no one else. But, of course, it was not the screen hero who was the real object of his campaign: it was the Prime Minister himself, and his coterie of ambitious money-grabbing young men among whom was included Ajitabh Bachchan, charged with laundering the illegal kickbacks from the defence purchases of the government. Faced with this challenge, the Rajiv cohort prevaricated. Amitabh Bachchan had put up a show of injured pride by resigning his Lok Sabha seat as soon as the charges of financial impropriety were made against his brother. This would have been a good opportunity for him to take his case to the electorate and clear his name; and with it, the cloud of suspicion that had gathered around the Prime Minister. But the risks were too great. Clearly, the high command knew enough about the popular mood in northern India to decide, finally, that a contest between V.P. Singh and Amitabh Bachchan in Allahabad would inevitably build up into a proxy war for the next general elections. The rulers of New Delhi developed cold feet; but resorting to a level of low cunning that has characterized so much of Congress politics in recent years, they kept up the pretence of renominating the film hero until the very last moment, in order to keep an obdurate V.P. Singh in the field. In the end, they sought to precipitate an anticlimax by choosing Sunil Shastri, a political lightweight uninvolved in any way with the notorious circle of Rajiv Gandhi.

Despite every effort by the Congress(I) to downplay the

8 *Frontier*, 20, 45 (25 June 1988).

significance of the by-elections, the central issue could not be kept under cover. All over northern India, the Lok Sabha by-elections turned into a referendum on the probity of the Rajiv government. As it turned out, except for the Pali seat in Rajasthan, the Congress(I) was unable to retain four seats in U.P., Gujarat, Jammu and Haryana. The polling was suspended in Faridabad because of violence, but everyone expects the Congress(I) to lose there anyway. The only other seat which the Congress(I) was able to win was in Meghalaya where the redoubtable Williamson Sangma, who wins elections on his own, now happens to be in that party.

All in all, the Lok Sabha by-election results are a clear pointer to the main direction in which politics will move in the next year and a half. Beyond doubt, there is strong suspicion in the popular mind of the worthlessness and corruption of the Rajiv Gandhi government. This feeling is more or less generalized, and cuts across the usual segmentations of the electorate by election managers and forecasters. It is also clear that the opposition knows that it is in with a very good chance of actually winning the next election, if it can stay united. A very prominent feature of these by-elections was the agreement of all opposition parties on a common candidate in every Lok Sabha seat. The results are clear; where the opposition has won, it has done so by huge margins. Kanshi Ram's candidature in Allahabad was double-edged; as the results show, his strong support among scheduled-caste voters probably cost the Congress(I) a significant portion of its traditional votes. What is also clear by now is that V.P. Singh will be the strongest candidate as opposition leader. Questions of programmatic unity, the position of the BJP, and the ever-enigmatic role of the parliamentary Left are of course matters that will not be settled in a day. But the scent of victory is the strongest unifier in opposition politics in India, and that is something which will now keep the opposition going until the next general elections.

Far more problematic is the question of what happens in the Congress(I). The threat of dissension, and even of a split, will keep hanging over Congress politics. Nothing dramatic may happen in the near future; but by winning Allahabad with such a large margin, V.P. Singh has fought back all attempts to silence and marginalize him, and has consolidated his position as the rival centre to which Congress members, disgruntled or disillusioned with the electoral prospects of Rajiv Gandhi, can flock. This fact will now remain unaltered until the next general elections. What Rajiv Gandhi will now do to build up a more reliable party organization or a more populist image for the government remains to be seen. But then, this young man's stock of political ideas, never plentiful, seems to have reached rock-bottom.

16 August 1988: Alliance-Making[9]

The first steps were taken last week in setting up the electoral alternative to the Rajiv Congress. This time, there was not the drama of eleven years ago, when a collective experience in India's prisons cemented the virtually spontaneous coming together of an opposition tormented by the Emergency regime. Nor was there the saintly hand of a patriarch-renouncer like J.P., keeping everybody in line, pushing below the surface the petty conflicts and jealousies that always threatened to erupt, and generally reminding the leaders of their responsibilities to the people. This time there has been a much more mundane process of alliance-making, involving a long series of negotiations and deals. The result — the National Front or Rashtriya Morcha of seven opposition parties — is perhaps a more realistic expression of the possibilities of opposition politics today, but it is also much less dramatic in its impact.

Three constituents of the Front are the Lok Dal, the Janata Party and the Jan Morcha. These parties have been riding the crest of the widespread disenchantment with the Rajiv Congress that appears to be sweeping across the northern regions of the country. The recent electoral reverses suffered by the Congress(I) have generally been at the hands of these parties. It is not so much what they represent in themselves that has made them the principal spokesmen of the opposition in northern India. It is rather their position as a counter-force to the Rajiv Congress that has given them their recent impetus. Initially, it was Devi Lal's resounding victory in Haryana last year. Then there was the series of by-election victories by insignificant Janata Party candidates in several Assembly and Parliamentary constituencies in U.P. and Bihar. And finally, of course, there

[9] *Frontier*, 21, 1 (20 August 1988).

was V.P. Singh's dramatic win in Allahabad two months ago. There is no doubt that the northern Indian component of the new Front is sensing a large-scale 'wave' in the Hindi belt, and it is this above all else which will keep the alliance going until the next general elections.

The other components are the Congress(S), the DMK, the Asom Gana Parishad and the Telugu Desam. Of these, the first does not count for much, now that Sharad Pawar has been co-opted with full honours in the Congress(I) in Maharashtra. The DMK has undoubtedly received a new lease of life with the demise of its seemingly invincible enemy M.G.R., and the sub-sequent squabbles between the two women claiming his legacy. The AGP and the Telugu Desam are still the principal political forces in their regional bases and will, for that reason, have an important participation in the Front. Besides, N.T. Rama Rao has sought to play the role of elder statesman in the alliance-making exercises, and has been named as chairman of the Front. There is, of course, a southern component of the Janata Party as well, but its supremacy in Karnataka has been recently damaged — perhaps irreparably — by Ramakrishna Hegde's troubles in containing the factionalism within his own party. Now that he has chosen to quit the Chief Ministership, Mr Hegde may well play a more active part in the national politics of the Front: whether this will be an element of strength or weakness remains to be seen.

No serious analyst will believe that the National Front, as it has come into being, is a credible alternative — in the sense of a politically viable organization with a feasible alternative pro-gramme. Relations between its own constituents are lacking in harmony — as reflected in the continued vagueness as to who is to be the parliamentary leader of the Front, and in persistent rumours that people like H.N. Bahuguna may be taken back into the Congress(I). Also, there is still no certainty about the relations between the Front and the two other principal segments of the opposition: namely, the BJP and the Left. If electoral calculations predominate, as they seem to be doing at the moment, an alliance with the Left may seem more profitable. This is because the anti-Rajiv 'wave' in the Hindi belt, if it does rise, may be expected to hold irrespective of whether the BJP joins the Front or not, whereas the support of the Left will mean several additional parliamentary seats in West Bengal and Kerala. But then, the Left still remains undecided in this matter. In principle, the CPI(M) has declared itself in favour of an opposition alliance excluding the BJP. But in the days to come, it is certainly going to be wooed by the Congress(I) and asked to stay out of such an alliance. On the other hand, there is also an opinion within the Left which says that the overthrow of the Rajiv regime is the principal parliamentary task, and the broadest possible opposition alliance is the order of the day. Since programmes, policies and ideology have taken a backseat anyway, it is the calculation of votes and seats which will finally decide the matter.

5 September 1988: Gagging the Press[10]

The secrecy in which the Defamation Bill was drafted, the haste with which it was sought to be cleared through Parliament, the utter incompetence of its phraseology, the contempt it showed for the most elementary principles of law, the juvenile malice with which it sought vengeance upon its enemy — the press — and finally, the unprecedented political mess in which it has landed those that it tried to protect — all this can only be described as the doings of men who have taken leave of their senses.

To follow the phraseology of the Bill itself, what are the 'facts of the matter'? The first fact is that there has been, in recent months, a spate of revelations in the press about the illegal doings of the handful of men and women who are at the helm of affairs in New Delhi today. The second fact is that, in spite of the strenuous and successful efforts of all government agencies to see to it that these revelations are not followed up by legal proceedings in court, there are clear signs that the people — meaning, a vast majority of the electorate — are sufficiently convinced that their present rulers are so crooked that they can no longer be trusted with the reins of government. These two basic facts have combined to produce the insane reaction called the Defamation Bill, 1988.

It is now clear that the Bill was drafted, both in secrecy and in haste, perhaps within the space of a week. It seems that it was not even discussed in the Cabinet before P. Chidambaram, the

---

[10] *Frontier*, 21, 4 (10 September 1988).

Minister of State for Home, sought to move the Bill in the Lok Sabha, with only a few hours' notice. As the provisions of the Bill became known, the members of the House, and soon the entire nation, were astounded by the conceit of those who thought that they could push through a law so glaringly inconsistent with every principle of freedom of speech.

The Bill introduces in the existing law of defamation a new concept called 'criminal imputation'. Under this, if a person makes an imputation 'falsely alleging' that someone has committed an offence, the aggrieved party can go to court, but the onus of establishing that the imputation is true will be on the accused. A criminal imputation will incur a punishment, 'in the case of the first offence', of imprisonment up to one year and a fine up to Rs 2000, and for 'a second or subsequent offence', of imprisonment up to two years and a fine up to Rs 5000.

The implications of this provision for the freedom of the press are obvious: they amount to its obliteration. For the Bill takes away the right of fair comment, which is the soul of press freedom. The new Bill, if it were to become law, would mean that one would have to have evidence sufficient to prove a person guilty in a court of law before one could make a fair comment on his or her activities. It would mean, in effect, that those who are guilty of paying or accepting commissions and kickbacks would first have to be brought to trial and convicted, before the press could gain the right to talk about the Bofors scandal. It would also mean that the printer or publisher of a newspaper, if once convicted of defamation, would subsequently be liable to the higher penalty if there is 'criminal imputation' in a second, completely unrelated, case. Anyone who has any knowledge of how newspapers work will realize that this would mean that most papers of any standing would simply have to close shop.

Mr Chidambaram defended his new Bill with a series of statements beginning 'Truth is . . .' and 'Truth is not . . . ' But he was unable to persuade anybody that the Bill was not meant to destroy the freedom of the press in order to protect corrupt persons in authority. In fact, much to the dismay of Rajiv Gandhi, not only the members of the opposition, but even the stalwarts of the establishment media were forced to throw up their hands and say that this was too much. Every organ of the press, including the venerable Editors' Guild, declared its opposition to the Bill, threatening an all-India newspaper strike on 6 September 1988. Faced with this un-precedented — and by all accounts, unanticipated — opposition, Rajiv Gandhi has finally deferred the motion of the Bill in the Rajya Sabha, and has constituted a ministerial committee to discuss 'the misgivings' of the press.

There is, of course, nothing to discuss. The 'fact of the matter' is as clear as daylight and we all know it. Rajiv Gandhi and his cronies are now a frightened lot. They have been unnerved by the spate of news items that have cast far more than reasonable doubt on their probity as public servants. They are dreading the prospect of more revelations.

19 September 1988: The Limits of Power[11]

The seven-party National Front of the opposition which was formally launched last week at a huge rally on Marina Beach, Madras, has declared that one of its first concerns will be the discrimination by the Centre against non-Congress(I)-ruled states. Opposition politics in India has always moved through instant reactions to instant issues. Undoubtedly, N.T. Rama Rao, a leading star of the National Front, had in mind the recent attack by the Prime Minister's security men on Telugu Desam legislators when he said that the federal polity had been 'twisted and warped for the aggrandizement of the Centre', and that 'the states had been reduced to beggary'. The allegation is wholly true, but although opposition politicians tend to see the matter as simply a case of discrimination against non-Congress(I)-ruled states, it is in fact an expression of a much more fundamental malady.

Take the Congress(I)-ruled states. Is the situation any different? If some of them at certain points of time seem to enjoy the special favours of fund-dispensing authorities in New Delhi, one can be sure that has to do with the immediate electoral or factional concerns of the ruling power group at the Centre. But there will be as many occasions when Congress(I)-ruled states have been discriminated against, when Congress(I) chief ministers have been thrown out and replaced with such casualness

---

11 *Frontier*, 21, 6 (24 September 1988).

that one would think the chief minister was a member of the Prime Minister's personal staff and not the elected leader of the people of the state. It was the people's realization of their collective non-existence as a state within the Indian Union, that brought about the groundswell which threw men like Rama Rao or Prafulla Mahanta into power. The lathi blows on Telugu Desam MLAs may have been particularly humiliating, or the delay in sending flood relief to Assam particularly crass, but there is no reason to think that the people in other states, in their collective role as constituent units of a federal union, are any better off.

The fact is not only that the original framework of federalism in India has been distorted beyond recognition. Just as there has been a consistent tendency towards the centralization of powers in the last twenty years, so also has there been the growth of entirely new forces and aspirations among the people of this country. An innocent call for a return to the days of Jawaharlal Nehru will not be the answer. The plain fact is that the original structure of federalism, as thought of by the makers of the Indian Constitution, is incapable of accommodating the entirely genuine desires of the peoples of this country to maintain their distinct identities as well as to live together. It is high time that those who claim to voice the resentment of the people against Congress(I) misrule give more thought to this fundamental malady. The need of the day is a call for a new federalism.

Already we have had experiments and innovations — entirely ad hoc and piecemeal — within the old structure that point to an entirely different arrangement. The Hill Council in Darjeeling, which has just been created as a result of the Gorkhaland agitation, has the legal stamp of the present provisions of the Constitution; but its content is wholly new, because for all practical purposes it introduces the concept of a state within a state. No matter how much Subrata Mukherjee may shout about the injured pride of Bengalis, there is nothing to despair in this. On the contrary, it is an innovation wholly to be welcomed, and worked upon, improved, and developed. This may in fact give us the forms of a multi-tiered federal structure, which may be the most useful way of giving to the aspirations of many recently developed cultural identities in India their legitimate and constructive place within the union of the Indian peoples.

Those to whom political power only means the pompous stamp of sovereignty and the iron rod of bureaucracy will of course see in this the signs of a loss of 'national integrity'. It is the duty of those who claim to be the opposition to see that a new and more flexible federal structure will strengthen rather than weaken the unity of our people. The real tragedy is that those who lead opposition politics today cannot see beyond their noses.

20 October 1988: Satanic? Or the Surrender of the Modern?[12]

Is the Government of India seeking directly to interfere with the right of free speech? Is it trying to control what will be written and what will be read? Is it trying to create a climate where no uncomfortable question or dangerous thought will raise its head?

On the face of it, this must be the explanation behind the decision by the government to ban Salman Rushdie's novel. The book was banned as soon as it was published, before most people had a chance to read it. In other words, even before its literary or other qualities could be judged, an executive fiat declared the book unfit to be bought or read. If this decision is accepted without protest, it will be tantamount to a death warrant on artists, writers and scientists in this country.

Who decides on the quality of a serious literary work? Who is to pronounce judgement on a writer's social or political views? The literary readership, or a political leader or bureaucrat? By banning *The Satanic Verses*, the Government of India has declared that if there is sufficient political opposition, a literary work, irrespective of its artistic merits, will not reach its intended readership.

The menace contained in this move hardly requires explication. Yet, this virtual truism now has to be stated afresh. This is because the principal argument that is being offered in support of the government's decision, is political realism. It is the old argument about a situation of emergency: the times are dangerous,

---

[12] *Ānandabājār patrikā*, 27 October 1988 (translated from the Bengali).

there are too many risks of outbreak of violence. At such times, one must above all be practical. There will be occasions in future for the pure contemplation of moral principles; now, one must tackle the immediate situation, if necessary even by conceding a little bit to the enemy. Those journalists — official hacks — who only a few days ago were forced to shut up when faced with the storm of protest over the Defamation Bill, are now declaiming on the principles of political realism. And listening to these lectures on the intricate methods of determining the volatility of a political situation, even many of the progressives have been left without an answer. Publicly, they are silent about the ban; in private, they will confess their anxieties: 'You never know, these communal matters are highly inflammable. It's best to stay out of them.'

The ban is not part of a planned authoritarian assault. It is the sign of extreme insecurity, when rulers appeal to realism and practicality to cover up their weakness. This politics of immediate solutions to immediate problems is shortsighted and vacuous, and more dangerous because it would have everyone ignore the consequences. It is being argued that if Rushdie's book had been allowed to be sold, there would have been riots. Interestingly, none of those who demanded the ban or imposed it had read the book. Syed Shahabuddin has made the weighty pronouncement that to tell that a drain is a drain, one does not need to jump into it. In his case, of course, the task was simple. He had heard it being said: 'Here is a drain.' Where did he hear it? From some time before *The Satanic Verses* was actually published, there were stories about it in the papers. Not literary reviews, but news stories: that is to say, sensational speculations, half-truths and assorted misrepresentations. That was sufficient grist to Shahabuddin's mill. His politics consists of sniffing around for drains. As soon as he finds one, he shouts: 'There it is, it's polluting everything. Clean it up.' Looking for impurities and cleaning them up: that is the politics of fundamentalism. No matter what the religion or ideology, it thrives on an obsessive and intolerant search for polluting influences. Shahabuddin needed a drain; he found it. If it hadn't been this one, he would have found something else. The cry went up immediately: 'We will not tolerate this satanic conspiracy. Ban the book.' The demand found a few supporters from among that group whose only identity in democratic India is that of being 'secular Muslims'. 'Secular', and hence part of the so-called nationalist mainstream, yet 'Muslim', and hence different. They have tried all these years to keep their distinct identity intact while swimming with the mainstream — with pathetic results. Of course, being the trusted advisers of the government on Muslim matters, their sense of political realism is especially sharp. They were the ones who persuaded the government that the communal situation in northern India was so serious that with the impending general elections, etc., etc. . . .

I have read *The Satanic Verses*. I was fortunate in having bought a copy soon after the book appeared, not knowing at that time, of course, that it would be banned the next day. Having begun reading it, I could not put it down. I pushed aside all other work and read the book at a stretch over three days. Soon, I will read it once more. A narrative that is meticulously crafted, that shows unparalleled skills in the use of language, that has a complex structure, that does not sweep one away in a flood of emotion but ignites one's intelligence, that conceals at every turn the possibility of discovering some unexpected meaning: I like read-ing books such as this. Needless to say, the work of an author like Rushdie, steeped in the traditions of Western literary moder-nism and with skills virtually unsurpassed today in the innovative use of English prose, is exceedingly sophisticated. Woven into the dramatic twists and turns of the narrative is Rushdie's run-ning conversation with other authors — comments, debates with Goethe, Dickens, Tolstoy, Joyce, Brecht, Borges, Marquez: I am sure I will notice many more when I read the book again. This is a serious book written with much effort and care: it deserves care and effort on the part of the reader.

Those who say that the book is meant to defame Prophet Muhammad are either lying (because they have not read the book), or they are being deceitful, or else they are plain ignorant. The subject of the novel is not the life of Prophet Muhammad; the subject is Salman Rushdie himself. One of the two principal characters of the story is Saladin Chamchawalla. Born in Bom-bay, his nationalist Congress-supporting father, like many others of his generation, believed that now that the sahibs had left, his son would become a sahib and run the country. The boy Saladin was sent off to England, to study in the sahibs' school. His effort to become a sahib was earnest. He thought he would churn the ocean of European civilization and drink the pure nectar of freethinking modernity, and in the process wipe out his inherited marks of race, nationality and culture. The other character is Gibreel Farishta. He is a superstar, known all over India for his roles in blockbuster mythologicals. He is in love with the good life, with luxury and modern technology, addicted in equal measure to Scotch whisky and the company of white women. But his words are pure *swadeshi,* reflecting his unshakeable conviction about the decay and imminent destruction of a shallow, materialistic, spiritually vacuous Western civilization.

Gibreel and Saladin are two sides of the same self — two sides of Indian modernity, the one inseparable from the other. Suddenly, by a stroke of providence, Gibreel acquires the powers of an angel, while the hapless Saladin becomes the embodiment of Satan. Now, Saladin is made to see through the facade of British liberalism and discover the reality of racial discrimination in the land of his dreams. He sees that in London neighbourhoods torn by race riots, he is just one of a thousand other Indians, Pakistanis, Bangladeshis, Caribbeans. And Gibreel? He decides to take his new role as an angel seriously. He proceeds to redeem Western society from its million sins. Gibreel, angel of god, is slowly transformed into Azreel, the angel of death. In his mad desire to purify the world, he ignites a devastating fire of violence, hatred and destruction.

Needless to say, this is not the whole story of *The Satanic Verses.* It is narrative that sustains this massive book of 547 pages, and even two long paragraphs cannot provide a summary. The section that has caused such an uproar actually occupies a small portion of the book. Both Gibreel and Saladin are Muslim. Having been reborn, they ask themselves, 'What is religion? What is truth? What is the good?' Buried for so long under the layers of their consciousness, the words of the Koran are now interrogated afresh. If the Mahound described in this novel is the Prophet Muhammad, I have to say that in Rushdie's telling of his story he appears as a political figure of immense nobility: noble, but human, tortured by doubt, uncertain about the complex claims of right and wrong, courageous enough to admit his mistakes. The twelve prostitutes over whom there is so much protest are, in the novel, hardly the 'wives' of the Mahound; they are just prostitutes. It is the vengeful Salman Farsi and the poet Baal who, seeking to bring Muhammad to disrepute, spread the rumour that they might be the wives of the Prophet. And of course, it is the madam of the brothel who seeks to make a little business out of religion. Mahound, who is otherwise forgiving even in his moment of triumph, cannot forgive these transgressors. Waiting for his execution, Baal, the eternal unbeliever (one can hardly fail to recognize here the hero of Brecht's first play), says to Muhammad: 'Whores and writers. We are the people you can't forgive.' Muhammad replies, 'Writers and whores. I see no difference here.'

The Satanic Verses is a story of the contradictions, anxieties and crisis of a rationalist consciousness in independent India. This consciousness is touched by the magical certainty of folk belief, but it can never accept folk religion as its own. (One can hear Rushdie's debate with Marquez on this subject.) The days of divine revelation are past. Whether awake or in our dreams, never again will we hear another prophet. At least, not unless we deceive ourselves. And if we do, there are two choices. We could, like Saladin Chamcha, shut our eyes and say, 'It's fine the way it is, don't upset things too much.' This is the deception of political realism. Or else, we could make a prophetic declaration that the world will have to be cleansed of the pollution of evil, and like Gibreel Farishta, send thousands of innocent people to their doom. This is the deception of fundamentalism. Two sides of the same self: the two sides of Indian modernity, the one inseparable from the other.

I have heard a few 'secular Muslims' complaining about why the minorities were being singled out as being overly sensitive. If a book like this had been written about Hinduism, they ask, would Hindus have tolerated it? The complaint is justified. Among the frightened and cowardly adherents of modernity in India, there are no differences between Hindus and Muslims. If today, a man called Michael Madhusudan Dutt were to write a book called *Meghnādbadh* and declare, 'I despise Rama and his rabble,' I have no doubt the book would be proscribed. It is the good fortune of Bengali literature that the colonial state of the nineteenth century banned books only when they went against colonial interests, and not at the request of their native subjects.

1 November 1988: Looking Back[13]

A small piece of news tucked away in a corner: an additional sessions judge in New Delhi has sentenced six persons to rigorous life terms for killing four people in the Delhi riots of November 1984. This is the first significant judicial verdict in what remains perhaps the worst incident of communal violence in independent India. What was more interesting was the judge's observation that he was awarding the minimum punishment for murder, since the assassination of Mrs Gandhi 'had sent shock waves across the country, causing anger and anguish and resulting in the clogging of a sense of proportion and rationale in the common masses.'

'Clogging' of a sense of proportion is an adequate, if somewhat infelicitous, metaphor to describe much of what is happening today in our politics, although whether 'the common masses' are the only ones to suffer from the malady is debatable. Four years have passed since the riots in Delhi, and the government still insists that there is no need to inquire into why and how they were caused and who were responsible: as though the wounds will heal simply by refusing to recognize that they are there. The fact remains, of course, that the wounds have not healed. They have multiplied and bled, and the events in Punjab, Haryana and Delhi in the last four years are ample reminder that, no matter how desperately those in power might wish, the people do not simply forgive and forget. Fear and insecurity have become for them part of the daily business of survival, and they simply do not trust the sweet, reassuring platitudes of those who claim to run the state. The people know that it is not simply 'anger and anguish' which can lead to the sort of organized killings that swept the capital in those bloody days in November 1984. They also know that the real culprits are being sheltered by those who are in power.

If there is anything which can characterize the mood of the 'common masses' in northern India today, it is a pervasive feeling of insecurity and distrust. Authority and legitimate leadership have virtually vanished. Nothing can be taken at face value and nobody taken on his word. A wave of communal violence is sweeping the towns of Uttar Pradesh, from Muzaffarnagar through Aligarh, Khatauli, Faizabad to Bahraich. Since no one can trust the authorities of the law to maintain order and protect lives, the rule is: 'each for himself as best as he can'. Every street and *muhalla* in the U.P. towns is armed and organized to defend, retaliate and attack in a warfare of the most elemental kind. And the state is keeping itself busy by banning demonstrations, imposing curfews, sending in more and more armed policemen over whom it has less and less control, while pretending that the problem will go away if only people can be stopped from talking about it. What we are witnessing in Uttar Pradesh today is a farcical illustration — farcical and horrific at the same time — of the 'withering away' of the state!

2 January 1989: All Options Open[14]

In the end, all the speculations about an open conflict over the party line and a change in the top leadership proved to be futile. The Party Congress of the CPI(M) ended last week in Trivandrum after confirming both E.M.S. Namboodiripad as general secretary and his supposedly controversial line as the agreed line of the party. Mr Namboodiripad held up his line as one of unbroken continuity since the party's foundation in 1964, and demonstrated its correctness by pointing out such diverse events as the presence in the Party Congress of fraternal delegations from both the Soviet and Chinese parties (the first time this has happened in the party's history), the recent cordiality in the meetings between Prime Minister Rajiv Gandhi and the Chinese leaders (which, said E.M.S., only confirmed the CPI(M)'s position in 1964 on the border dispute), and the realization by the CPI that the Congress(I) was a force to be opposed and CPI(M) an ally. Continuity is a virtue which most communist parties treasure, particularly a party which has had a completely unchanged leadership since the death of Jawaharlal Nehru.

But despite the assertion of continuity and consensus, the speeches and resolutions at the Party Congress bear clear signs of a papering over of differences. There is no doubt that the

[14] *Frontier*, 21, 21 (7 January 1989).

disagreement over electoral strategy has not been sorted out: it has merely been shelved for the time being. The main political resolution proclaims the party's intention to forge a broad unity of the 'left, democratic and secular' forces in the country in order to oust the Congress(I) government. However, a lot of persuasion is still going on within the party to assure members that this line is not going to become an instrument to prop up the Rajiv government, should it fall in a crisis. This is revealed by the fact that the inclusion of 'secular' needed to be tied with an explanation that the communal forces in India were directly serving the interests of imperialist powers, and matched with the declaration that the Congress(I) was nevertheless the principal enemy of the Indian people. Clearly, many members are not completely reassured; and Mr Namboodiripad not only had to explain the differences between the situation in 1977–9 when the Janata came to power and the situation prevailing today when a purely secular opposition stands the chance of replacing the Congress(I), but he also had B.T. Ranadive chide the delegates from West Bengal for not appreciating the dangers of the communal forces in the country. In the end, the resolution adopted basically concedes that the specific question of electoral alliances will be taken up as and when the situation demands. In other words, all opinions within the party may argue that its options have been left open.

It is interesting that, whereas the Akali Dal and Telugu Desam are regarded by the CPI(M) as solidly secular allies in the fight for an alternative to the Congress(I) based on a socio-economic programme, and while there is much soul-searching about the failure of a Left advance in northern India, the only radical movement which has made the most significant headway into the heart of the Bihar countryside in recent years — against the fiercest opposition from both landlords and the state administration — has been officially declared by the CPI(M) as an 'enemy of the Left'. Perhaps this is the true indicator of the seriousness with which the terms 'left', 'secular', 'democratic', etc. are taken by the parliamentary communists. These terms have come to bear entirely different meanings for them, and are used as signals for identifying, in Aesopian language, the specific electoral parties with which open or secret understandings may be arrived at for electoral purposes. If there are sections among the CPI(M) members who are still suspicious about the intentions of their leaders and about the significance of their newly adopted political line, they have good reasons for their suspicion.

16 January 1989: Unite to Divide[15]

While public attention is now focused on Tamil Nadu where the election campaign is hotting up, there were other signs last week of the endless tangles in which opposition politics has found itself. All this time the assumption was that the National Front led by V.P. Singh would be the principal alliance around which the opposition would organize itself in order to oust the government of Rajiv Gandhi. Of course, a spanner was thrown into the works early on by Chandra Shekhar, who refused to go along with the decision to merge some of the party identities in order to go into the Front. But no one takes Chandra Shekhar seriously these days, and although his intransigence did mean some problems for the Janata government in Karnataka, this was never seen as an insurmountable problem for opposition alliance-making.

The problem was not with the middle, but with the two extremes of the opposition — the BJP on the one side and the Left on the other. V.P. Singh has been trying his utmost to have both sides go along with the National Front. He has offered all sorts of formulae so that both could contribute their respective electoral advantages to the Front, without unduly compromising on their publicly declared hostility towards each other. The calculations for the National Front are simple. Having the Left with it may not immediately contribute very much in terms of winning seats in Parliament, because in the areas where the Left has electoral strength — especially in West Bengal and Kerala — it will win or lose on its own, without gaining very much from the alliance. The advantage to the Front is rather in terms of keeping the Left away from the Congress(I), and of neutralizing any attempt the latter might make to project a 'left' image in its campaign. It has been clear for some time that Rajiv Gandhi's advisers have rediscovered

15 *Frontier*, 21, 23 (21 January 1989).

the electoral usefulness of a left-leaning campaign, something which his mother had used with such deadly perfection. On the other hand, the BJP is a very significant electoral force in a lot of parliamentary seats in northern India, and the existence or otherwise of an electoral understanding with it may decide the fate of at least fifty seats in four or five states in the Hindi belt. Mr Singh, it seems, has tried out several methods to have the Front retain both advantages, including seat adjustments on a state-by-state basis so that the Left need not be seen as running on the same platform with the BJP in those states where the latter has strength.

But the CPI(M) in particular, having recently adopted in its Party Congress a political resolution which pronounced communalism to be at least as grave a danger to the country as the misrule of the Congress(I), took a leading part last week in a move to launch a 'national campaign for a left democratic programme'. Along with the CPI, the RSP, and the Forward Bloc, the CPI(M) leaders teamed up with the indestructible H.N. Bahuguna to remind the nation that politics is not simply about winning elections but about ideology and programmes. The object of the 'campaign', these leaders said, was not to set up another front but to 'radicalize the national political situation' by drawing attention to the question of 'national unity' and to the crucial issue of India's foreign policy. They criticized the National Front, and its leader V.P. Singh, for not taking these two issues seriously. Naturally enough, they also singled out the BJP as an enemy of this 'left democratic programme' and said categorically that there was no question this time of reviving 'the spirit of 1977'.

It is curious that whenever Mr Bahuguna is down and out, he suddenly reappears as bearing the conscience of the Left. That has been his method of finding his way back into favour with the Congress(I). For the CPI(M), the double game played by its all-India leaders has been clear for some time. While its rank and file is largely committed to the struggle against a corrupt and brutal regime, exemplified so tragically by the murder of Safdar Hashmi, its national leaders are jockeying for bargaining advantage in the horse race for power. In Tamil Nadu, they have teamed up with the DMK and a faction of the Muslim League, while at the national level they talk endlessly of the great communal danger and of the infinite wisdom of Rajiv Gandhi's foreign policy. While the new 'national campaign' was so forthright in its criticism of V.P. Singh's ideological vagueness, Jyoti Basu declared in Calcutta that, come what may, the Left would in the end support the National Front in the next elections. All in all, therefore, the scenario remains unclear. And doubtless, Rajiv Gandhi and his advisers will spare no effort to keep the opposition as confused as ever.

3 April 1989: Conceal and Be Damned[16]

The Thakkar Commission report as placed before Parliament has been called a damp squib. It is, and it isn't. True, it contains virtually no sensational disclosures apart from the references to R.K. Dhawan already published in the *Indian Express* report which, of course, was what started the entire hullabaloo anyway. The reasons for Justice Thakkar's damning observation that the 'needle of suspicion' pointed towards Mr Dhawan have not been elaborated with any substantive evidence beyond what was already known from the extracts leaked out earlier. It was clear even then that the insinuations levelled against Mrs Gandhi's confidential secretary by Justice Thakkar did not, notwithstanding the honourable judge's florid prose, add up to a credible indictment; it is still clear that there is a great deal of mystery about the former Prime Minister's assassination that has hardly been touched upon.

Justice Thakkar had recommended that Mr Dhawan's role be thoroughly investigated. After the Commission's report was tabled in Parliament, Mr Buta Singh announced that this had in fact been done, and that the special investigation team had cleared Mr Dhawan of all suspicions of complicity in the crime or in the conspiracy. Curiously, however, Justice Thakkar's own evidence, on the basis of which he had identified the 'needle of suspicion', had come from earlier interrogations of Mr Dhawan conducted by the same investigation team headed by S. Anandaram. The special investigation team's later report, which has supposedly discounted all of Justice Thakkar's suspicions, has not been made public.

16 *Frontier*, 21, 34 (8 April 1989).

Not only that: despite Rajiv Gandhi's boastful announcement that the entire report of the Commission would be placed before Parliament and thoroughly discussed so that 'the truth would be out', it now turns out that only two of the five volumes of the original report have seen the light of day. When this was pointed out by opposition members, the government resorted to the old plea that the remaining portions of the report could not be made public for 'reasons of national security'. It was, of course, under the same plea that a law had been pushed through Parliament to prevent publication of the report; and it was only after the furore caused by the *Indian Express* leak three weeks ago that the government had relented. Now it is clear that the government has many more things to hide.

Pushed into a corner by the countrywide uproar over the leaked extracts of the report, Rajiv Gandhi's attempt to come clean has boomeranged. The suspicion has deepened in the public mind that the story of Mrs Gandhi's assassination did not end with the executions of Satwant and Beant Singh, and that there was a much more deep-rooted conspiracy whose details Rajiv Gandhi's government is at pains to conceal. The matter has been made even murkier by the government's indecisive, indeed panicky, handling of the consequences of the *Indian Express* story. After three days of heavy-handed attempts by the government to throttle the demands of the opposition and to manipulate the rumour mill in order to identify the person who may have leaked the report, the Prime Minister suddenly announced — apparently without even consulting his ministers — that the report would be published in full. Now that this promise has been breached, even the strongest Rajiv Gandhi loyalists are at a loss to defend their position.

In the meantime, Mr Dhawan continues to occupy his new official position among Mr Gandhi's advisers, while no formal move has yet been made against any of Mrs Gandhi's former security chiefs whose lapses Justice Thakkar had forcefully, and quite predictably, condemned.

Since politics in the nation's capital has for long assumed the character of medieval palace intrigue, rumours, speculations, insinuations and innuendos have become the very stuff of politics. But despite their fleeting existence, rumours also leave a deep residue of conviction in the popular mind, and this has nothing to do with the tenability or otherwise of specific suspicions or accusations. The full details of the conspiracy behind Mrs Gandhi's assassination may not be revealed for a long time to come; but the people of this country have already formed their judgement on the utter falsity of the present government's pretensions to probity, cleanliness and efficiency in public life.

3 July 1989: Cynical Moves[17]

Early in the morning on 25 June 1988, terrorists fired into a public gathering of the local RSS *shakha* in Moga town in Punjab and killed 25 people. The day before, in different parts of Punjab, some 24 people were killed in terrorist actions, including the Superintendent of Police of Tarn Taran. A few days before that, a massive bomb blast in a crowded waiting hall at New Delhi railway station killed another 30 people. So what is new? People have become inured to incidents such as these. Punjab is not a subject that provokes any serious discussion any more, because everything that anyone had to say has been said. This is the classic situation of a permanent state of siege: a permanent insurgency pitted against a permanent counter-insurgency.

The government, of course, keeps making its periodic claims of 'success'. The government, in this case, means the triumvirate of the Governor S.S. Ray, the Union Home Minister Buta Singh and the Prime Minister. A police state is best run by a small political leadership who bear no popular responsibility. An apparent lull in terrorist incidents, or a set of 'encounter deaths' or the capture of a 'dreaded terrorist' by security forces, immediately prompts a government claim that the back of terrorism has been broken. If the terrorists strike in Delhi, the government claims that they are on the run and are only hitting out in desperation. When they strike back in Punjab, the government issues a sobering reminder that the stamping out of terrorism takes years, even decades.

Opposition responses too have by now fallen into a set pattern. Blame the government for its failures, praise the people for their courage and good sense, remind everyone that nothing can be

17 *Frontier*, 21, 47 (8 July 1989).

set right without a 'political solution'. In the five years that have passed since Operation Blue Star, it is of course the political solution that has been promised time and again. It is that solution which now seems more distant than ever.

In the meantime, the last hope for a negotiated settlement — the Unified Akali Dal President Simranjit Singh Mann — is now appearing daily in a New Delhi courtroom, facing charges of conspiracy to assassinate Indira Gandhi. The series of rumours about an impending change in the Governorship of Punjab has also abated. Nothing new, it seems, is likely to happen in Punjab in the next few months, except a repetition of the same hopeless pattern.

All of this points to the true significance of a recent announcement by a senior Congress member, that Punjab will be the main issue in the forthcoming general elections. Rajiv Gandhi in his recent speeches has taken to screeching, and one of the things he has been screeching is an accusation that the entire opposition is in league with the Khalistanis. Punjab, it seems, will be allowed to bleed for some time longer, only to enable it to become a credible example for the Congress(I) campaign that the nation is still in danger. The utter cynicism which runs through ruling class politics in India today is best exemplified by the speculation, seriously debated in supposedly 'informed' circles, that the elections for a new Parliament will be held on the fifth anniversary of Indira Gandhi's death!

7 August 1989: Getting Organized?[18]

When the cause has a moral fervour, even the dullest foot-dragger can turn out a brilliant tactician. So many times in the last three years, the opposition has seemed little more than a rag-tag bunch of factious old men, mouthing antiquated slogans and moved only by petty jealousies. And then, all of a sudden, some particularly heinous injustice committed by Rajiv Gandhi's government — and there have been many such crimes — has galvanized them into unity and action. The effect of the mass resignations by opposition members of the Lok Sabha two weeks ago was electrifying, throwing the ruling party into panic and

[18] *Frontier*, 21, 52 (12 August 1989).

confusion. Now the time has come to consolidate and prepare for the next round, which is where the opposition finds the going much tougher.

The official campaign machinery of the government and the ruling party has, of course, swung into action. If the opposition to Rajiv Gandhi has a one-point programme — opposition to Rajiv Gandhi — so does the official campaign have a one-point programme, namely to hammer home the argument that the opposition can never unite. It is a tactic which the ruling Congress party has always used. For, the simple arithmetic of parliamentary elections in India is that if the opposition does unite across the board, the Congress can never hope to win a majority of seats and form a government. The opposition knows this, and so all talk of unity ultimately boils down to a simple question: can the opposition agree enough to put up just one candidate for each seat?

No matter what the media pundits might say, there is little doubt that the opposition this time has had a much longer spell of preparations and talking-among-themselves than at any previous general election in India. Their principal point of moral criticism against the Rajiv Gandhi government, sharpened through a long period of public debate, has now been focused on one simple and well-known issue: corruption in high places. After all, the great turnaround elections always hinge on questions of ethical judgement. Unlike previous elections, and especially unlike 1977, it now also has an unquestioned candidate for the post of Prime Minister. The question of alliances and seat adjustments has been considered off and on for a long time, and since everyone knows that will be the crucial arithmetic that will decide their fate, the discussions in the matter have been conducted on a level of hard-nosed realism. On all these counts, it would appear that the opposition is, in a fundamental sense, far better prepared to face the next elections than it has ever been before.

The question that is being asked is: can this unity last? That is the question which Rajiv Gandhi's media minions are throwing at the public. Surprisingly, the same question is not asked of the Congress(I) itself. Has there been unity in the Congress(I)? How has it been achieved? In the states where it is out of power, the disunity and factiousness in its ranks are so stark that they do not even have to be pointed out. Where it is in power, the same disunity and factiousness make the life of every Congress(I) chief minister as anxious and painful as a spell in purgatory. Even at the Centre, there have been more changes in ministerial positions in the last four years than anyone can remember. And even a monumental majority in Parliament has had to be artificially kept in place by the enactment of an anti-defection law. So what unity are we talking about anyway?

The Indian voters have now been hardened enough by experience not to ask for the moon. They seem to know very well what elections can and cannot achieve. The continuity in government policy, which in essence means continuity in the conditions of power for the ruling classes, is not fundamentally affected by changes in governments and ministers. What the people do wish to assert is their right to say, 'We have had enough of you lot.'

21 August 1989: Gohpur Again[19]

No trick is too low for today's cynical practitioners of the political game of squeezing the last drop out of a corrupt and cynical system. This is most apparent in the contentious field of centre–state relations. The players in this particular game consist not only of the Union and state governments, but also of groups and movements claiming to represent the aspirations to statehood of peoples who do not have a distinct political identity within the Indian federation. Given all that has happened over this issue in the last few years — in Punjab, Assam, Darjeeling, Jharkhand, to name only the most well-known cases — one would have thought the time had come for all those who claim to lead our nation to put their heads together to devise a suitable political framework for the proper working out of Indian federalism. That the present constitutional order is grossly inadequate to provide for the aspirations to autonomy of new cultural solidarities and nationalities has never been more obvious.

Yet what we are witnessing is a sickening display of unscrupulous manipulation and low cunning. The incidents over the last two weeks in the remote area of Gohpur on the Assam–Arunachal border constitute a particularly unsavoury instance.

[19] *Frontier*, 22, 2 (26 August 1989).

What first attracted national headlines was an announcement from Itanagar that the Arunachal police, with the help of the CRP, had recovered more than a hundred bodies of victims of group clashes at Gohpur in Assam, bordering Arunachal Pradesh. The report added that most of the victims were Bodo women and children, and that the death figures were probably much higher. The scale of violence seemed very large, and immediately the official propaganda machinery orchestrated from New Delhi went into full swing. Another instance of 'Assamese chauvinism', the chorus went up. Further proof of the incompetence of the AGP government! The AICC even made an official demand to the Prime Minister that the Assam government be dismissed and President's Rule declared in the state.

It gradually transpired that the event in question was of a different order altogether. Gohpur has been a sensitive place for ethnic relations for a long time. It was the scene of considerable violence in February 1983, at the time of the disputed Assam Assembly elections. The incidents this time were precipitated, it appears, with the killing of a non-tribal by an alleged Bodo militant. The total number of those killed in the ethnic clashes that followed was somewhere around fifteen, and most of the victims were non-tribals. It was the overenthusiastic Arunachal Chief Minister Gegong Apang who was mainly responsible for distorting and exaggerating the incident out of all proportion and creating a first-rate crisis. He was undoubtedly emboldened by the postures of his senior party leaders in New Delhi, led by the Prime Minister himself, to create as much trouble as possible for the non-Congress(I) state governments in the run-up to the next general elections. A further compulsion was introduced by the forthcoming talks on 28 August 1989 between representatives of the All Bodo Students Union and the Assam government, supervised by the Union government. Since the leaders in Delhi have shown that they are prepared to concede to all parties who can create the maximum trouble, especially if a non-Congress(I) government can be cut down to size in the process, one can hardly blame the Bodo agitators for choosing the tactics they have adopted. The fact that thousands of innocent people are being rendered homeless, their properties burnt or looted, and that dozens are being killed every week simply to keep up the tempo of the agitation bothers nobody at all. It does not take too much skill in political analysis to predict that a lot more blood will flow in Assam in the next few months before anything like a 'solution' to the Bodo problem is found. When the very existence of a 'problem' serves the purpose, who wants a solution?

18 September 1989: Dirty Game[20]

As the general elections draw nearer, a great number of issues that would otherwise have been regarded as of merely regional importance are increasingly becoming entangled in the cobweb of national politics. No part of the country is free of this process. In the non-Congress(I) states, for instance, the Union government, along with whatever help it can get from the Governors, the local Congress(I) machinery, and of course its own captive media, is out to create as much trouble as possible. A relentless campaign is on against Devi Lal for one. The plot to buy up a number of Janata Dal MLAs in Haryana having failed, it was Siddhartha Ray who stepped in with a series of letters charging Devi Lal with having interfered with the functioning of the Punjab government on the occasion of the *Bharat bandh*. In Assam, the Bodo agitation seems to have the silent, and not-so-silent, blessings of New Delhi. In Andhra Pradesh, Mr Rama Rao is being pressurized from all possible quarters. In West Bengal, several Congress(I) leaders have demanded that President's Rule be imposed in view of a threatening law and order situation. In Tamil Nadu, there were alarming reports that the Congress(I) was preparing for a major show of violence against the DMK on the day of the *bandh*: fortunately nothing happened, perhaps only because of the advance publicity.

This is not to say, of course, that the non-Congress(I) governments have nothing to answer for. Whether it is Haryana or West Bengal or Andhra Pradesh, there is much in the way these states are being ruled that smacks of inefficiency, arbitrariness, sectarianism, corruption and the authoritarian use of governmental and party power. The point is, however, that the criticism of these injustices and failings, inasmuch as it is being taken up by the Congress(I), is motivated exclusively by considerations that have to do with the next general elections, with a general helping hand being provided by the dirty tricks department of the central government. Corruption and autocratic functioning being the central issues threatening the future of the Rajiv Gandhi regime, the attitude seems to be to proclaim: 'We are not the only ones; everybody else is just as bad.'

Turning to the Congress(I)-ruled states, the situation is similar. In Jammu and Kashmir, where Farooq Abdullah rules as a pliable proxy for the Congress(I), what was previously a vast reservoir of regional grievances on which Mr Abdullah's father had thrived despite the machinations of New Delhi, is now being rapidly channelized into a purely communal politics. Once Mr Abdullah decided to abandon his natural constituency for what he thought was a comfortable sinecure offered to him by Delhi, this was virtually a foregone conclusion. In other states, like U.P. or Bihar or Madhya Pradesh, the political picture is dominated by the jockeying for positions within the Congress(I). Many forces are at work here. There are first the calculations of which groups will get what share of the nominations for the parliamentary elections. Following upon that, there is the need to demonstrate one's indispensability for the Congress(I)'s electoral success in the state. Finally, there is a subtle but nonetheless perceptible calculation, which is weighing the options and probabilities of a Congress(I) disaster in the general elections, and thus opening up avenues of communication with 'the other side'.

While all this is likely to continue in the next couple of months — the period of preparation — it is by no means certain that this will have any necessary bearing upon the results of the next elections. There have been in recent years several occasions when the voters have, without any obvious prompting, acted collectively to produce a 'wave'. There are many reasons to believe that the forthcoming elections might become one where the one exclusive issue will be a referendum on Rajiv Gandhi. If that does turn out to be the case, regional calculations will not figure in the minds of the voter at all. The only question which he or she will want to answer is: 'Do we want to give Rajiv Gandhi another term as Prime Minister?' No matter what the opinion polls say, perhaps most people have already decided.

6 November 1989: From Despair to Hope[21]

When Rajiv Gandhi announced to his startled Cabinet colleagues that he had decided to call the general elections ahead of schedule, he is said to have explained that the campaign arrangements were already complete. Two weeks later, it is now clear that what he meant was that his ad boys had finalized the plans for the media blitz now sweeping the country, exhorting voters to count the number of times their hearts beat for India. One more example, if example was indeed required, of the sources of political authority and wisdom from which the Prime Minister draws sustenance for his rule: they lie not in his party or in the democratic processes of national life, but in his inner circle of family, schoolboy network and assorted conmen. With a little more than two weeks to go for the elections, the ruling Congress(I) has not yet managed to release its election manifesto. But then, what is the use of a party manifesto when the ad men have decided that the only way to secure votes for the Congress(I) is to strike terror in the hearts of the voters?

Terror there is in abundance. Not only in the full-page ads in national dailies and in the millions of posters, hoardings and audio-visual presentations that will soon flood the length and breadth of the country, but also in the actual course of events on the political scene.

The daily killings continue in Punjab and Kashmir, as they have for so many months. In the rest of northern India, the communal situation is on the edge of a precipice. After a series of sparks in different towns of U.P., Rajasthan and Madhya Pradesh, the fire was lit in Bhagalpur in Bihar; and after some forty deaths in cold-blooded rioting, the area still continues to be under curfew. The Vishwa Hindu Parishad is going ahead with its highly provocative programme of the *Ramshila yajna* on 9 November, and the Union government has refused to take a clear position in the matter. There are reports of secret negotiations between the Union Home Minister Buta Singh and the VHP organizers — offering, it seems, covert encouragement. V.P. Singh, after having warned at least a month ago that the Congress(I) would engineer communal riots all over the country

21 *Frontier*, 22, 13 (11 November 1989).

before seeking a fresh mandate, is desperately appealing to the VHP to withdraw its programme, but to no avail. If one follows the basic principle of criminal investigation and looks for the party which has the most to gain from a crime, there can be no doubt about which one is the strongest suspect in this grisly and cynical story of political criminality. And yet, notwithstanding the atmosphere of surcharged communal tension, Rajiv Gandhi had no compunctions about inaugurating his election campaign in Ayodhya, 'the birth place of Rama' as he proudly announced, and promising to lead the struggle for *Ram Rajya*.

The silver lining is that despite these cold-blooded and cynical manipulations of base passions, the Congress(I) has been seriously frustrated in its attempt to establish an early lead in the campaign race. If the motive behind the sudden announcement of elections was to catch the opposition napping, the move has clearly failed. For once, the opposition has shown itself able to sort out its differences, arrive at workable understandings, and put up common candidates against the Congress(I) for most of the seats. There has been no alliance between the National Front and the BJP — in fact, the political differences have been clearly marked — but this has not pushed them into the obvious trap laid by the ruling party, of putting candidates against each other and dividing the opposition votes. What has come to the surface most dramatically is the state of discord and uncertainty in the Congress(I) ranks, expressed most surprisingly in the refusal by K.C. Pant, the Defence Minister, to accept the nominations offered to him by the party. There are even stronger indications that senior leaders of the party are only biding their time, hoping to catch their Prime Minister at a vulnerable moment.

The most hopeful sign is the steady assertion of a popular mood, strong enough, it seems, to openly proclaim its rejection of an arbitrary, corrupt, wilful and utterly unprincipled regime.

28 November 1989: Promises and Anxieties[22]

The similarities with 1977 are close enough to be uncanny. In three-fourths of the country, from Gujarat in the west to Haryana and Delhi in the north to West Bengal and Orissa in the east,

[22] *Frontier*, 22, 16 (2 December 1989).

the Congress(I) has been virtually routed. In the four southern states, not only has this wave been resisted, it has been reversed. The result is that the Congress(I), having enjoyed an unprecedented 400-plus bonanza in the previous Lok Sabha, is now down to about 200 seats, leaving it with virtually no chance of forming a government even with the help of its electoral allies. From three-fourths of the country, the verdict of the electorate has been clear: it is an emphatic defeat of the Congress(I).

The political activity will in the meantime shift to New Delhi where the President, Mr Venkataraman, will have to make the momentous decision in a situation which has been unprecedented at the national level in this country: how to form a workable government out of a hung Parliament? Two small differences from 1977 have produced this unprecedented situation: first, the Congress rout is not as complete in the north as it was in 1977, so that it has secured about forty additional seats; and second, what is now the BJP had merged with the Janata Party in 1977, so that, taken together, the Janata Party then had an absolute majority on its own. This time, the non-Congress Members of Parliament are divided into three distinct blocs — the National Front (which is now virtually identical with the Janata Dal as far as the Lok Sabha is concerned), the BJP and the Left. The only possibility for a government now seems to be a National Front government supported from outside by both the BJP and the Left. The initial responses from the leaders of all three blocs suggest that they are in fact working towards this course of action.

The election results have now produced another opportunity — only the second time in Indian history — for a non-Congress government at the Centre. The earlier experience was bitterly disappointing, and it has taken the electorate ten years to be persuaded that the opposition deserves to be given another chance. The responsibility that has been bestowed upon the three non-Congress blocs in Parliament is huge. The ideological differences between them have been many, but in so far as they have been thrown together in common criticism of Congress(I) misrule, it now devolves upon them to work out a common programme on which basis a National Front government might work. The possibility for this is not as remote as is often made out. After all, the entire opposition had agreed over the last five

years that the evils of the Rajiv Gandhi regime lay not so much
in its declared policies, whether on internal or external matters,
but in the excessive over-centralization of powers, the arbitrariness of a coterie rule, the unwillingness to make itself account-
able to the people, and the cynical manipulation of people and
of issues by the use of money, muscle-power and the media.
These evils provide a large enough target for any non-Congress
government to work upon. A more effective federal system, a
more open style of government, greater responsiveness to popular demands, and the cleansing of political institutions of the
squalid atmosphere of sycophancy, corruption and highhandedness that has resulted from despotic dynastic rule — these goals
can well form the immediate programme of such a government.
It is therefore not true that nothing can be done on which the
entire non-Congress spectrum in Indian politics can agree. The
people seem to have placed, even if cautiously, this trust in the
anti-Congress parties. It is now up to them to fulfil this trust.

The issue of communalism has dominated the scene, at least
in northern India, in the weeks preceding the general elections.
Unless one takes an utterly cynical view of politics and asserts
that the Indian people are inherently communal-minded, or
that they are mere playthings in the hands of communal agitators, there can be only one interpretation of the north Indian
results. The people have expressed their condemnation of the
way in which the Congress(I) has handled the communalism
issue. Here too they have placed their trust in the opposition.
The new government, even if it has to depend for its survival
on the two opposed groups — the BJP and the Left — will
enjoy a great deal of goodwill from the people, at least in the
initial phase. This will probably be the first major test which
will prove whether or not a non-Congress government can
really work in Indian politics.

The people have demonstrated that they, at least, are not afraid
to take risks for the sake of change. Whether the political leaders
will do the same remains to be seen.

12

The National Front and After

18 December 1989: Taking Over[1]

V.P. Singh's first press conference as Prime Minister was predictably undramatic. He did not make any startling revelations either on policy or on personnel matters. He was careful in his choice of words and eager to avoid any unnecessary controversy. In a way, it was indicative of the mood of cautious optimism in which the new government has begun its work.

No doubt, on the home front, Mr Singh made a significant gesture on Punjab by choosing to visit Amritsar and take a trip through the city streets in an open jeep. The spontaneous goodwill he was clearly successful in eliciting from the people makes for a new beginning. More than any specific political demands, it is the feeling of distrust and alienation among the people of Punjab which has made peace in that part of the country seem like an impossible dream. The Prime Minister has begun by using the occasion of a change of regimes in Delhi to send out the signal that the new government is prepared to begin afresh. The change of governors in Punjab, the all-party meeting on 17 December and the appointment of Air Chief Marshal Arjan Singh as Lieutenant-Governor of Delhi are all part of that exercise. It is true that nothing concrete has emerged yet, and it would be foolhardy to think that the conflicting political trends and leadership tussles among different sections of the Akali movement will vanish simply by virtue of the electoral victories of the Mann group. Nevertheless, a new chapter has certainly opened in what has so far been the grim story of Punjab.

On Kashmir, however, the auguries are far more disquieting. The appointment of Mufti Muhammad Sayeed as Union Home Minister was immediately greeted by the kidnapping of his

[1] *Frontier*, 22, 19 (23 December 1989).

daughter in Srinagar. After several days of tense negotiations, an exchange was arranged in which five activists of the Jammu and Kashmir Liberation Front were released from prison. What the incident showed was the depth of popular animosity about 'Indian' rule in Kashmir, and the extent to which, by aligning itself with the Congress(I), the regime of Farooq Abdullah had alienated itself from its historical legacy of being the true voice of the people of Kashmir. Clearly, the northern-most state of India will rank high among the 'problems' which Mr Singh's government has inherited from Rajiv Gandhi.

On the economy, too, the prognostics are grim. The budget exercise is being prolonged, and Madhu Dandavate, the Union Finance Minister, has already announced that there will be a vote on account until such time as the new government is prepared with a statement on the overall condition of the economy. Given the mindless spending spree in which Rajiv Gandhi and his men had indulged, the state of public finances, both domestic and external, is critical. The new government is in an unenviable position. It cannot simply tighten up and say that we cannot spend until our finances are in better shape: the political expectations are too pressing. It will have to be a complicated balancing act.

The silver lining is that as far as the 'support from outside' factor is concerned, neither the BJP nor the Left parties have so far said or done anything that might embarrass the government. For some time at least, V.P. Singh will have the support and goodwill of a large section of political opinion in the country. For how long will depend on the performance of the government.

9 July 1990: The Politics of Economics[2]

With Kashmir going the way of Punjab, no one expects the National Front government to produce any dramatic results any more. It seems to have been taken for granted that yet another part of the country will now fester and bleed, with nobody knowing what to do with it. Kashmir having been relegated to the inside pages, the news from the capital last

2 *Frontier*, 22, 48 (14 July 1990).

week was dominated by economics. Shorn of jargon, it was really politics by another means.

The issue was the government's new industrial policy, which was discussed and apparently adopted by the Cabinet. When the Industries Minister Ajit Singh announced the policy a few weeks ago, there was considerable confusion, since it seemed to run in an opposite direction from the new Planning Commission's thinking. The Congress(I) was, of course, quick to pounce on the issue, declaring that the National Front government was preparing to sell the country to the multinationals. The stand was hardly credible, since the new policy seemed to follow with perfect consistency the direction taken by Rajiv Gandhi's government during its own term in office.

More dramatic opposition came, however, from the irrepressible Chandra Shekhar. He criticized the new policy as one calculated to please the World Bank and the multinationals. It would not ease the foreign currency situation at all, but exacerbate it. It would bring in wasteful and unhealthy investment by the multinationals in the luxury sector. He was particularly critical of the lessening of importance of the public sector, which he said had to be revived and strengthened, not abandoned, if self-reliance was to be achieved.

Chandra Sekhar's arguments immediately received the support of the CPI and the CPI(M). Even the BJP seemed to echo his sentiments about the undesirable entry of multinationals. More interesting was the support he received from Devi Lal, then recuperating in Bangalore. This too seemed to follow the expected alignments within the Janata Dal. Curiously, however, the unpredictable patriarch of Haryana did a sudden *volte-face*, claiming two days later that the policy was not as disastrous as Chandra Shekhar was making it out to be, that in fact it was the best possible move in the present circumstances.

Devi Lal has now queered the pitch. No one knows how he plans to move when he returns to Delhi next week. The confusion over this was compounded by his statement on Ramakrishna Hegde's resignation from the Planning Commission. This in itself was a tortuous affair, although it had nothing to do with the controversy over economic policy. Mr Hegde offered to resign because he had apparently been censured by the Kuldip Singh Commission, appointed by the previous government to investigate the telephone tapping affair in Bangalore. V.P. Singh first asked Mr Hegde to continue. Then, on second thoughts, he accepted his resignation.

It is possible that there will be factional realignments within the Janata Dal in the next few weeks. New general secretaries are to be chosen, and Om Prakash Chauthala, disgraced and ousted from his seat in Haryana despite his father Devi Lal's clout, is in the running. The outside supporters of the Dal, without whose cooperation the National Front government cannot survive, are also becoming restive. The BJP, unhappy with the removal of Jagmohan from Kashmir, has begun to threaten the government for its 'anti-Hindu' policy over the Ayodhya issue. The Left has been particularly critical over the economic policy of the government. While the policy itself was approved by the Cabinet, differences of opinion seem to persist, since old-time socialists like George Fernandes and Sharad Yadav do not share the views of liberalizers like Ajit Singh and Arun Nehru.

23 July 1990: Stronger, but Weaker[3]

It had to be the irrepressible Devi Lal who would do it. Ever since the National Front government took office, it has been clear that the danger to its stability lay not where minority governments usually flounder — the uncertain support of allied parties outside the government. Rather, this government was most likely to be endangered from within. Initially, it had seemed that the truculent Chandra Shekhar, who had kept himself out of a ministerial position in a fit of pique, was the danger man. Only two weeks ago, it was Chandra Shekhar who launched the major attack against the new industrial policy of the government. At the time, Devi Lal was undergoing treatment in a clinic in Bangalore.

Immediately on his return to Delhi, however, Devi Lal got going. When he first came to Delhi in November 1989, persuading himself that as Deputy Prime Minister he would supervise the affairs of the new government as a sort of senior statesman and father-figure, he arranged to hand over his satrapy in Haryana to his son Om Prakash Chauthala. There was a great deal of eyebrow-raising about this in the press as well as within the Janata Dal, because talk of 'dynastic rule' was still very much in the air. But to the patriarch from Haryana this seemed the most natural procedure of transfer of power. The real difficulty arose when Mr Chauthala, seeking election to the Haryana Assembly in order to meet the basic legal qualification to continue as Chief Minister (another needless encumbrance invented by effete urban minds, Devi Lal surely thought), perpetrated the most ham-handed attempt at rigging an election in recent electoral history. The hue and cry was so strong that Devi Lal had to concede that Chauthala must step down until investigations into the Meham poll violence were completed.

Most people underestimated how much of a personal blow this was to the senior citizen from Haryana. It was, so to speak, a challenge to the very core of his authority. The investigations, as usual, were slow to get off the ground. Mr Chauthala, in the meantime, became a candidate in another by-election and won a seat in the Assembly. Devi Lal, impatient in his efforts to secure a legitimate political position for his son, interceded with the Prime Minister to make him a general secretary of the Janata Dal. If there were any other agreements at this meeting, they will perhaps long remain secrets. Immediately after this, in a swift stroke of political organization, the Haryana MLAs met in Delhi, elected Mr Chauthala their leader, the current Chief Minister resigned, and Devi Lal's son was sworn in again as Chief Minister.

All hell broke loose after this. Beginning with Arun Nehru and Arif Mohammed Khan, as many as sixteen ministers sent in their resignations from the Union Cabinet. Finally, to take the crisis to its peak, V.P. Singh himself sent in a letter of resignation to the party president. For three days, the capital was on tenterhooks, fearing the collapse of the government. Devi Lal, intractable as ever, refused to budge. In the end, the truth of the matter was forced to come out in the open. The entire spectrum of opinion and personalities in the National Front, including such sworn enemies as Chandra Shekhar, had to declare that V.P. Singh must stay and Chauthala resign. There could have been no other solution, and after two days of recalcitrance Devi Lal had to give way.

V.P. Singh has now established what should have been obvious from the very beginning: that the political credibility of this government will stand or fall with the credibility of V.P. Singh. By precipitating the drama of his resignation, he has now proved to all his indispensability. There are fears, of course, that Devi Lal will strike back. Chandra Shekhar, never reconciled to the reality of V.P. Singh's pre-eminence, is probably only biding his time. The question of Arun Nehru and Arif Mohammed Khan has now become a new element in the complex calculations of political viability, for their loyalty to the present leadership has come under a cloud. But the crisis has proved that the true centre of stability is the Prime Minister himself.

What is thus a strength is also, not surprisingly, the principal weakness of this government. It is not ideology or organization or an agreement on policy that keeps the government going. There will be constant jerks and irritations in its wayward journey. Above all, it will be the quality of leadership of one man which will decide whether this experiment in non-Congress government will succeed or flounder.

10 September 1990: We Have Heard This Before[4]

When the interests of dominant minorities are threatened, the reactions are always the same.

A hundred years ago, when the demand was made that, to enable Indians to sit for the examinations to the Indian Civil Service, the age limit of applicants be raised and arrangements be made for examinations to be held in India, British civil servants were aghast. 'That would bring disaster,' they said. 'We could never maintain the efficiency of the service. Indians cannot have the same abilities as graduates of British universities. Besides, these jobs will be cornered by a tiny elite among Indians. What good will that do to the vast majority?' Historians today consider these opinions as reflecting the racial prejudices of the then rulers of India.

Fifty years ago, when the demand to abolish *zamindari* was being debated, landlords raised similar arguments. The demand was discriminatory, they said. First, to take property away from one class and give it to another violated the universal right of property. Second, not all *zamindars* were wealthy or oppressive. There were many who were owners of small landed property whose incomes

4 *Ānandabājār patrikā*, 14 September 1990 (translated from the Bengali).

barely provided them with a livelihood. The only class that would profit from the abolition of *zamindari* was the rich peasantry. This class was poorly educated, with no tradition of assuming social leadership or responsibility. If they had power, rich peasants would be far more oppressive than *zamindars* ever were. The poor peasant would hardly be better off. Third, the demand was politically motivated. It would produce conflict between classes and hatred and disorder in society. If the anti-reservationists of today take a look at the debates in the provincial legislatures of Bengal, Bihar or U.P. half a century ago, they will be astonished. Whether they will be embarrassed as well, I cannot tell.

It is often true that the more substantial peasants were the ones who gained the most from the abolition of *zamindari*. It is also true that they are the ones who have in many regions become the oppressive rich farmers of today. But we do not for that reason claim that the abolition of *zamindari* was wrong. On the contrary, we often condemn the Congress governments of the time for having paid compensation to *zamindars,* and for allowing the loopholes in law which enabled landlords to retain their hold over much of their possessions. Of course, we forget which classes of the future were to profit from those loopholes.

The same arguments are now being repeated in the debate over reservation of jobs for backward castes in the Central government services. Three objections have been raised to the proposal. First, disregarding the criterion of merit, jobs are being reserved for one section of applicants: this is both discriminatory and harmful to administrtive efficiency. Second, it is not true that everyone from the upper castes is privileged or that everyone from the lower castes is disadvantaged. If jobs are reserved by caste, the better-off among the lower castes will grab them; those who are truly disadvantaged will not gain in any way. If jobs have to be reserved, it should be done by economic criteria, not by caste. Third, a politically motivated move such as this will only create new conflicts between castes. Unlike education or land reforms which are the real answers to caste discrimination, this proposal will only increase disparities, not remove them.

The same arguments, but in different contexts. The debate must therefore be carried out all over again.

Take first the question of merit. It does not require much knowledge of economic theory to see that under conditions of free competition, those who have greater initial endowments will in the end capture the market. The observation holds for the education market too. Where recruitment is by open competitive examination, if it is found that successful applicants come predominantly from a small section of society, then surely the conclusion cannot be that their merit is a natural gift. There must be social reasons for systematic disparities in 'merit'. The report of the Mandal Commission shows that of Class I positions in the Central services, only 7.14 per cent are held by those from the scheduled castes or tribes (despite a reservation for them of 22.5 per cent). Other backward castes hold 2.59 per cent. Of Class II posts, scheduled castes and tribes have only 13.66 per cent. Of Class III and IV jobs, however, they hold 31 per cent, well above the reserved quota. Obviously, the upper castes are not particularly interested in these lowly jobs. Hence, the division of labour in the administrative apparatus of our modern state looks much like that recommended by the *varna* system of the scriptures.

Yet this is a division of labour produced by an assessment of educational merit. And it is not as if we do not know why such a result has been produced. Yes, there has been an expansion of secondary and higher education in independent India, but this expansion has brought into existence two separate educational systems. The more the educated upper castes have been ousted from landed property and turned themselves into the urban middle classes, the more strenuously have they built up their own institutions for producing professionals with 'merit'. The consequence has been that the system of public education catering to the rest of the population has been entirely dissociated from the production of 'merit'. This disparity has been less the result of state patronage and more that of the enterprise, expenditure and infinite energy of the urban middle classes. Every city and town in India is now part of this structure, beginning with nursery schools. These institutions have better teaching, better facilities; the costs are also much higher. Needless to say, there is also far greater homogeneity in the class backgrounds of students. Every urban resident in India knows that if one can manage to put one's child into one of these 'English-medium' schools, he or she would get a headstart in the race to acquire 'merit'. Disparities in educational achievement, therefore, begin from the primary stage of schooling.

Where there is such extreme disparity in access to education, it is easy to see what open competitive examinations will perpetuate. If educational achievement is the only merit that will be tested, surely those who come from educated middle class families and who have had the privilege of going into the elite schools will be the ones to qualify. Others will not stand a chance. If the criterion of merit is to be applied fairly, there should not only be expansion of education but also equalization of educational opportunities, at least up to the secondary level. In every country of the world where there is universal secondary education, the principle is not only that every child must go to school, but that, with rare exceptions, they will go to the same *kind* of school. This is not some coercive diktat of socialist regimes. Even the United States follows exactly the same system. Except for a handful who go to private or denominational schools, all children in that holy land of modern capitalism and meritocracy are educated through a universal system of public schooling. If in India today it is ruled that all children, irrespective of class, will have to attend their neighbourhood schools, I suppose middle-class parents in their despair will decide to renounce the world and retire to monastic life. There is no political force in the country which can bring about such a democratic revolution in education.

If jobs are reserved for those from socially and educationally backward castes, it is obvious that they will go to the relatively better-off sections among those castes. What else could we expect? Only those from relatively prosperous lower caste families will have the minimum educational qualifications for getting even the reserved places in the Class I and II services, over which there is so much competition. The alternative proposal of reservation by economic criteria is entirely irrelevant to the problem of caste discrimination. If that proposal is aimed at reserving places for those who, irrespective of caste, fall below a certain level of income, then we are hardly likely to find many who will be from a backward caste, from a low-income family, and at the same have the minimum educational qualifications for the job. Clearly, these reserved positions will then go overwhelmingly to low-income upper-caste applicants. That will only reinforce the present caste imbalance in the professional middle class; the lower castes will again be denied entry into that exclusive circle.

Hidden behind the cloud of political slogans is a very simple fact. Is it at all correct to say that the demand for reservations is the result of the lack of spread of education or the incompleteness of land reforms? To me, the truth seems to be the exact opposite. It is in fact because of the spread, however tardy, of education in rural areas and of land reforms, no matter how inadequate, that there has now grown a class of prosperous peasants in the countryside. They have even acquired some economic and political power at the local levels. Their children are now making a bid to find a place among the urban middle classes which inhabit the central institutions of power in society. This has nothing to do with the removal of poverty in the country at large. The Central government services, over which there is such conflict today, actually comprise only about ten per cent of the total employment in the organized sector of the economy. If one takes the Class I and II positions, they account for less than five per cent. Not even an idiot will claim that by distributing these jobs the problem of poverty will be affected in any way. It is in fact the class differentiation among the peasantry and among the middle castes, brought about in the rural areas in the last few decades by economic changes and the expansion of education, that is now producing the assault on the citadels occupied for so long by the educated urban middle classes. The real question is: will the institutions of administrative, professional and cultural power remain under the dominance of the upper castes, or will others have to be given a place? That is what the fight is all about.

It is apparent that caste conflicts will grow. Those who were complaining the most about the possibility of conflict are the ones who have now taken to violence. This is a conflict that took place in the south of the country a few decades ago. In most parts of southern India, the social dominance of the upper castes has crumbled. The conflict has now emerged in a big way in the north. To complain of political motives in this connection is strange, to say the least. Could any decision of such consequence for the structures of power in the country have been taken without strong political motivations? Were there no political motives behind the fact that the Mandal Commission report had only gathered dust in the last ten years? In terms of politics, the truth is that the National Front government has taken a daring risk. It is a tough task indeed to incur the wrath of the urban upper and middle classes and still remain in power.

The expressions of wrath are frightening. There are few things more ugly than the flaunting of the cultural superiority of dominant minorities. I am no longer surprised when I hear of the parents of anti-reservationist student agitators waxing nostalgic about the golden age of the ICS. I can see in front of my eyes the first political movement in independent India whose campaign is in English, whose slogans are in English, whose ideology too, I presume, is articulated in English. I can also see despicable vulgarities of which only the privileged are capable, from ridiculing the Chief Minister of Bihar on the size of his family to shining shoes for the benefit of news photographers. These are perhaps the most sublime examples of the perversities of a merit-producing education.

There is no doubt that there will be conflict. There is also no doubt that no political party and no elected government in India will ever succeed in overturning the recent decision to reserve government jobs for backward castes. Of course, there will now appear innumerable loopholes in the regulations: in whose interest, it hardly needs to be elaborated. And it is my presumption that future historians will judge the anti-reservationists of today in exactly the same way that present-day historians judge British imperialists or Indian *zamindars*. It may be that I am being excessively optimistic. Only the future acts of the present generation of educated youth can decide whether my presumption will prove to be correct.

10 November 1990: The People Betrayed[5]

There are times when the perversities of the parliamentary system can produce results that are completely contradictory even to the electorally expressed wishes of the people. Such a time has now come with the installation of Chandra Shekhar's government.

The withdrawal of support by the BJP immediately after Mr Advani's burlesque act was stopped, had sealed the fate of the National Front government. If V.P. Singh still insisted that he would test his majority in the Lok Sabha, it was because he wished, in effect, to use the occasion to open his campaign for the next elections. With V.P. Singh's government gone, the only options would seem to have been a Congress(I) minority government or fresh elections. The Congress(I), however, chose an even more roundabout way to get back the reins of power without actually taking the responsibility of running a government. It chose to rule by proxy.

Mr Chandra Shekhar's allergy towards V.P. Singh was never concealed: it was written on his face. He agreed with expected alacrity to be the pawn in Rajiv Gandhi's game. Projected by the Congress(I) as the one man who could save the country from going into another general election within a year, Chandra Shekhar, in association with the ever-unpredictable Devi Lal, first attempted to effect a change in the leadership of the Janata Dal. When that attempt failed, they chose to form a breakaway group which would stake its claim to government with Congress(I) support. A rehearsal was carried out in Gujarat where the Chimanbhai Patel ministry had also lost its majority after the withdrawal of BJP support. Chimanbhai was given support by the Congress(I). The same pattern has now been repeated in New Delhi.

There is something grotesque in the sight of a breakaway group of uncertain status, comprising barely one-tenth of the members of the Lok Sabha, forming a government with the outside support of the largest single party in the House. What is even more ridiculous is that all the members in Chandra Shekhar's group had been elected only a year ago on an expressly anti-Congress(I) platform. Rajiv Gandhi has managed to satisfy all his needs at present. Having made delightfully vague utterances right through the political crisis of the last two months and not having taken the responsibility of a decisive intervention, he now finds that he cannot afford to go into elections even after the collapse of the latest experiment with a non-Congress government. Yet it is necessary for him to gain some control over the administrative apparatus before the elections finally come. He will now be able to do this without actually bearing any responsibility for the performance of this ramshackle government.

It is curious that the first legislative move of Rajiv Gandhi immediately after he was elected to power in 1984 was to bring an anti-defection law. He has now resorted precisely to the well-tested means of engineering defections in order to instal his proxy government. Whatever the technical considerations in the application of the anti-defection law — and these will probably be contested for some time in the case of the Janata Dal split — there is no doubt that it is the author of the anti-defection law who has now flouted its very spirit in order to gain his own objectives.

No one believes that the Chandra Shekhar government will stay for any length of time. The BJP has demanded immediate elections: clearly, it wishes to cash in on the *Hindutva* madness for whatever it is worth. V.P. Singh's Janata Dal has announced its programme of 'going to the people' on the issues that brought about its fall. The Left, having stayed with V.P. Singh despite a few mild flutters, is for the moment resolved to make anti-communalism and social justice the main issues for a national campaign. The Congress(I) knows that this government will not last. Its problem is to decide when it will be ready to face the electorate: a volatile atmosphere in which basic political issues are being debated is not a congenial condition in which Rajiv Gandhi's skills can flourish.

The uncertainty will therefore continue. The people will have to press on for some more time before they are given a chance to make a decision.

13

The Centre Crumbles

25 March 1991: Business Or Politics?[1]

Perhaps the most significant index of the professionalization of political careers in India today was provided by one of the last acts of this short-lived Parliament. When it became clear to all that there was no alternative but to go back and face the electorate all over again, the esteemed Members of our Parliament rushed through in record time a Bill to secure for themselves a lifelong pension and other perquisites. A.K. Roy, the Marxist Coordination Council member from Dhanbad, did try and remind the so-called leaders of the people that they were using, for purely personal gratification, the powers given to them by the Constitution to supervise the finances of the government. But Mr Roy was peremptorily silenced by virtually every other member of the House.

For many, politics is now a business, like speculating in the share markets. It is a risky business where you can go bust all of a sudden, but where you can also make a fortune if things go all right. The purely individualized fortune-hunting political career is best exemplified by that disreputable bunch that styled itself the Janata Dal (Socialist). Backroom manoeuvres and deals had brought them to power under the most extraordinary circumstances. When Chandra Shekhar decided to turn a patently impossible situation into a moral victory, the Janata Dal(S) members, disappointed at having their days in power cut short, did not however give up on their attempts to pursue their business. Om Prakash Chauthala, in one of those incredible two-hour performances, reclaimed the Chief Minister's chair in Haryana for the third time in a year and a half. Chimanbhai Patel and Mulayam Singh Yadav have made it known that they

[1] *Frontier*, 23, 33 (30 March 1991).

will strike a deal with anybody and on any terms to stay in power in Gujarat and Uttar Pradesh. And Chandra Shekhar himself has said that since 'everything is possible in politics', no alliances and agreements can be ruled out. It is said that Chandra Shekhar's strategy is to have as many of his people elected as possible, no matter which parties they happen to join or seek support from. Should the numbers game become important in the next Parliament, he would then be in a position once again to strike a bargain.

There is a very strong opinion in the ruling establishments in the country that this is what politics should be. Avoid issues, avoid political debate, avoid popular movements. Politics is a matter of bargains and compromises between organized interests. The Congress(I), which represents more than any other party the dominant ethos of the ruling classes, has stated this very clearly in its revived slogan of 'stability'. This party has no stand on the Ayodhya dispute, nor does it have a clear position on the question of reservations. It decries the fact that so much heat should be generated in political controversy. Why don't you let Rajiv Gandhi's bright boys run the government? The fact is, of course, that there is nothing stable about the Congress(I) except its supreme leader, which position is hereditary. At every other rung of the leadership, the situation is as unstable as can be. There have been more changes of ministers and chief ministers — all the result of factional intrigue and court politics — in Congress(I) governments than anywhere else. What the Congress(I) means by stability and orderly government is simply that the politics be taken out of politics.

The issues of communalism and reservations are likely to be the most strongly discussed topics in the next elections. It must be said that no matter how limited or distorted the form, certain basic questions about power and justice have once again emerged in popular consciousness. The value in terms of the power of the people to intervene in the political process is considerable. No matter how much the backroom strategists may decry such populist politics, mobilization of the people around issues is the only way to keep the polity from falling entirely into the clutches of self-seeking and unprincipled political speculators.

8 April 1991: What Stability?[2]

It is a major paradox of Indian politics since 1979 that the more strident the cry of 'stability', the more pronounced have been the tendencies towards regionalism. The Congress(I), which took over in that year of collapse of the Janata experiment the role of the principal political organization of the all-India ruling classes, fought and won the general elections on the slogan of 'stability'. This was Indira Gandhi in a new incarnation; for, ten years before when she first took the hustings by storm, her cry was not stability but 'change'. From her fight against the 'Syndicate' to the 20-point programme, she managed to give to her politics the edge of a radical rhetoric. In the process she also created a new centre.

From 1980, it is this new centre which the all-India political establishment has sought to protect. Right through that decade, the Congress(I) dynasty — mother and son — brought about a concentration of power unparalleled in the history of India. On the one hand, it was a decade of selective economic liberalization — selective in its choice of targets, now breaking the power of this monopoly house, now favouring that monopoly house. On the other hand, the political institutions of representative democracy were systematically destroyed. Even the ruling party, the Congress(I), virtually ceased to have any effective centre of power anywhere other than at the very top. Congress chief ministers were appointed and dismissed at the whim of the Gandhis. All Congress candidates for Parliament, assemblies or even local bodies were selected in Delhi. The institution of the state Governor was reduced to that of a police agent appointed from New Delhi. Federalism was in a shambles.

It was in the 1980s again that the new regionalism also began. Punjab and Assam were the most dramatic examples, followed by Jammu and Kashmir. They have all reached a stage where the normal processes of democratic politics seem to have been suspended permanently. But there were other examples. Regional parties came to power in Andhra and Assam, while Tamil Nadu has for a long time developed its own local party system. As the Andhra and Tamil Nadu cases show, whether in or out of power, a regional party is a permanently viable entity, surviving on local

2 *Frontier*, 23, 35 (13 April 1991).

interests and solidarities but making suitable alliances with all-India organizations. The Left groups in Kerala, West Bengal and Tripura are again at core similar groupings of regional interests.

The topsy-turvy politics of the last year has brought this paradox even more sharply into prominence. The Congress(I) is once again shouting 'stability'. But having split the opposition Janata Dal once, it is now trying to strike deals with the fragments of the Janata(S). In Gujarat, Chimanbhai Patel has floated a new regional party simply to keep his alliance going with the Congress(I). The same might have happened in U.P., but Mulayam Singh Yadav showed once again that in the game of conmanship Rajiv's bright boys are still novices. In Haryana, it was Bansi Lal yesterday, it is Bhajan Lal today, it may be Devi Lal tomorrow. In the north-eastern states, the Congress(I) has changed its chief ministers so often that no one can be sure which local force is actually with the all-India party. In Tamil Nadu, the Congress(I)'s seat-sharing arrangement is a matter of formal agreement. So what is this stability that the Congress(I) talks about? It too is only an unstable collection of regional forces.

The issue of real federalism should have emerged as a major question in the forthcoming elections. Some of the most positive — although incomplete and half-hearted — steps taken in the brief period of the National Front government related to the creation of some new procedures to give more effective powers to the federal units. The irony is that the Left is all for more federalism when it suits its party interest, but is for central rule and 'stability' when it goes against it, as it does at the moment in Punjab. It is such unprincipled opposition politics which continues to give sustenance to the Congress(I) slogan of 'stability'.

27 May 1991: Waiting Game[3]

There is no end to the bizarre curiosities Indian democracy is capable of producing. The swearing-in of Rajiv Gandhi after the assassination of his mother was one of the most unbelievable confirmations of the fact that a monarchical mode of political leadership can develop even within what is ostensibly a republic. The attempt by the Congress leaders to persuade Mrs Sonia

[3] *Frontier*, 23, 42 (1 June 1991).

Gandhi to succeed her assassinated husband is only further confirmation of this trend. Paradoxically, however, the shocking death of Rajiv Gandhi has also produced the circumstances in which this extra-constitutional monarchical system can be buried once for all.

The successive tragedies that have befallen the Nehru–Gandhi family are not unrelated to the fact that the Congress system since the era of Indira Gandhi has consistently emulated the form of monarchical rule. It is not only that the real exercise of power in both party and government was centralized; the very style of rule sought to produce the impression that power flowed only from one source. Even the most trivial policy decision required approval from the top; every state programme was packaged as a special gift of benevolence of the supreme leader. Within the hierarchy of power, it produced the most abject protestations of feudal loyalty and sycophancy.

It is curious that the Nehru–Gandhi family, whose legitimacy within the Indian elite rests on its claims to a thoroughly modernist social vision and lifestyle, should have become willing accomplices if not the actual perpetrators of a system of political leadership which is totally contradictory to the modern forms of exercise of power. The superiority of the modern state — its institutions of representative politics and rational bureaucracy — consists in the fact that power does not flow from one source. Rather, it is distributed over the entire field of social life. This is how the exercise of power is made economic and efficient.

It was a corollary of the monarchical form of power that the violence of the Indian state — a systematic and often brutal violence of the state machinery — should have been perceived as a violence carried out personally by Indira or Rajiv Gandhi. Their assassinations were also personalized acts of violent retribution. The real tragedy of their deaths lay in the surrender by the ruling Congress party of all the efficiencies and advantages of the modern institutions of power which it had built up over a hundred years. Now, with the sudden death of Rajiv Gandhi, the total bankruptcy of its organization is staring the party in the face.

The fact that the assassination has taken place in the middle of the parliamentary elections has made the task doubly difficult for the Congress. On the one hand, there is unconcealed glee that the party will actually gain from its tragedy by drawing upon the 'sympathy' of the voters. On the other hand, there is the fear that unless it can put its own house in order in a very short time, the voters may not be persuaded that the Congress is still in business. The two contradictory pulls have, at the time of writing, landed the Congress in a state of paralysis.

The two other elements on the national political scene — the BJP and the National Front–Left alliance — are waiting for the Congress to make its move. And Mr Chandra Shekhar, who thrives on political confusion, is undoubtedly hoping that the next Parliament will be even more confused than the last one so that his considerable skills at manipulative politics will find fresh pastures.

10 June 1991: Getting Along With Panic[4]

The immediate aftermath of the assassination of Rajiv Gandhi saw attacks by Congress(I) supporters all over the country on the party's political opponents. In Kerala, their target was the Left Front, in Tamil Nadu the DMK, in Andhra the Telugu Desam, in West Bengal and Tripura the CPI(M), in northern India it was the BJP and the Janata Dal. Part of the frustration of Congress(I) supporters could have stemmed from the mystery surrounding the identity of Rajiv Gandhi's killers. But the situation was made far worse by dozens of irresponsible statements from senior Congress(I) leaders, accusing opposition politicians and parties by name and charging them with the responsibility for the murder. The most serious consequences of these acts of political vandalism were in Andhra and Tripura: in the former state, N.T. Rama Rao went on a hunger strike which was forcibly and hamhandedly broken by the Congress(I) government, while in the latter the CPI(M) has withdrawn from the Lok Sabha elections alleging widespread violence and terrorization by the Congress(I).

One institution which has contributed a great deal to the uncertainties and confusion is the Election Commission itself. The very appointment of T.N. Seshan to the post had raised eyebrows. The pomposity and highhandedness of his methods became apparent almost as soon as the election process went

[4] *Frontier*, 23, 44 (15 June 1991).

under way. Following Rajiv Gandhi's death, the Election Commission announced the next morning a postponement of elections by three weeks. No political parties were consulted. Mr Seshan then went on to take a series of unprecedented decisions — the countermanding of elections in six Lok Sabha constituencies, and the ordering of re-polls a full two weeks after polling had taken place. There are now open allegations by a number of political parties that the Election Commission is acting at the behest of the Congress(I) and some ministers of the Chandra Shekhar government.

If panic and confusion have marked the Congress(I) and its supporters, those who make tall claims about responsible and serious politics have not entirely escaped either. A few days after Rajiv Gandhi's death, the CPI(M) leader E.M.S. Namboodiripad wrote an open letter to the Congress(I) suggesting that it rethink its attitude towards the Left. Other leaders of the CPI(M) had to rush in to clarify that the Left was still aligned with the National Front and was going to remain faithful to that alliance. What prompted the veteran communist to do what he did will probably never be known, but whether it was panic or a 'shrewd tactical move', all it has achieved is further confusion about alignment and principles.

Perhaps the most panicky reactions have come from those sinecurist members of the country's political establishment — the national communists. The real possibility of the end of the Nehru–Gandhi dynasty has hit them with such a terrible shock that some have suggested immediate cancellation of elections and the formation of a national government; others have called for wholesale changes in the Constitution. The most piquant has been the observation by several of these students of political physiognomy that Priyanka's jaw shows the same boldness and determination as Indira's did. Why blame only the Indian peasant for nourishing a fondness for kings and princesses?

24 June 1991: Ten Parliaments[5]

A Congress(I) ministry has assumed office in New Delhi. It was not a particularly smooth affair. Apart from the fact that it is a

5 *Frontier*, 23, 46 (29 June 1991).

minority government which does not have an explicit promise of support from any quarter, the manner in which it decided upon the Prime Minister and the unseemly delays in distributing portfolios do not augur well for the cohesiveness of the ministry. At the time of writing, certain important departments such as Defence and Industry are without a minister, and all seems to have been held up for Mr Sharad Pawar's striking an agreement with Mr Narasimha Rao.

Perhaps the most significant aspect of the ministry-making exercise has been the demonstration of the continued grip of the so-called 'Rajiv coterie' on the Congress(I). Belying predictions of the emergence of a new 'syndicate' consisting of powerful regional bosses, the coterie not only managed to overwhelm Sharad Pawar's much-advertised attempt to force an election of the party leader but also imposed itself on the new Cabinet. M.L. Fotedar, Ghulam Nabi Azad and Sitaram Kesri, none of them members of the Lok Sabha, have now occupied senior Cabinet-rank posts, and Sharad Pawar is still out in the cold.

One effect of the coterie's reassertion has been the fizzling out of all speculations about coalitions and alliances. Namboodiripad, Surjeet and Basu are now looking downright silly after their panicky protestations of support; the coteric-ruled Congress(I) has now made it clear that it is not terribly worried about support and will go ahead with its owns plans; no one has the courage now to bring down the government and take the blame for precipitating yet another mid-term election.

The plans are also emerging bit by bit. In Punjab and Kashmir, it will be more of the same: continued occupation by the security forces, continued killings, continued recriminations against 'hostile forces across the border' and no political initiative. On the economy, not merely the IMF loan with the full range of 'conditionalities' but a host of relaxations of legal and bureaucratic controls on direct foreign investment. There is no doubt that this moment is going to be seized by all the proponents of 'new industrialization'; and the bitter pill of devaluation, expenditure-cutting and inflation will be given the sugar coating of export-led growth and foreign investments. It will be a pretty sight indeed to see Nehruvians, Lohiaites and public-sector Marxists voting to usher in the full range of World Bank–IMF sponsored economic reforms.

In domestic politics, no matter how hard the Congress(I) may wish that the problem will simply go away, the mosque–temple issue will remain the single most divisive dispute. The BJP, having been swept into power in India's most populous state on the promise of building the temple at the very spot where Rama is alleged to have been born, is unlikely to kill the goose which laid the golden egg. It is a most convenient issue which will now acquire all the overtones of a centre–state confrontation; and we may now hear the BJP speak from Lucknow in the same language that the CPI(M) speaks in Calcutta.

The new Parliament will certainly be one of the most interesting in the history of post-independence India.

22 July 1991: Coup[6]

It is nothing short of a *coup d'état*. Whatever the composition of the circle which is now running the country, it has managed to hijack the central organs of government and is hurtling India on a course which would never have been approved of if the normal procedures of democracy had been allowed to function. But that is often the characteristic of representative democracies — to produce 'democratic' results which are totally contradictory to the balance of democratic opinion.

The plan unfolded in the last days of the Chandra Shekhar government, when the cry went up that the economy was facing a crisis. In fact, it was then that the announcement was made that there was no alternative to the IMF loan. The period of the elections and the subsequent formation of the Narasimha Rao ministry is still dotted with many mysteries, including the assassination of Rajiv Gandhi, the attempts by the President to form a 'national government', and the victory of Narasimha Rao over Sharad Pawar.

Immediately after the inauguration of the government, the question of the economy took centre stage. Manmohan Singh, a government economist who has held key advisory positions since Mrs Gandhi's days in the 1970s, was chosen to be Finance Minister; and the people who were said to be negotiating with

[6] *Frontier*, 23, 50 (27 July 1991).

the IMF during Yashwant Sinha's brief tenure were kept on. Indeed, it seemed as if the small group of government economists who were said to comprise the 'liberalization' lobby in government had taken complete charge, and had found new allies among former left-wingers including the new Finance Minister himself.

The campaign was now taken up in right earnest by the media. The crisis of the economy and the inevitability of an IMF loan was the principal theme, but the need for 'hard decisions' and a complete restructuring of an 'outmoded' system was the refrain. It soon transpired that the 'structural reforms' would be an unavoidable part of the conditions the IMF would demand, and since the decision had already been made that the IMF loan was inevitable, there was no way the 'reforms' could be avoided either. A series of policy decisions and pronouncements, beginning with a two-stage (three-stage?) devaluation of the rupee and a new trade policy, was followed by warnings that the new fiscal policy would cut down government expenditure and subsidies and the new industrial policy would mean a removal of government controls and an invitation to direct foreign investment.

It is a strange negotiating tactic which first announces that we have no alternative to the IMF loan and then proceeds to negotiate. What is left to negotiate? The more credible answer is that there is a lobby in the ruling establishment which has made the balance of payments crisis a pretext to ram through massive changes in the institutional structure of the Indian economy. These are changes which have no sanction in democratic opinion.

The point about 'reforms' of this kind is, of course, that there is no going back. Once institutional changes of such far-reaching magnitude are initiated, they will have to be continued. There are almost no previous instances of these kinds of changes being implemented in a liberal democracy. Given a peculiar set of circumstances, a coup has taken place in Indian democracy. If the democratic procedures assert themselves, whether inside or outside Parliament, there could be more serious attempts to subvert the democratic institutions altogether. After all, the announcement has already been made by the leaders of the coup: 'We have no choice.'

25 March 1996: Of Obsolete Modernities and Unborn Democracies[7]

Given the virtual certainty of a hung Parliament after the forth-coming general elections, a general sense of panic appears to have seized the country. There are, of course, many reasons for anxiety. Many seem to believe that without a stable govern-ment at the Centre, the financial, administrative and defence systems of the country will collapse. Others are worried that if no party gets a majority in Parliament, the sordid game of party-splitting and buying MPs could reach such unplumbed depths that government in general would lose all moral auth-ority. Indeed, if the events at the time of the fall of the V.P. Singh government and the formation of the Chandra Shekhar regime are any precedent, and if the process of the Rao govern-ment transforming itself from a minority to a majority in Par-liament is kept in mind, there is much reason to be apprehensive about what might happen in New Delhi after these elections. Some commentators have also reminded us of what happened after the 1991 elections: an unstable government with uncertain control over the economy will provide yet another opportunity for the international financial institutions to ram their medicines down the throat of the Indian economy.

On the other hand, it is also not clear that we will have a stable government of acceptable quality, even if one of the three contending forces in national politics manages to get a majority in Parliament. If the Congress gets a majority, it will only mean a worsening of all the processes of decay that had seized the central political structures of Indian politics in the last five years. The Congress as an all-India political organization is now daily crumbling from the inside. There is no reason to think that a victory in these elections will arrest that process of disintegration. As for the Bharatiya Janata Party, the prospect of its winning a majority and forming a government at the Centre is like a nightmare for a large section of the Indian people. And as far as the National Front–Left Front combination is concerned, the elements of agreement within this 'third force' are so narrow

[7] Bātil ādhunikatā, anāgata ganatantra', *Bāromās*, 17, 2 (April 1996), pp. 13–15 (translated from the Bengali).

and weak that, apart from the slogan of 'social justice', there seems to be little that will convince anyone that this assortment of parties could run a government on the basis of a credible minimum programme.

It is this general sense of uncertainty among voters all over the country that is reflected in the prospects of a hung Parliament. There is simply no party today that can command the confidence of a majority of the people of India. It is noticeable that whereas in earlier elections, anyone trying to make a casual prediction of the number of seats the various parties might win would usually end up with a total of 600 or more seats, this time no one seems to be able to account for more than 350 or 400 seats.

If one studies the recent history of Indian politics a little closely, it will become clear that this state of uncertainty has not emerged overnight. In the days of Rajiv Gandhi's rule, it might have seemed as though the political centre, with the government enjoying a huge majority and the chain of command ending up in a tightly focused centre of authority, was strong and fully in control. In actual fact, the countrywide organization of the Congress as the all-India ruling party was already in an advanced stage of decay. This process had started as early as the first phase of Indira Gandhi's dominance after the 1971 elections. In her successful attempt to re-establish Congress hegemony, she had embarked on a policy of centralization of powers, both in government and in the party organization. As a result, the space that had existed in the Nehru era for relatively independent exercise of power by Congress leaders at state and district levels was now completely taken away from them. The differentiated and flexible structure of both government and party organization, with powerful Congress leaders ruling at state and district levels — which was so much a characteristic of the old Congress system — now disappeared under Indira Gandhi, and after her, under her son. Every time a Congress leader had differences with the central leadership, he or she would now either leave the party or go into the political wilderness. This process has now reached a stage where even though the Congress is in power at the Centre, it does not rule in most of the states of India.

At this moment, there is no clear or stable pattern in the central structures of party politics in India. It is not the case that if the

Congress fails to win a majority, some other party or alliance will make a smooth entry into power. The two-party structure which is supposed to characterize a parliamentary system of the British type is at present completely absent in all-India politics. It is this absence that is being read as a sign of general political instability.

If one looks at the states, on the other hand, the picture is very different. In most states, a two-party or two-front system has attained a fair degree of permanence. If one party loses, the other gains a majority and forms the government. In most of the states of India, there is not a trace of the kind of uncertainty that hangs over New Delhi.

What is the significance of this fact? My interpretation is that the centre of gravity of Indian politics has decisively shifted from the central level to that of the states. The negotiations between various class and group interests, which are the stuff of democratic politics, are now most effectively conducted in the states. Each state has now developed, after five decades of electoral democracy, its own party structure that fits the effective structures of power as they exist in that state. Indeed, regions that have their own political identities but which do not have the status of separate states — such as the various regions of Uttar Pradesh or the Jharkhand region, or the Darjeeling hills in West Bengal — have also developed their own distinct party systems.

If one considers the nature of democratic politics, there is nothing surprising about these developments. Fifty years ago, when a new structure of electoral democracy was created in this country, the actual proportion of the country's population which effectively participated in it was extremely small. Today, there are numerous groups that are able to make their demands heard in the democratic arena: groups which, even twenty years ago, would have gone entirely unnoticed. The more the processes of democracy have deepened in India, the more has its centre of gravity moved downwards.

One can cite several kinds of evidence in support of this observation. At one time, it was virtually a truism to say that state policy in India in relation to large industry was laid down by the central government. Today, it has become clear that in the matter of new industrial investments, not only by domestic capital but also by foreign investors, a great deal depends on the enterprise and resourcefulness of the state governments. For several years now, state governments have taken the initiative in attracting investments, even by sending delegations abroad. And yet, on paper it is still the central government which lays down policy for large industry. That things are somewhat different in reality is not because of any constitutional or administrative change. It is because those who make industrial investments have discovered that their projects will effectively work only when they have managed to steer them through the ground-level realities at the state and local levels. Their practical sense for business tells them that effective political power is now so structured that it must be negotiated at those lower levels.

There is no doubt that this democratization of the political institutions has pushed many of the older institutions of civil society into a tight corner. We have heard persistent complaints for some time that the modern institutions of civic life that were built in India since the days of British rule are now in a state of collapse; that party and caste politics has brought ruin to our schools, colleges and universities, our cultural institutions, our voluntary organizations, our hospitals, our sporting clubs. These sentiments are widespread in educated middle-class circles in India today. This is the reason why, when an Election Commissioner or a judge of the Supreme Court declares that he will rid the public institutions of this country of the muck and grime of politics and turn the walls of Indian cities into sparkling and sanitized suburban facades, he is enthusiastically applauded by the educated.

The question is: can our civic institutions be revived by whitewashing the walls of our cities? Or will it only strengthen the anti-democratic prejudices of our elite? I believe this conflict has sharpened in recent years — on the one hand, the decay of our old institutions of modernity in the face of the growing demands of democratic politics; and, on the other, the attempt, in the name of institutional modernization, to erect fortifications against democracy.

There is much reason to be concerned about the way in which anti-democratic attitudes have slowly and almost imperceptibly seeped into the country's most articulate, conscious and well-educated circles. These sentiments had erupted at the time of the agitations against the Mandal Commission recommendations. But there are many other symptoms of this phenomenon. It can

be seen in one aspect of that collective malady called *Hindutva*
— not the one which charged, pickaxe and shovel in hand and
'Jai Sri Ram' in their voices, to break the mosque in Ayodhya,
but rather the one which explains in rational and sophisticated
words its impatient dream of turning India into a world power.
It is, as I said, among the articulate and educated that the anti-
democratic attitudes are the stongest. Similar sentiments also
seem to be building up among those who are frustrated by what
they see as unwarranted political obstacles to their project of rapid
economic liberalization.

Of course, it is not the case that the effects of democratization
are always desirable or acceptable. It is also true that institutional
reform is necessary. The question is: can we bring about these
reforms only by beating the breast over the collapse of moral
values, or wallowing in nostalgia for some long-lost golden age?
Listening these days to many political analysts on the Left, it
almost seems as though the Nehru era was a utopia of self-
reliance, secularism and even socialism. They have forgotten that
at that time the Leftists were — I believe, for entirely justified
reasons — Nehru's most trenchant critics.

Faced with the political uncertainties of the present, many
do not want to admit that those institutions which are now
facing collapse have actually exhausted their vitality and usefulness. They can never be revived by trying to go back to the
old ways. Rather, the task for tomorrow is to build new civic
institutions that are consonant with the demands of an expand-
ing democracy. It seems reasonable to suppose that such institutions will first evolve at local and regional levels. Perhaps
even at this moment, such institutions are actually taking shape
in various parts of the country. It may take a long time for a
new structure of democratic institutions to assume clear forms
at the central level of Indian politics. Perhaps what we now
refer to as the 'central level' may be very differently organized
and located under the new democratic arrangements. Until
then, we will simply have to put up with the laments, the
breast-beating and the snivels of nostalgia.

14

Secularism and Toleration

There is little doubt that in the last two or three years, we have seen a genuine renewal of both thinking and activism among left-democratic forces in India on the question of the fight for secularism. An important element of the new thinking is the re-examination of the theoretical and historical foundations of the liberal-democratic state in India, and of its relation to the history and theory of the modern state in Europe and the Americas.

An interesting point of entry into the problem is provided by the parallels recently drawn between the rise of fascism in Europe in the 1920s and 1930s, and that of the Hindu right in India in the last few years. Sumit Sarkar, among others, has noted some of the chilling similarities.[1] But a more careful look at precisely this comparison will, I think, lead us to ask a basic and somewhat unsettling question: is secularism an adequate, or even appropriate, ground on which to meet the political challenge of Hindu majoritarianism?

The Nazi campaigns against Jews and other minority groups did not call for an abandonment of the secular principles of the state in Germany. If anything, Nazi rule was accompanied by an attempt to de-Christianize public life and to undermine the influence of the Catholic as well as the various Protestant Churches. Fascist ideology did not seek the union of state and religion in Italy, where the presence of a large peasant population and the hold of Catholicism might be supposed to have provided an opportune condition for such a demand — and this despite the virtually open collaboration of the Roman Church with Mussolini's regime. Nazi Germany and fascist Italy are, of course, only two examples of a feature that has been noticed many times in

[1] Sumit Sarkar, 'The Fascism of the Sangh Parivar', *Economic and Political Weekly*, 30 January 1993, pp. 163–7; Jan Breman, 'The Hindu Right: Comparisons with Nazi Germany', *Times of India*, 15 March 1993.

the career of the modern state in many countries of the world: namely, that state policies of religious intolerance, or of discrimination against religious and other ethnic minorities, do not necessarily require the collapsing of state and religion, nor do they presuppose the existence of theocratic institutions.

The point is relevant in the context of the current politics of the Hindu right in India. It is necessary to ask why the political leadership of that movement chooses so meticulously to describe its adversaries as 'pseudo-secularists', conceding thereby its approval of the ideal as such of the secular state. None of the serious political statements made by that leadership contains any advocacy of theocratic institutions; and, notwithstanding the exuberance of a few sadhus celebrating their sudden rise to political prominence, it is unlikely that a conception of the 'Hindu Rashtra' will be seriously propagated which will include, for instance, a principle that the laws of the state be in conformity with this or that *saṃhitā* or even with the general spirit of the *Dharmaśāstra*. In this sense, the leading element in the current movement of the Hindu right can be said to have undergone a considerable shift in position from, let us say, that of the Hindu Mahasabha at the time of the debate over the Hindu Code Bill some forty years ago. Its position is also quite unlike that of most contemporary Islamic fundamentalist movements, which explicitly reject the theoretical separation of state and religion as 'western' and un-Islamic. It is similarly unlike the fundamentalist strand within the Sikh movements in recent years. The majoritarianism of the Hindu right, it seems to me, is perfectly at peace with the institutional procedures of the 'western' or 'modern' state.

Indeed, the mature, and most formidable, statement of the new political conception of 'Hindutva' is unlikely to pit itself at all against the idea of the secular state. The persuasive power, and even the emotional charge, that the Hindutva campaign appears to have gained in recent years does not depend on its demanding legislative enforcement of ritual or scriptural injunctions, a role for religious institutions in legislative or judicial processes, compulsory religious instruction, state support for religious bodies, censorship of science, literature and art in order to safeguard religious dogma, or any other similar demand undermining the secular character of the existing Indian state. This is not to say that in the frenzied mêlée produced by the Hindutva brigade such noises would not be made; the point is that anti-secular demands of this type are not crucial to the political thrust, or even the public appeal, of the campaign.

Indeed, in its most sophisticated forms, the campaign of the Hindu right often seeks to mobilize on its behalf the will of an interventionist modernizing state, in order to erase the presence of religious or ethnic particularisms from the domains of law or public life, and to supply, in the name of 'national culture', a homogenized content to the notion of citizenship. In this role, the Hindu right in fact seeks to project itself as a principled modernist critic of Islamic or Sikh fundamentalism, and to accuse the 'pseudo-secularists' of preaching tolerance for religious obscurantism and bigotry. The most recent example of this is the Allahabad High Court pronouncement on divorce practices among Muslims by a judge well known for his views on the constitutional sanctity of Lord Rama.

Thus, the comparison with fascism in Europe points to the very real possibility of a Hindu right locating itself quite firmly within the domain of the modernizing state, and using all of the ideological resources of that state to lead the charge against people who do not conform to its version of the 'national culture'. From this position, the Hindu right can not only deflect accusations of being anti-secular, but can even use the arguments for interventionist secularization to promote intolerance and violence against minorities.

As a matter of fact, the comparison with Nazi Germany also extends to the exact point that provides the Hindutva campaign with its venomous charge: as Sarkar notes, ' . . . the Muslim here becomes the near exact equivalent of the Jew.' The very fact of belonging to this minority religious community is sufficient to put a question mark against the status of a Muslim as a citizen of India. The term 'communal', in this twisted language, is reserved for the Muslim, whereas the 'pseudo-secular' is the Hindu who defends the right of the Muslim citizen. (Note once more that the term 'secular' itself is not made a target of attack.) Similarly, on the vexed question of migrants from Bangladesh, the Hindu immigrant is by definition a 'refugee' while the Muslim is an 'infiltrator'. A whole series of stereotypical features, now sickeningly familiar in their repetitiveness, are then adduced in order to declare as dubious the historical, civil and political status of the

Muslim within the Indian state. In short, the current campaign of the Hindu right is directed not against the principle of the secular state, but rather towards mobilizing the legal powers of that state in order to systematically persecute and terrorize a specific religious minority within its population.

The question then is as follows: is the defence of secularism an appropriate ground for meeting the challenge of the Hindu right? Or should it be fought where the attack is being made, i.e. should the response be a defence of the duty of the democratic state to ensure policies of religious toleration? The question is important because it reminds us that not all aggressive majoritarianisms pose the same sort of problem in the context of the democratic state: Islamic fundamentalism in Pakistan or Bangladesh, or Sinhala chauvinism in Sri Lanka do not necessarily have available to them the same political strategies as the majoritarian politics of the Hindu right in India. It also warns us of the very real theoretical possibility that secularization and religious toleration may sometimes work at cross-purposes.[2] It is necessary therefore to be clear about what is implied by these concepts.

Meaning of Secularism

At the very outset, let us face up to a point that will be invariably made in any discussion on 'secularism' in India: namely that in the Indian context the word has very different meanings from

---

[2] Ashis Nandy makes a distinction between religion-as-faith, by which he means a way of life that is operationally plural and tolerant, and religion-as-ideology which identifies and enumerates populations of followers fighting for non-religious, usually political and economic, interests. He then suggests, quite correctly, that the politics of secularism is part of the same process of formation of modern state practices which promotes religion-as-ideology. Nandy's conclusion is that rather than relying on secularism of a modernized elite we should 'explore the philosophy, the symbolism and the theology of tolerance in the various faiths of the citizens and hope that the state systems in South Asia may learn something about religious tolerance from everyday Hinduism, Islam, Buddhism, and/or Sikhism. . . . ': 'The Politics of Secularism and the Recovery of Religious Tolerance', in Veena Das, ed., *Mirrors of Violence: Communities, Riots and Survivors in South Asia* (Delhi: Oxford University Press, 1990), pp. 69–93. I am raising the same doubt about whether secularism necessarily ensures toleration, but, unlike Nandy, I am here looking for political possibilities *within* the domain of the modern state institutions as they now exist in India.

its standard use in the English language. This fact is sometimes cited as confirmation of the 'inevitable' difference in the meanings of a concept in two dissimilar cultures. ('India is not Europe: secularism in India cannot mean the same thing as it does in Europe.') At other times, it is used to underline the 'inevitable' shortcomings of the modern state in India. ('There cannot be a secular state in India because Indians have an incorrect concept of secularism.')

Of course, it could also be argued that this comparison with European conceptions is irrelevant if our purpose is to intervene in the Indian debate on the subject. What does it matter if secularism means something else in European and American political discourse? As long as there are reasonably clear and commonly agreed referents for the word in the Indian context, we should go ahead and address ourselves to the specifically Indian meaning of secularism.

Unfortunately, the matter cannot be settled that easily. The Indian meanings of secularism did not emerge in ignorance of the European or American meanings of the word. I also think that in its current usage in India, with apparently well-defined 'Indian' referents, the loud and often acrimonious Indian debate on secularism is never entirely innocent of its Western genealogies. To pretend that the Indian meaning of secularism has marked out a conceptual world all of its own, untroubled by its differences with Western secularism, is to take an ideological position which refuses either to recognize or to justify its own grounds.

In fact, I wish to make an even stronger argument. Commenting upon Raymond Williams's justly famous *Keywords*, Quentin Skinner has pointed out that a concept takes on a new meaning not when (as one would usually suppose) arguments that it should be applied to a new circumstance succeed, but rather when such arguments fail.[3] Thus, if one is to consider the 'new' meaning acquired by the word 'secularism' in India, it is not as though the plea of the advocates of secularism that the concept bears application to modern Indian state and society

[3] Quentin Skinner, 'Language and Political Change', in Terence Ball, James Farr and Russell L. Hanson, eds, *Political Innovation and Conceptual Change* (Cambridge: Cambridge University Press, 1989), pp. 6–23.

has won general acceptance, and that the concept has thereby taken on a new meaning. If that had been the case, the 'original' meaning of the word as understood in its standard sense in the West would have remained unmutilated; it would only have widened its range of referents by including within it the specific circumstances of the Indian situation. The reason why arguments have to be made about 'secularism' having a new *meaning* in India is because there are serious difficulties in applying the standard meaning of the word to the Indian circumstances. The 'original' concept, in other words, will not easily admit the Indian case within its range of referents.

This, of course, could be a good pretext for insisting that Indians have their own concept of secularism which is different from the Western concept bearing the same name; that, it could be argued, is exactly why the Western concept cannot be applied to the Indian case. The argument then would be about a difference in concepts: if the concept is different, the question of referential equivalence cannot be a very crucial issue. At the most, it would be a matter of family resemblances, but conceptually Western secularism and Indian secularism would inhabit entirely autonomous discursive domains.

That, it is needless to say, is hardly the case. We could begin by asking why, in all recent discussions in India on the relation between religion and the state, the central concept is named by the English words 'secular' and 'secularism', or in the Indian languages, by neologisms such as *dharma-nirapeksatā* which are translations of those English words and are clearly meant to refer to the range of meanings indicated by the English terms. As far as I know, there does not exist in any Indian language a term for 'secular' or 'secularism' which is standardly used in talking about the role of religion in the modern state and society, and whose meaning can be immediately explicated without having recourse to the English terms.

What this implies is that although the use of *dharma* in *dharma-nirapeksatā* or *mazhab* in *ghair-mazhabi* might open up conceptual or referential possibilities in Indian discourse which were unavailable to the concept of secularism in the West, the continued use of an awkward neologism, besides of course the continued use of the English term itself, indicates that the more stable and well-defined reference for the concept lies in the Western political discourse about the modern state.[4] In fact, it is clear from the discussions among the Indian political and intellectual elite at least from the 1920s that the proponents of the secular state in India never had any doubt at all about the meaning of the concept of secularism; all the doubts were about whether that concept would find a congenial field of application in the Indian social and political context. The continued use of the term 'secularism' is, it seems to me, an expression of the desire of the modernizing elite to see the 'original' meaning of the concept actualized in India. The resort to 'new meanings' is, to invoke Skinner's point once more, a mark of the failure of this attempt.

It might prove instructive to do a 'history of ideas' exercise for the use of the word 'secularism' in Indian political discourse in the last hundred years, but this is not the place for it. What is important for our purposes is a discussion of how the nationalist project of putting an end to colonial rule and inaugurating an independent nation-state became implicated, from its very birth, in a contradictory movement with regard to the modernist mission of secularization.

British Rule, Nationalism, and the Separation of State and Religion

Ignoring the details of a complicated history, it would not be widely off the mark to say that by the latter half of the nineteenth century, the British power in India had arrived at a reasonably firm policy of not involving the state in matters of religion. It tried to keep neutral on disputes over religion, and was particularly careful not to be seen as promoting Christianity. Immediately after the assumption of power by the Crown in 1858, the most significant step was taken in instituting equality before the law

[4] Even in the mid-1960s, Ziya-ul Hasan Faruqi was complaining about the use of *ghair-mazhabi* and *la-dini*. '*Ghayr mazhabi* means something contrary to religious commandments and *la dini* is irreligious or atheistic. . . . The common man was very easily led to conclude that the Indian state was against religion. It is, however, gratifying to see that the Urdu papers have started to transliterate the word "secular" . . .': 'Indian Muslims and the Ideology of the Secular State', in Donald Eugene Smith, ed., *South Asian Politics and Religion* (Princeton: Princeton University Press, 1966), pp. 138–49.

by enacting uniform codes of civil and criminal law. The area left out, however, was that of personal law which continued to be governed by the respective religious laws as recognized and interpreted by the courts. The reason why personal law was not brought within the scope of a uniform civil code was, precisely, the reluctance of the colonial state to intervene in matters close to the very heart of religious doctrine and practice. In the matter of religious endowments, while the British power in its early years took over many of the functions of patronage and administration previously carried out by Indian rulers, by the middle of the nineteenth century it largely renounced those responsibilities and handed them over to local trusts and committees.

As far as the modernizing efforts of the Indian elite are concerned, the nineteenth-century attempts at 'social reform' by soliciting the legal intervention of the colonial state are well known. In the second half of the nineteenth century, however, the rise of nationalism led to a refusal on the part of the Indian elite to let the colonial state enter into areas that were regarded as crucial to the cultural identity of the nation. This did not mean a halt to the project of 'reform': all it meant was a shift in the agency of reform — from the legal authority of the colonial state to the moral authority of the national community.[5] This shift is crucial: not so much because of its apparent coincidence with the policy of non-intervention of the colonial state in matters of religion in the late nineteenth century, but because of the underlying assumption in nationalist thinking about the role of state legislation in religion — legal intervention in the cause of religious reform was not undesirable *per se*, but it was undesirable when the state was colonial.

As it happened, there was considerable change in the social beliefs and practices of the sections that came to constitute the new middle class in the period leading up to independence in 1947. Not only was there change in the actual practices surrounding family and personal relations, and even in many religious practices, without there being any significant change in the laws of the state, but, perhaps more important, there was an overwhelming tide in the dominant attitudes among these sections

[5] I have discussed the point more elaborately in *The Nation and its Fragments: Colonial and Postcolonial Histories* (Princeton: Princeton University Press, 1993).

in favour of the legitimacy of 'social reform'. These reformist opinions affected the educated sections in virtually all parts of the country, and found a voice in most religious and caste communities.

One of the dramatic results of this cumulation of reformist desire within the nationalist middle class was the sudden spate of new legislation on religious and social matters immediately after independence. This is actually an extremely significant episode in the development of the nation-state in India, and its deeply problematic nature has been seldom noticed in the current debates over secularism. It needs to be described in some detail.

Religious Reform and the Nation-State

Even as the provisions of the new Constitution of India were being discussed in the Constituent Assembly, some of the provincial legislatures had begun to enact laws for the reform of religious institutions and practices. One of the most significant of these was the Madras *Devadasis* (Prevention of Dedication) Act, 1947, which outlawed the institution of dedicating young girls to temple deities, and prohibited 'dancing by a woman . . . in the precincts of any temple or other religious institution, or in any procession of a Hindu deity, idol or object of worship. . . . '[6] Equally important was the Madras Temple Entry Authorization Act, 1947, which made it a punishable offence to prevent any person on the ground of untouchability from entering or worshipping in a Hindu temple. This act was immediately followed by similar legislation in the Central Provinces, Bihar, Bombay and other provinces, and finally by the temple entry provisions in the Constitution of India.

Although in the course of the debates over these enactments, views were often expressed about the need to 'remove a blot on the Hindu religion', it was clearly possible to justify some of the laws on purely secular grounds. Thus, the *devadasi* system could be declared unlawful on the ground that it was a form of bondage or of enforced prostitution. Similarly, 'temple entry' was sometimes defended by extending the argument that the denial of

---

[6] Cited in Donald Eugene Smith, *India as a Secular State* (Princeton: Princeton University Press, 1963), p. 239.

access to public places on the ground of untouchability was unlawful. However, a contradiction appeared in this 'civil rights' argument since all places of worship were not necessarily thrown open to all citizens; only Hindu temples were declared open for all Hindus, and non-Hindus could be, and actually still are, denied entry. But even more problematically, the right of worship 'of all classes and sections of Hindus' at 'Hindu religious institutions of public character', as Article 25(2) of the Constitution has it, necessarily implies that the state has to take up the onus of interpreting even doctrinal and ritual injunctions in order to assert the *religious* legitimacy of forms of worship that would not be discriminatory in terms of caste.[7]

Still more difficult to justify on non-religious grounds was a reformist law like the Madras Animal and Bird Sacrifices Abolition Act, 1950. The view that animal sacrifices were repugnant and represented a primitive form of worship was clearly the product of a very specific religious interpretation of *religious* ritual, and could be described as a sectional opinion even among Hindus. (It might even be described as a view that was biased against the religious practices of the lower castes, especially in southern India.) Yet in bringing about this 'purification' of the Hindu religion, the legislative wing of the state was seen as the appropriate instrument.

The period after independence also saw, apart from reformist legislation of this kind, an enormous increase in the involvement of the state administration in the management of the affairs of Hindu temples. The most significant enabling legislation in this regard was the Madras Hindu Religious and Charitable Endowments Act, 1951, which created an entire department of government devoted to the administration of Hindu religious

---

[7] In fact, the courts, recognizing that the right of a religious denomination 'to manage its own affairs in matters of religion' [Article 26(b)] could come into conflict with the right of the state to throw open Hindu temples to all classes of Hindus [Article 25(2)(b)], have had to come up with ingenious, and often extremely arbitrary, arrangements in order to strike a compromise between the two provisions. Some of these judgements are referred to in Smith, *India as a Secular State*, pp. 242–3. For a detailed account of a case illustrating the extent of judicial involvement in the interpretation of religious doctrine and ritual, see Arjun Appadurai, *Worship and Conflict under Colonial Rule: A South Indian Case* (Cambridge: Cambridge University Press, 1981), pp. 36–50.

endowments.[8] The legal argument here is, of course, that the religious denomination concerned still retains the right to manage its own affairs in matters of religion, while the secular matters concerned with the management of the property of the endowment is taken over by the state. But this is a separation of functions that is impossible to maintain in practice. Thus, if the administrators choose to spend the endowment funds on opening hospitals or universities rather than on more elaborate ceremonies or on religious instruction, then the choice will affect the way in which the religious affairs of the endowment are managed. The issue has given rise to several disputes in court about the specific demarcation between the religious and the secular functions, and to further legislation, in Madras as well as in other parts of India. The resulting situation led one commentator in the early 1960s to remark that 'the commissioner for Hindu religious endowments, a public servant of the secular state, today exercises far greater authority over Hindu religion in Madras state than the Archbishop of Canterbury does over the Church of England.'[9]

Once again, it is possible to provide a non-religious ground for state intervention in the administration of religious establishments, namely prevention of misappropriation of endowment funds and ensuring the proper supervision of what is after all a public property. But what has been envisaged and actually

[8] Actually, the increased role of the government in controlling the administration of Hindu temples in Madras began with the Religious Endowments Acts of 1925 and 1927. It is interesting to note that there was nationalist opposition to the move at the time: S. Satyamurthi said during the debates in the provincial legislature in 1923 that 'the blighting hand of this Government will also fall tight on our temples and *maths*, with the result that they will also become part of the great machinery which the Hon'ble Minister and his colleagues are blackening every day.' During the debates preceding the 1951 Act, on the other hand, T.S.S. Rajan, the Law Minister, said: ' . . . the fear of interfering with religious institutions has always been there with an alien Government but with us it is very different. Ours may be called a secular Government, and so it is. But it does not absolve us from protecting the funds of the institutions which are meant for the service of the people.' For an account of these changes in law, see Chandra Y. Mudaliar, *The Secular State and Religious Institutions in India: A Study of the Administration of Hindu Public Religious Trusts in Madras* (Wiesbaden: Fritz Steiner Verlag, 1974).

[9] Smith, *India as a Secular State*, p. 246.

practised since independence goes well beyond this strictly negative role of the state. Clearly, the prevailing views about the
reform of Hindu religion saw it as entirely fitting that the representative and administrative wings of the state should take up
the responsibility of managing Hindu temples in, as it were, the
'public interest' of the general body of Hindus.

The reformist agenda was, of course, carried out most com-
prehensively during the making of the Constitution and subsequently in the enactment in 1955 of what is known as the
Hindu Code Bill.[10] During the discussions, objections were
raised that in seeking to change personal law, the state was
encroaching upon an area protected by the right to religious
freedom. B.R. Ambedkar's reply to these objections summed
up the general attitude of the reformist leadership:

The religious conceptions in this country are so vast that they cover
every aspect of life from birth to death. There is nothing which is not
religion and if personal law is to be saved I am sure about it that in
social matters we will come to a standstill . . . There is nothing extraordinary in saying that we ought to strive hereafter to limit the definition
of religion in such a manner that we shall not extend it beyond beliefs
and such rituals as may be connected with ceremonials which are
essentially religious. It is not necessary that the sort of laws, for instance,
laws relating to tenancy or laws relating to succession, should be governed by religion. . . . I personally do not understand why religion
should be given this vast expansive jurisdiction so as to cover the whole
of life and to prevent the legislature from encroaching upon that field.[11]

Impelled by this reformist urge, the Indian Parliament proceeded to cut through the immensely complicated web of local
and sectarian variations that enveloped the corpus known as
'Hindu law' as it had emerged through the colonial courts, and
to lay down a single code of personal law for all Hindu citizens.
Many of the new provisions were far-reaching in their departure
from traditional brahmanical principles. Thus, the new code
legalized inter-caste marriage; it legalized divorce and prohibited

---

[10] Actually, a series of laws called the Hindu Marriage Bill, the Hindu
Succession Bill, the Hindu Minority and Guardianship Bill and the Hindu
Adoptions and Maintenance Bill.

[11] *Constituent Assembly Debates* (New Delhi: Government of India, 1946–50),
vol. 7, p. 781.

polygamy; it gave to the daughter the same rights of inheritance as the son, and permitted the adoption of daughters as well as of sons. In justifying these changes, the proponents of reform not only made the argument that 'tradition' could not remain stagnant and needed to be reinterpreted in the light of changing conditions, but they also had to engage in the exercise of deciding what was or was not essential to 'Hindu religion'. Once again, the anomaly has provoked comments from critical observers: 'An official of the secular state [the law minister] became an interpreter of Hindu religion, quoting and expounding the ancient Sanskrit scriptures in defence of his bills.'[12]

Clearly, it is necessary here to understand the force and internal consistency of the nationalist-modernist project which sought, in one and the same move, to rationalize the domain of religious discourse and to secularize the public domain of personal law. It would be little more than reactionary to rail against the 'western-educated Hindu' who is scandalized by the profusion of avaricious and corrupt priests at Hindu temples, and who, influenced by Christian ideas of service and piety, rides roughshod over the 'traditional Hindu notions' that a religious gift was never made for any specific purpose; that the priest entrusted with the management of a temple could for all practical purposes treat the property and its proceeds as matters within his personal jurisdiction; and that, unlike the Christian church, a temple was a place 'in which the idol condescends to receive visitors, who are expected to bring offerings with them, like subjects presenting themselves before a maharaja.'[13] More serious, of course, is the criticism that by using the state as the agency of what was very often only religious reform, the political leadership of the new nation-state flagrantly violated the principle of separation of state and religion.[14] This is a matter we will now consider in

---

[12] Smith, *India as a Secular State*, pp. 281–2.

[13] See, for instance, J. Duncan M. Derrett, 'The Reform of Hindu Religious Endowments', in Smith, ed., *South Asian Politics and Religion*, pp. 311–36.

[14] The two most comprehensive studies on the subject of the secular state in India make this point. V.P. Luthera in *The Concept of the Secular State and India* (Calcutta: Oxford University Press, 1964) concludes that India should not properly be regarded as a secular state. D.E. Smith in *India as a Secular State* disagrees, arguing that Luthera bases his conclusion on too narrow a definition of the secular state, but nevertheless points out the numerous anomalies in the current situation.

detail, but it is nevertheless necessary to point out that the violation of this principle of the secular state was justified precisely by the desire to secularize.

Anomalies of the Secular State

What are the characteristics of the secular state? Three principles are usually mentioned in the liberal-democratic doctrine on this subject.[15] The first is the principle of *liberty* which requires that the state permit the practice of any religion, within the limits set by certain other basic rights which the state is also required to protect. The second is the principle of *equality* which requires that the state not give preference to one religion over another. The third is the principle of *neutrality* which is best described as the requirement that the state not give preference to the religious over the non-religious, and which leads, in combination with the liberty and equality principles, to what is known in US constitutional law as the 'wall of separation' doctrine: namely, that the state not involve itself with religious affairs or organizations.[16]

Looking now at the doctrine of the secular state as it has evolved in practice in India, it is clear that whereas all three principles have been invoked to justify the secular state, their application has been contradictory and has led to major anomalies. The principle of liberty, which implies a right of freedom of religion, has been incorporated in the Constitution which gives to every citizen — subject to public order, morality and health — not only the equal right to freedom of conscience but

[15] For a recent exchange on this matter, see Robert Audi, 'The Separation of Church and State and the Obligations of Citizenship', *Philosophy and Public Affairs*, 18, 3 (Summer 1989), pp. 259–96; Paul J. Weithman, 'Separation of Church and State: Some Questions for Professor Audi', *Philosophy and Public Affairs*, 20, 1 (Winter 1991), pp. 52–65; Robert Audi, 'Religious Commitment and Secular Reason: A Reply to Professor Weithman', *Philosophy and Public Affairs*, 20, 1 (Winter 1991), pp. 66–76.

[16] The US Supreme Court defined the doctrine as follows: 'Neither a state nor the federal government can set up a church. Neither can pass laws which aid one religion, aid all religions, or prefer one religion over another. . . . Neither a state nor the federal government can, openly or secretly, participate in the affairs of any religious organization or groups and vice versa.' *Everson* v. *Board of Education*. 330 U.S. 1 (1947), cited in Smith, *India as a Secular State*, pp. 125–6.

also, quite specifically, 'the right freely to profess, practise and propagate religion'. It also gives 'to every religious denomination or any section thereof' certain collective rights of religion. Besides, it specifically mentions the right of 'all minorities, whether based on religion or language', to establish and administer their own educational institutions. Limiting these rights of freedom of religion, however, is the right of the state to regulate 'any economic, financial, political or other secular activity which may be associated with religious practice', to provide for social welfare and reform and to throw open Hindu religious institutions to all sections of Hindus. This limit to the liberty principle is what enabled the extensive reform under state auspices of Hindu personal law, and of the administration of Hindu temples.

The liberal-democratic doctrine of freedom of religion does recognize, of course, that this right will be limited by other basic human rights. Thus, for instance, it would be perfectly justified for the state to deny that — let us say — human sacrifice or causing injury to human beings, or as we have already noted in the case of *devadasis*, enforced servitude to a deity or temple, constitutes permissible religious practice. However, it is also recognized that there are many grey areas where it is difficult to lay down the limit. A case very often cited in this connection is the legal prohibition of polygamy even when it may be sanctioned by a particular religion: the argument that polygamy necessarily violates other basic human rights is often thought of as problematical.

But no matter where this limit is drawn, it is surely required by the idea of the secular state that the liberty principle be limited only by the need to protect some other *universal* basic right, and not by appeal to a particular interpretation of religious doctrine. This, as we have mentioned before, has not been possible in India. The urge to undertake by legislation the reform of Hindu personal law and Hindu religious institutions made it difficult for the state not to transgress into the area of religious reform itself. Both the legislature and the courts were led into the exercise of interpreting religious doctrine on religious grounds. Thus, in deciding the legally permissible limits of state regulation of religious institutions, it became necessary to identify those practices that were *essentially* of a religious character; but, in accordance with the judicial procedures of a modern state, this decision could not be left to the religious denomination itself but had to be determined 'as an objective question' by the courts.[17] It can be easily seen that this could lead to the entanglement of the state in a series of disputes that are mainly religious in character.

It could, of course, be argued that given the dual character of personal law — inherited from the colonial period as religious law that had been recognized and codified as the laws of the state — and in the absence of appropriate institutions of the Hindu religion through which religious reform could be organized and carried out outside the arena of the state, there was no alternative to state intervention in this matter. Which other agency was there with the requisite power and legitimacy to undertake the reform of religious practices? The force and persuasiveness of this argument for the modernist leadership of independent India can hardly be overstated. The desire was in fact to initiate a process of rational interpretation of religious doctrine, and to find a representative and credible institutional process for the reform of religious practice. That the use of state legislation to achieve this modernist purpose must come into conflict with another modernist principle, of the freedom of religion, is one of the anomalies of the secular state in India.

The second principle — that of equality — is also explicitly recognized in the Indian Constitution which prohibits the state from discriminating against any citizen on the basis only of religion or caste, except when it makes special provisions for the advancement of socially and educationally backward classes or for scheduled castes and scheduled tribes. Such special provisions in the form of reserved quotas in employment and education, or of reserved seats in representative bodies, have of course led to much controversy in India in the last few decades. But these disputes about the validity of positive discrimination in favour of underprivileged castes or tribes have almost never taken the form of a dispute about equality on the ground of religion. Indeed, although the institution of caste itself is supposed to derive its basis from the doctrines of the brahmanical religion, the recent debates in the political arena about caste discrimination usually do not make any appeals at all to religious doctrines. There is only one significant way in which the question of

[17] *Durgah Committee* v. *Hussain, A.* 1961 S.C. 1402 *(1415)*, cited in Durga Das Basu, *Constitutional Law of India* (New Delhi: Prentice-Hall of India, 1977), p. 84.

positive discrimination in favour of scheduled castes is circum-
scribed by religion: in order to qualify as a member of a scheduled
caste, a person must profess to be either Hindu or Sikh; a public
declaration of the adoption of any other religion would lead to
disqualification. However, in some recent provisions relating to
'other backward classes', especially in the much-disputed recommendations of the Mandal Commission, attempts have been
made to go beyond this limitation.

The problem with the equality principle which concerns us
more directly is the way in which it has been affected by the
project of reforming Hindu religion by state legislation. All the
legislative and administrative measures we have mentioned before concern the institutions and practices of the Hindus, including the reform of personal laws and of religious endowments.
That this was discriminatory was argued in the 1950s by the
socially conservative sections of Hindu opinion, and by political
parties like the Hindu Mahasabha which were opposed to the
idea of reform itself. But the fact that the use of state legislation
to bring about reforms in only the religion of the majority was
creating a serious anomaly in the very notion of equal citizenship,
was pointed out by only a few lone voices within the progressive
sections. One such belonged to J.B. Kripalani, the socialist leader,
who argued: 'If we are a democratic state, I submit we must make
laws not for one community alone. . . . It is not the Mahasabhites
who alone are communal: it is the government also that is communal, whatever it may say.' Elaborating, he said,

If they [the Members of Parliament] single out the Hindu community
for their reforming zeal, they cannot escape the charge of being communalists in the sense that they favour the Hindu community and are
indifferent to the good of the Muslim community or the Catholic community. . . . Whether the marriage bill favours the Hindu community
or places it at a disadvantage, both ways, it becomes a communal
measure.[18]

The basic problem here was obvious. If it was accepted that
the state could intervene in religious institutions or practices in
order to protect other social and economic rights, then what was
the ground for intervening only in the affairs of one religious
community and not of others? Clearly, the first principle — that

[18] Cited in Smith, *India as a Secular State*, pp. 286, 288.

of freedom of religion — could not be invoked here only for the minority communities when it had been set aside in the case of the majority community.

The problem has been got around by resorting to what is essentially a pragmatic argument. It is suggested that, for historical reasons, there is a certain lag in the readiness of the different communities to accept reforms intended to rationalize the domain of personal law. In any case, if equality of citizenship is what is desired, it already stands compromised by the very system of religion-based personal laws inherited from colonial times. What should be done, therefore, is to first declare the desirability of replacing the separate personal laws by a uniform civil code; but to proceed towards this objective in a pragmatic way, respecting the sensitivity of the religious communities about their freedom of religion, and going ahead with state-sponsored reforms only when the communities themselves are ready to accept them. Accordingly, there is an item in the non-justiciable Directive Principles of the Constitution which declares that the state should endeavour to provide a uniform civil code for all citizens. On the other hand, those claiming to speak on behalf of the minority communities tend to take a firm stand in the freedom of religion principle, and to deny that the state should have any right at all to interfere in their religious affairs. The anomaly has, in the last few years, provided some of the most potent ammunition to the Hindu right in its campaign against what it describes as the 'appeasement' of minorities.

It would not be irrelevant to mention here that there have also occurred, among the minority religious communities in India, not entirely dissimilar movements for the reform of religious laws and institutions. In the earlier decades of this century, there were organized attempts, for instance, to put an end to local customary practices among Muslim communities in various parts of India and replace them with a uniform Muslim personal law. This campaign, led in particular by the Jamiyat al-ulama-i Hind of Deoband — well known for its closeness to the Indian National Congress — was directed against the recognition by the courts of special marriage and inheritance practices among communities such as the Mapilla of southern India, the Memon of western India, and various groups in Rajasthan and Punjab. The argument given was not only that such practices were 'un-Islamic'; specific criticisms were also made about how these customs were backward and iniquitous, especially in the matter of the treatment of women. The preamble to a Bill to change the customary succession law of the Mapilla, for instance, said, using a rhetoric not unlike what would be used later for the reform of Hindu law, 'The Muhammadan community now feels the incongruity of the usage and looks upon the prevailing custom as a discredit to their religion and to their community.'[19]

The reform campaigns led to a series of new laws in various provinces and in the central legislature, such as the Mapilla Succession Act 1918, the Cutchi Memons Act 1920 and 1938, and the NWFP Muslim Personal Law (Shari'at) Application Act 1935 (which was the first time that the terms 'Muslim personal law' and Shari'at were used interchangeably in law). The culmination of these campaigns for a uniform set of personal laws for all Muslims in India was reached with the passing of the so-called Shari'at Act by the Central legislature in 1937. Interestingly, it was because of the persistent efforts of Muhammad Ali Jinnah, whose political standing was in this case exceeded by his prestige as a legal luminary, that only certain sections of this Act were required to be applied compulsorily to all Muslims; on other matters its provisions were optional.

The logic of completing the process of uniform application of Muslim personal law has continued in independent India. The optional clauses in the 1937 Act have been removed. The Act has been applied to areas that were earlier excluded: especially the princely states that merged with India after 1947, the latest in that series being Cooch Behar where the local customary law for Muslims was superseded by the Shari'at laws through legislation by the Left Front government of West Bengal in 1980.

Thus, even while resisting the idea of a uniform civil code on the ground that this would be a fundamental encroachment on the freedom of religion and destructive of the cultural identity of religious minorities, the Muslim leadership in India has not shunned state intervention altogether. One notices, in fact, the same attempt to seek rationalization and uniformity as one sees in the case of Hindu personal law or Hindu religious institutions.

---

[19] Cited in Tahir Mahmood, *Muslim Personal Law: Role of the State in the Indian Subcontinent* (Nagpur: All India Reporter, 1983), p. 21.

The crucial difference after 1947 is, of course, that unlike the majority community, the minorities are unwilling to grant to a legislature elected by universal suffrage the power to legislate the reform of their religions. On the other hand, there do not exist any other institutions which have the representative legitimacy to supervise such a process of reform. That, to put it in a nutshell, is the present impasse on the equality principle.

The third principle we have mentioned of the secular state — that of the separation of state and religion — has also been recognized in the Constitution, which declares that there shall be no official state religion, no religious instruction in state schools, and no taxes to support any particular religion. But, as we have seen, the state has become entangled in the affairs of religion in numerous ways. This was the case even in colonial times; but the degree and extent of the entanglement, paradoxically, has increased since independence. Nor is this involvement limited only to the sorts of cases we have mentioned before, which were the results of state-sponsored religious reform. Many of the older systems of state patronage of religious institutions, carried out by the colonial government or by the princely states, still continue under the present regime. Thus, Article 290A of the Constitution makes a specific provision of money to be paid every year by the governments of Kerala and Tamil Nadu to the Travancore Devaswom Fund. Article 28(2) says that although there will be no religious instruction in educational institutions wholly maintained out of state funds, this would not apply to those institutions where the original endowment or trust requires that religious instruction be given. Under this provision, Benaras Hindu University and Aligarh Muslim University, both central universities, do impart religious instruction. Besides, there are numerous educational institutions all over the country run by religious denominations which receive state financial aid.

The conclusion is inescapable that the 'wall of separation' doctrine of US constitutional law can hardly be applied to the present Indian situation (as indeed it cannot in the case of many European democracies; but there at least it could be argued that the entanglements are politically insignificant, and often obsolete remnants of older legal conventions). This is precisely the ground on which the argument is sometimes made that 'Indian secularism' has to have a different meaning from 'Western secularism'.

What is suggested in fact is that the cultural and historical realities of the Indian situation call for a *different* relationship between state and civil society than what is regarded as normative in Western political discourse, at least in the matter of religion. Sometimes it is said that in Indian conditions, the neutrality principle cannot apply; the state will necessarily have to involve itself in the affairs of religion. What must be regarded as normative here is an extension of the equality principle, i.e. that the state should favour all religions equally. This argument, however, cannot offer a defence for the selective intervention of the state in reforming the personal laws only of the majority community. On the other hand, arguments are also made about secularism having 'many meanings',[20] suggesting thereby that a democratic state must be expected to protect cultural diversity and the right of people to follow their own culture. The difficulty is that this demand cannot be easily squared with the homogenizing secular desire for, let us say, a uniform civil code.

Where we end up then is a quandary. The desire for a secular state must concede defeat even as it claims to have discovered new meanings of secularism. On the other hand, the respect for cultural diversity and different ways of life finds it impossible to articulate itself in the unitary rationalism of the language of rights. It seems to me that there is no viable way out of this problem within the given contours of liberal-democratic theory, which must define the relation between the relatively autonomous domains of state and civil society always in terms of individual rights. As has been noticed for many other aspects of the emerging forms of non-Western modernity, this is one more instance where the supposedly universal forms of the modern state turn out to be inadequate for the post-colonial world.

To reconfigure the problem posed by the career of the secular state in India, we will need to locate it on a somewhat different conceptual ground. In the remainder of this paper, I will suggest the outlines of an alternative theoretical argument which holds the promise of taking us outside the dilemmas of the secular-modernist discourse. In this, I will not take the easy route of appealing to an 'Indian exception'. In other words, I will not trot out yet another version of the 'new meaning of secularism'

[20] Sumit Sarkar, 'The Fascism of the Sangh Parivar'.

argument. But to avoid that route, I must locate my problem on a ground which will include, at one and the same time, the history of the rise of the modern state in both its Western and non-Western forms. I will attempt to do this by invoking Michel Foucault.

Liberal-Democratic Conundrum

But before I do that, let me briefly refer to the current state of the debate over minority rights in liberal political theory, and why I think the problem posed by the Indian situation will not find any satisfactory answers within the terms of that debate. A reference to this theoretical corpus is necessary because, first, left-democratic thinking in India on secularism and minority rights shares many of its premises with liberal-democratic thought; and second, the legally instituted processes of the state and the public domain in India have clearly avowed affiliations to the conceptual world of liberal political theory. Pointing out the limits of liberal thought will also allow me, then, to make the suggestion that political practice in India must seek to develop new institutional sites that cut across the divide between state sovereignty on the one hand and people's rights on the other.

To begin with, liberal political theory in its strict sense cannot recognize the validity of any collective rights of cultural groups. Liberalism must hold as a fundamental principle the idea that the state, and indeed all public institutions, will treat all citizens equally, regardless of race, sex, religion or other cultural particularities. It is only when everyone is treated equally, liberals will argue, that the basic needs of people, shared universally by all, can be adequately and fairly satisfied. These universal needs will include not only 'material' goods such as livelihood, health care or education, but also 'cultural' goods such as religious freedom, free speech, free association, etc. But in order to guarantee freedom and equality at the same time, the locus of rights must be the individual citizen, the bearer of universal needs; to recognize rights that belong only to particular cultural groups within the body of citizens is to destroy both equality and freedom.

Needless to say, this purist version of the liberal doctrine is regarded as unduly rigid and narrow by many who otherwise identify with the values of liberal-democratic politics. But the attempts to make room, within the doctrines of liberalism, for some recognition of collective cultural identities have not yielded solutions that enjoy wide acceptance. I cannot enter here into the details of this controversy which, spurred on by the challenge of 'multiculturalism' in many Western countries, has emerged as perhaps the liveliest area of debate in contemporary liberal philosophy. A mention only of the principal modes of argument, insofar as they are relevant to the problems posed by the Indian situation, will have to suffice.

One response to the problem of fundamental moral disagreements caused by a plurality of conflicting — and sometimes incommensurable — cultural values, is to seek an extension of the principle of neutrality in order to preclude such conflicts from the political arena. The argument here is that, just as in the case of religion, the existence of fundamentally divergent moral values in society would imply that there is no rational way in which reasonable people might resolve the dispute; and since the state should not arbitrarily favour one set of beliefs over another, it must not be asked to intervene in such conflicts. John Rawls and Thomas Nagel, among others, have made arguments of this kind, seeking thereby to extend the notions of state impartiality and religious toleration to other areas of moral disagreement.[21]

Not all liberals, however, like the deep scepticism and 'epistemic abstinence' implied in this view.[22] More relevant for us, however, is the criticism made from within liberal theory that these attempts to cope with diversity by taking the disputes off the political agenda are 'increasingly evasive. They offer a false impartiality in place of social recognition of the persistence of fundamental conflicts of value in our society.'[23] If this is a judgement that can be made for societies where the 'wall of separation' doctrine is solidly established, the remoteness of

---

[21] John Rawls, 'Justice as Fairness: Political not Metaphysical', *Philosophy and Public Affairs*, 14 (1985), pp. 248–51; John Rawls, 'The Priority of the Right and Ideas of the Good', *Philosophy and Public Affairs*, 17 (1988), pp. 260–4; Thomas Nagel, 'Moral Conflict and Political Legitimacy', *Philosophy and Public Affairs*, 16(1987), pp. 218–40.

[22] For instance, Joseph Raz, 'Facing Diversity: The Case of Epistemic Abstinence', *Philosophy and Public Affairs*, 19 (1990), pp. 3–46.

[23] Amy Gutmann and Dennis Thompson, 'Moral Conflict and Political Consensus', *Ethics*, 101 (October 1990), pp. 64–88.

these arguments from the realities of the Indian situation hardly needs to emphasized.

However, rather than evade the question of cultural diversity, some theorists have attempted to take up the 'justice as fairness' idea developed by liberals such as John Rawls and Ronald Dworkin, and extend it to cultural groups. Justice, according to this argument, requires that undeserved or 'morally arbitrary' disadvantages should be removed or compensated for. If such disadvantages attach to persons because they were born into particular minority cultural groups, then liberal equality itself must demand that individual rights be differentially allocated on the basis of culture. Will Kymlicka has made such a case for the recognition of the rights of cultural minorities whose very survival as distinct groups is in question.[24]

We should note, of course, that the examples usually given in this liberal literature to illustrate the need for minority cultural rights are those of the indigenous peoples of North America and Australia. But in principle there is no reason why the argument about 'being disadvantaged' should be restricted only to such indubitable cases of endangered cultural groups; it should apply to any group that can be reasonably defined as a cultural minority within a given political entity. And this is where its problems as a liberal theory become insuperable. Could a collective cultural right be used as an instrument to perpetuate thoroughly illiberal practices within the group? Would individual members of such groups have the right to leave the group? If an individual right of exit is granted, would that not in effect undermine the right of the group to preserve its identity? On the other hand, if a right of exit is denied, would we still have a liberal society?[25]

Clearly, it is extremely hard to justify the granting of substantively different collective rights to cultural groups on the basis of liberalism's commitment to procedural equality and universal citizenship. Several recent attempts to make a case for special rights for cultural minorities and oppressed groups, have

[24] Will Kymlicka, *Liberalism, Community and Culture* (Oxford: Oxford University Press, 1989).

[25] See, for example, the following exchange: Chandran Kukathas, 'Are there any Cultural Rights?' and Will Kymlicka, 'The Rights of Minority Cultures', *Political Theory*, 20, 1 (February 1992), pp. 105–46; Kukathas, 'Cultural Rights Again', *Political Theory*, 20, 4 (November 1992), pp. 674–80.

consequently gone on to question the idea of universal citizenship itself: in doing this, the arguments come fairly close to upholding some sort of cultural relativism. The charge that is made against universal citizenship is not merely that it forces everyone into a single homogeneous cultural mould, thus threatening the distinct identities of minority groups; but that the homogeneous mould itself is by no means a neutral one, being invariably the culture of the dominant group, so that it is not everybody but only the minorities and the disadvantaged who are forced to forego their cultural identities. That being the case, neither universalism nor neutrality can have any moral priority over the rights of cultural groups to protect their autonomous existence.

Once again, arguments such as this go well beyond the recognized limits of the liberal doctrine; and even those who are sympathetic to the demands for the protection of plural cultural identities feel compelled to assert that the recognition of difference cannot mean the abandonment of all commitment to a universalist framework of reason.[26] Usually, therefore, the 'challenge of multiculturalism' is sought to be met by asserting the value of diversity itself for the flowering of culture, and making room for divergent ways of life *within* a fundamentally agreed set of universalist values. Even when one expects recognition of one's 'right to culture', therefore, one must always be prepared to act within a culture of rights and thus give reasons for insisting on being different.[27]

None of these liberal arguments seems to have enough strength to come to grips with the problems posed by the Indian situation. Apart from resorting to platitudes about the value of diversity, respect for other ways of life, and the need for furthering understanding between different cultures, they do not provide any means for relocating the institutions of

[26] See, for example, Charles Taylor, *Multiculturalism and 'The Politics of Recognition'* (Princeton: Princeton University Press, 1992); Amy Gutmann, 'The Challenge of Multiculturalism in Political Ethics', *Philosophy and Public Affairs*, 22 (1993), pp. 73–206.

[27] Rajeev Bhargava has sought to make the case for the rights of minorities in India in these terms. See 'The Right to Culture', in K.N. Panikkar, ed., *Communalism in India: History, Politics and Culture* (New Delhi: Manohar, 1991), pp. 165–72.

rights or refashioning the practices of identity in order to get out of what often appears to be a political impasse.

Governmentality

I make use of Foucault's idea of governmentality not because I think it is conceptually neat or free of difficulties. Nor is the way in which I will use the idea here one that, as far as I know, Foucault has advanced himself. I could have, therefore, gone on from the preceding paragraph to set out my own scheme for re-problematizing the issue of secularism in India, without making this gesture towards Foucault. The reason I think the reference is necessary, however, is that by invoking Foucault I will be better able to emphasize the need to shift our focus from the rigid framework laid out by the concepts of sovereignty and right, to the constantly shifting *strategic* locations of the politics of identity and difference.

Foucault's idea of governmentality[28] reminds us, first, that cutting across the liberal divide between state and civil society there is a very specific form of power that entrenches itself in modern society, having as its goal the well-being of a population, its mode of reasoning a certain instrumental notion of economy, and its apparatus an elaborate network of surveillance. True, there have been other attempts at conceptualizing this ubiquitous form of modern power: most notably in Max Weber's theory of rationalization and bureaucracy, or more recently in the writings of the Frankfurt School, and in our own time in those of Jürgen Habermas. However, unlike Weberian sociology, Foucault's idea of governmentality does not lend itself to appropriation by a liberal doctrine characterizing the state as a domain of coercion ('monopoly of legitimate violence') and civil society as the zone of freedom. The idea of governmentality — and this is its second important feature — insists that by exercising itself through forms of representation, and hence by offering itself as an aspect of the self-disciplining of the very population over which it is

---

[28] See, in particular, Michel Foucault, 'Governmentality', in Graham Burchell, Colin Gordon and Peter Miller, eds, *The Foucault Effect: Studies in Governmentality* (Chicago: University of Chicago Press, 1991), pp. 87–104; and 'Politics and Reason', in Foucault, *Politics, Philosophy, Culture: Interviews and Other Writings 1977–1984* (New York: Routledge, 1988), pp. 57–85.

exercised, the modern form of power, whether inside or outside the domain of the state, is capable of allowing for an immensely flexible braiding of coercion and consent.

If we bear in mind these features of the modern regime of power, it will be easier for us to grasp what is at stake in the politics of secularization. It is naive to think of secularization as simply the onward march of rationality, devoid of coercion and power struggles. Even if secularization as a process of the decreasing significance of religion in public life is connected with such 'objective' social processes as mechanization or the segmentation of social relationships (as sociologists such as Bryan Wilson have argued),[29] it does not necessarily evoke a uniform set of responses from all groups. Indeed, contrary phenomena such as religious revivalism, fundamentalism, and the rise of new cults have sometimes also been explained as the consequence of the same processes of mechanization or segmentation. Similarly, arguments about the need to hold on to a universalist framework of reason even as one acknowledges the fact of difference ('deliberative universalism' or 'discourse ethics') tend to sound like pious homilies because they ignore the strategic context of power in which identity or difference is often asserted.

The limit of liberal-rationalist theory is reached when one is forced to acknowledge that, within the specific strategic configuration of a power contestation, what is asserted in a collective cultural right is in fact *the right not to offer a reason for being different.* Thus, when a minority group demands a cultural right, it in fact says, 'We have our own reasons for doing things the way we do, but since you don't share the fundamentals of our world-view, you will never come to understand or appreciate those reasons. Therefore, leave us alone and let us mind our own business.' If this demand is admitted, it amounts in effect to a concession to cultural relativism.

But the matter does not necessarily end there. Foucault's notion of governmentality leads us to examine the other aspect of this strategic contestation. Why is the demand made in the language of rights? Why are the ideas of autonomy and freedom invoked? Even

---

[29] Bryan Wilson, *Religion in Secular Society* (London: Watts, 1966); Wilson, *Religion in Sociological Perspective* (Oxford: Oxford University Press, 1982). Also, David Martin, *A General Theory of Secularization* (Oxford: Basil Blackwell, 1978).

as one asserts a basic incommensurability in frameworks of reason, why does one nevertheless say, 'We have our own reasons'?

Consider then the two aspects of the process that Foucault describes as the 'governmentalization of the state': juridical sovereignty on the one hand, governmental technology on the other. In his account of this process in Western Europe since the eighteenth century, Foucault tends to suggest that the second aspect completely envelops and contains the first.[30] That is to say, in distributing itself throughout the social body by means of the technologies of governmental power, the modern regime no longer retains a distinct aspect of sovereignty. I do not think, however, that this is a necessary implication of Foucault's argument. On the contrary, I find it more useful — especially of course in situations where the sway of governmental power is far from general — to look for a disjuncture between the two aspects, and thus to identify the sites of application of power where governmentality is unable to successfully encompass sovereignty.

The assertion of minority cultural rights occurs on precisely such a site. It is because of a contestation on the ground of sovereignty that the right is asserted *against governmentality*. To say 'We will not give reasons for not being like you' is to resist entering that deliberative or discursive space where the technologies of governmentality operate. But then, in a situation like this, the only way to resist submitting to the powers of sovereignty is literally to declare oneself unreasonable.

Toleration and Democracy

It is necessary for me to clarify here that in the remainder of this paper, I will be concerned exclusively with finding a defensible argument for minority cultural rights in the given legal–political

[30] 'Maybe what is really important for our modernity — that is, for our present — is not so much the *étatisation* of society, as the "governmentalization" of the state. . . . This governmentalization of the state is a singularly paradoxical phenomenon, since if in fact the problems of governmentality and the techniques of government have become the only political issue, the only real space for political struggle and contestation, this is because the governmentalization of the state is at the same time what has permitted the state to survive, and it is possible to suppose that if the state is what it is today, this is so precisely thanks to this governmentality, which is at once internal and external to the state . . . ': Foucault, 'Governmentality', p. 103.

situation prevailing in India. I am not therefore proposing an abstract institutional scheme for the protection of minority rights in general. Nor will I be concerned with hypothetical questions such as: 'If your proposal is put into practice, what will happen to national unity?' I am not arguing from the position of the state; consequently, the problem as I see it, is not what the state, or those who think and act on behalf on the state, can grant to the minorities. My problem is to find a defensible ground for a strategic politics, both within and outside the field defined by the institutions of the state, in which a minority group, or one who is prepared to think from the position of a minority group, can engage in India today.

When a group asserts a right against governmentality, i.e. a right not to offer reasons for being different, can it expect others to respect its autonomy and be tolerant of its 'unreasonable' ways? The liberal understanding of toleration will have serious problems with such a request. If toleration is the willing acceptance of something of which one disapproves, then it is usually justified on one of three grounds: a contractualist argument (persons entering into the social contract cannot know beforehand which religion they will end up having, and hence will agree to mutual toleration),[31] a consequentialist argument (the consequences of acting tolerantly are better than those of acting intolerantly),[32] or an argument about respect for persons.[33] We have already pointed out the inappropriateness of a contractualist solution to the problems posed by the Indian situation. The consequentialist argument is precisely what is used when it is said that one must go slow on the universal civil code. But this is only a pragmatic argument for toleration, based on a tactical consideration about the costs of imposing what is otherwise the right thing to do. As such, it always remains vulnerable to righteous moral attack.

The principle of respect for persons does provide a moral

---

[31] The most well known such argument is in John Rawls, *A Theory of Justice* (London: Oxford University Press, 1971), pp. 205–21.

[32] See, for instance, Preston King, *Toleration* (London: George, Allen and Unwin, 1976); D.D. Raphael, 'The Intolerable', in Susan Mendus, ed., *Justifying Toleration: Conceptual and Historical Perspectives* (Cambridge: Cambridge University Press, 1988), pp. 137–53.

[33] For instance, Joseph Raz, 'Autonomy, Toleration and the Harm Principle', in Mendus, ed., *Justifying Toleration*, pp. 155–75.

argument for toleration. It acknowledges the right of the toler-ated, and construes toleration as something that can be claimed as an entitlement. It also sets limits to toleration and thereby resolves the problem of justifying something of which one dis-approves: toleration is required by the principle of respect for persons, but practices which fail to show respect for persons need not be tolerated. Applying this principle to the case of minority cultural rights, one can easily see where the difficulty will arise. If a group is intolerant towards its own members and shows inadequate respect for persons, how can it claim tolerance from others? If indeed the group chooses not to enter into a reasonable dialogue with others on the validity of its practices, how can it claim respect for its ways?

Once again, I think that the strategic location of the contest-ation over cultural rights is crucial. The assertion of a right to be different does not exhaust all of the points where the contestation is grounded. Equally important is the other half of the assertion: 'We have our own reasons for doing things the way we do.' This implies the existence of a field of reasons, of processes through which reasons can be exchanged and validated, even if such pro-cesses are open only to those who share the viewpoint of the group. The existence of this autonomous discursive field may only be implied and not activated, but the implication is a neces-sary part of the assertion of cultural autonomy as a matter of *right*.[34]

The liberal doctrine tends to treat the question of collective rights of cultural minorities from a position of externality. Thus, its usual stand on tolerating cultural groups with illiberal practices is to advocate some sort of right of exit for individual dissident members. (One is reminded of the insistence of the liberal Jinnah that not all sections of the Shari'at Bill should apply compulsorily

---

[34] In some ways, this is the obverse of the implication which Ashis Nandy derives from his Gandhian conception of tolerance. His 'religious' conception of tolerance 'must impute to other faiths the same spirit of tolerance. Whether a large enough proportion of those belonging to the other religious traditions show in practice and at a particular point of time and place the same tolerance or not is a secondary matter. Because it is the imputation or presumption of tolerance in others, not its existence, which defines one's own tolerance. . . . ' Nandy, 'The Politics of Secularism'. My search is in the other direction. I am looking for a 'political' conception of tolerance which will set out the practical conditions I must meet in order to demand and expect tolerance from others.

to all Muslims.) The argument I am advancing would, however, give a very different construction to the concept of toleration. Toleration here would require one to accept that there will be political contexts where a group could insist on its right not to give reasons for doing things differently, provided it explains itself adequately in its own chosen forum. In other words, toleration here would be premised on autonomy and respect for persons, but it would be sensitive to the varying political salience of the institutional contexts in which reasons are debated.

To return to the specificities of the Indian situation, then, my approach would not call for any axiomatic approval to a uniform civil code for all citizens. Rather, it would start from the historically given reality of separate religion-based personal laws and the intricate involvement of state agencies in the affairs of religious institutions. Here, equal citizenship already stands qualified by the legal recognition of religious differences; the 'wall of separation' doctrine cannot be strictly applied either. Given the inapplicability of the neutrality principle, therefore, it becomes necessary to find a criterion by which state involvement, when it occurs in the domain of religion, can appear to the members of a religious group as both legitimate and fair. It seems to me that toleration, as described above, can supply us with this criterion.

Let us construct an argument for someone who is prepared to defend the cultural rights of minority religious groups in India. The 'minority group', she will say, is not the invention of some perverse sectarian imagination: it is an actually existing category of Indian citizenship — constitutionally defined, legally administered and politically invoked at every opportunity. Some people in India happen to be born into minority groups; a few others choose to enter them by conversion. In either case, many aspects of the status of such people as legal and political subjects are defined by the fact that they belong to minority groups. If there is any perversity in this, our advocate will point out, it lies in the specific compulsion of the history of the Indian state and its nationalist politics. That being so, one could not fairly be asked to simply forget one's status as belonging to a minority. What must be conceded instead is one's right to negotiate that status in the public arena.

Addressing the general body of citizens from her position

within the minority group, then, our advocate will demand toleration for the beliefs of the group. On the other hand, addressing other members of her group, she will demand that the group publicly seek and obtain from its members consent for its practices, insofar as those practices have regulative power over the members. She will point out that if the group was to demand and expect toleration from others, it would have to satisfy the condition of representativeness. Our advocate will therefore demand more open and democratic debate within her community. Even if it is true, she will say, that the validity of the practices of the religious group can be discussed and judged only in its own forums, those institutions must satisfy the same criteria of publicity and representativeness that members of the group demand of all public institutions having regulatory functions. That, she will insist, is a necessary implication of engaging in the politics of collective rights.

She will not of course claim to have a blueprint of the form of representative institutions which her community might develop, and she will certainly resist any attempt by the state to legislate into existence representative bodies for minority groups as prerequisites for the protection of minority rights. The appropriate representative bodies, she will know, could only achieve their actual form through a political process carried out primarily within each minority group. But by resisting, on the one hand, the normalizing attempt of the national state to define, classify and fix the identity of minorities on their behalf (the minorities, while constituting a legally distinct category of citizens, can only be acted upon by the general body of citizens; they cannot represent themselves), and demanding, on the other, that regulative powers within the community be established on a more democratic and internally representative basis, our protagonist will try to engage in a strategic politics that is neither integrationist nor separatist. She will in fact locate herself precisely at that cusp where she can face, on the one side, the assimilationist powers of governmental technology and resist, on the grounds of autonomy and self-representation, its universalist idea of citizenship; and, on the other side, struggle, once again on the grounds of autonomy and self-representation, for the emergence of more representative public institutions and practices within her community.

Needless to say, there will be many objections to her politics, even from her own comrades. Would not her disavowal of the idea of universal citizenship mean a splitting up of national society into mutually exclusive and rigidly separated ethnic groups? To this question, our protagonist could give the abstract answer that universal citizenship is merely the form offered by the bourgeois-liberal state to ensure the legal–political conditions for the deployment and exploitation of differences in civil society; universal citizenship normalizes the reproduction of differences by pretending that everyone is the same. More concretely, she could point out that nowhere has the sway of universal citizenship meant the end of either ethnic difference or discrimination on cultural grounds. The lines of difference and discrimination dissolve at some points, only to reappear at others. What is problematic here is not so much the existence of bounded categories of population, which the classificatory devices of modern governmental technologies will inevitably impose, but rather the inability of people to negotiate, through a continuous and democratic process of self-representation, the actual content of those categories. That is the new politics that one must try to initiate within the old forms of the modern state.

She will also be asked whether, by discounting universal citizenship, she is not throwing away the possibility of using the emancipatory potential of the ideas of liberty and equality. After all, does not the liberal-secular idea of equal rights still hold out the most powerful ideological means to fight against unjust and often tyrannical practices within many religious communities, especially regarding the treatment of women? To this, the answer will be that it is not a choice of one or the other. To pursue a strategic politics of demanding toleration, one would not need to oppose the liberal-secular principles of the modern state. One would, however, need to rearrange one's strategic priorities. One would be rather more sceptical of the promise that an interventionist secular state would, by legislation or judicial decisions, bring about progressive reform within minority religious groups. Instead, one would tend to favour the harder option, which rests on the belief that if the struggle is for progressive change in social practices sanctioned by religion, then that struggle must be launched and won within the religious communities themselves. There are no historical shortcuts here.

A strategic politics of demanding toleration does not require one to regurgitate the tired slogans about the universality of discursive reason. Instead, it takes seriously the possibility that at particular conjunctures and on specific issues, there could occur an honest refusal to engage in reasonable discourse. But it does not, for that reason, need to fully subscribe to a theory of cultural relativism. Indeed, it could claim to be agnostic in this matter. All it needs to do is to locate itself at those specific points where universal discourse is resisted (remembering that those points could not exhaust the whole field of politics: e.g. those who will refuse to discuss their rules of marriage or inheritance in a general legislative body might be perfectly willing to debate in that forum the rates of income tax or the policy of public health); and then engage in a two-fold struggle — resist homogenization from the outside, and push for democratization inside. That, in brief, would be a strategic politics of toleration.

Contrary to the apprehensions of many who think of minority religious groups as inherently authoritarian and opposed to the democratization of their religious institutions, it is unlikely, I think, that the principal impediment to the opening of such processes within the religious communities will come from the minority groups themselves. There is considerable historical evidence to suggest that when collective cultural rights have been asserted on behalf of minority religious groups in India, they have often been backed by the claim of popular consent through democratic processes. Thus, the campaign in the 1920s for reform in the management of Sikh gurdwaras was accompanied by the Akali demand that Sikh shrines and religious establishments be handed over to elected bodies. Indeed, the campaign was successful in forcing a reluctant colonial government to provide, in the Sikh Gurdwaras and Shrines Bill 1925, for a committee elected by all adult Sikhs, men and women, to take over the management of Sikh religious places.[35] The Shiromani Gurdwara Prabandhak Committee was perhaps the first legally constituted public body in colonial India for which the principle of universal suffrage was recognized. It is also important to note that the so-called 'traditional' *ulema* in India,

---

[35] For this history, see Mohinder Singh, *The Akali Movement* (Delhi: Macmillan, 1978).

when campaigning in the 1920s for the reform of Muslim religious institutions, demanded from the colonial government that officially appointed bodies such as Wakf committees be replaced by representative bodies elected by local Muslims.[36] The persuasive force of the claim for representativeness is often irresistible in the politics of collective rights.

The more serious opposition to this proposal is likely to come from those who will see in the representative public institutions of the religious communities, a threat to the sovereign powers of the state. If such institutions are to be given any role in the regulation of the lives and activities of its members, then their very stature as elected bodies representative of their constituents will be construed as diminishing the sovereignty of the state. I can hear the murmurs already: 'Remember how the SGPC was used to provide legitimacy to Sikh separatism? Imagine what will happen if Muslims get their own parliament!' The deadweight of juridical sovereignty cannot be easily pushed aside even by those who otherwise subscribe to ideas of autonomy and self-regulating civil social institutions.

I do not, therefore, make these proposals for a reconfiguration of the problem of secularism in India and a redefinition of the concept of toleration with any degree of optimism. All I can hope for is that, faced with a potentially disastrous political impasse, some at least will prefer to err on the side of democracy.

[36] Tahir Mahmood, *Muslim Personal Law*, pp. 66–7.

15

Talking about our Modernity in Two Languages

I had promised the editors that I would do an English version of something I had written in Bengali. Here it is. But I cannot offer it without considerable qualification.

In September 1994 I delivered in Calcutta a public lecture in memory of a student of mine who had died the year before of an incurable kidney ailment. The subject of that talk was 'Our Modernity'.[1] Needless to say, my intention was to problematize the much-talked-about notion of modernity by focusing on the pronoun 'our'. One implication of using the pronoun was to suggest that there might be modernities that were not ours. If we could have 'our' modernity, then others could just as well have 'their' modernities. It could be the case, I said, that what others think of as modern, we have found unacceptable, whereas what we have cherished as valuable elements of our modernity, others do not consider to be modern at all. By playing upon the distinction between 'us' and 'them', I was hoping to lead the discussion into an area where I could question commonsensical notions about the existence of certain universally held values of modernity, and suggest that modernity was a contextually located and enormously contested idea.

In that lecture I did not go into any explicit discussion of whom I meant when I said 'our'. I had assumed that when I played with the range of meanings available to the terms 'we' and 'they' in the particular context in which I was talking, my Calcutta audience would follow me the whole way. When I said 'our', we — I and my audience — would have meant, depending on the

[1] The Srijnan Halder Memorial Lecture, 1994, delivered in Bengali in Calcutta on 3 September 1994. Published as 'Āmāder ādhunikatā', *Yogasūtra*, October 1994, pp. 71–86. English translation published in *The Present History of West Bengal: Essays in Political Criticism*, chapter 12, pp. 193–210.

context, Indians, or Bengalis, or perhaps more specifically the Indian or the Bengali middle class, or perhaps in an even more limited sense the literati or intelligentsia of the last hundred years or so a group possessing an articulate historical consciousness of being modern, and what is more, of being modern in a way that was, in significant ways, different from 'their' modernity. By 'them', there could have been little ambiguity about what we meant. We meant the modern West, sometimes more specifically modern Europe. We were aware of course of the many debates and disagreements within Western thought about the meanings of modernity; we also knew that not everything in contemporary Western society was necessarily modern. But we nevertheless felt it meaningful to hold on to a certain notion of Western modernity as something that was 'theirs', with reference to which we needed to define 'our' modernity.

In assuming this complicity between me and my audience, I was not being unjustifiably hopeful. There was, I knew, a fairly well established tradition of talking about 'ours' and 'theirs' in exactly this way in the immediate intellectual tradition to which both I and most of my audience belonged. This was, of course, the nationalist tradition of social and historical thinking that had emerged, in Bengal along with other parts of India, over more than a hundred years; a tradition built up for the most part by bilingual intellectuals who were conversant with the rhetorics and modes of thought of the modern West as well of their own indigenous cultures. Speaking as I was to a roomful of listeners having practically the same intellectual background as myself — most of them being teachers and researchers in the social sciences, and many of them indeed being my colleagues or former students — I had no doubt that my gesture of inclusiveness would easily draw my audience into a comfortable enclosure of shared texts, shared memories and shared languages.

I propose now to give my readers in English a glimpse of that space, and to let them hear some of those conversations. For a substantial part of this lecture, now, you will have to imagine yourself transported to an uncomfortably warm September evening in Calcutta, looking into a somewhat dingy room crammed with nearly a hundred people, and listening — let us say — to a simultaneous English translation of my Bengali lecture. After you have heard me out in this way, I will pose to you a problem for which I have no answer.

Conceptualizing Our Modernity

I began my talk that evening by going directly into a nineteenth century account of the consequences of modernity.

In 1873, Rajnarayan Basu had attempted a comparative evaluation of *Se kāl ār e kāl* [Those Days and These Days].[2] By 'those days' and 'these days', he meant the period before and after the full-fledged introduction of English education in India. The word *ādhunik*, in the sense in which we now use it in Bengali to mean 'modern' was not in use in the nineteenth century. The word then used was *nabya* [new]: the 'new' was that which was inextricably linked to Western education and thought. The other word that was much in use was *unnati*, an equivalent of the nineteenth-century European concept of 'improvement' or 'progress', an idea we will today designate by the word *pragati*.

Rajnarayan Basu, needless to say, was educated in the *nabya* or new manner; he was a social reformer and very much in favour of modern ideas. Comparing 'those days' with 'these days', he spoke of seven areas where there had been either improvement or decline. These seven areas were health, education, livelihood, social life, virtue, polity and religion. His discussion on these seven subjects is marked by the recurrence of some familiar themes. Thus, for instance, the notion that whereas people of 'those days' were simple, caring, compassionate and genuinely religious, religion now is mere festivity and pomp, and people have become cunning, devious, selfish and ungrateful:

Talking to people nowadays, it is hard to decide what their true feelings are . . . Before, if there was a guest in the house, people were eager to have him stay a few days more. Before, people even pawned their belongings in order to be hospitable to their guests. Nowadays, guests look for the first opportunity to leave. (Basu, p. 82)

Rajnarayan gives several such examples of changes in the quality of sociability.

But the subject on which Rajnarayan spends the longest time

2 Rajnarayan Basu, *Se kāl ār e kāl*, Brajendranath Bandyopadhyay and Sajanikanta Das, eds (Calcutta: Bangiya Sahitya Parishat, 1956).

in comparing 'those days' with 'these days' is that of the *śarīr*, the body. I wish to present this matter a little elaborately, because in it lies a rather curious aspect of our modernity.

Ask anyone and he will say, 'My father and grandfather were very strong men.' Compared with men of those days, men now have virtually no strength at all . . . If people who were alive a hundred years ago were to come back today, they would certainly be surprised to see how short in stature we have become. We used to hear in our childhood of women who chased away bandits. These days, leave alone women, we do not even hear of men with such courage. Men these days cannot even chase away a jackal. (Basu, pp. 37–8)

On the whole, people — and Rajnarayan adds here, 'especially *bhadralok*', respectable people — have now become feeble, sickly and short-lived.

Let us pause for a minute to consider what this means. If by 'these days' we mean the modern age, the age of a new civilization inaugurated under English rule, then is the consequence of that modernity a decline in the health of the people? On ethics, religion, sociability and such other spiritual matters, there could conceivably be some scope for argument. But how could the thought occur to someone that in that most mundane of worldly matters — our biological existence — people of the present age have become weaker and more short-lived than people of an earlier age?

If my historian friends are awake at this moment, they will of course point out straightaway that we are talking here of 1873, when modern medicine and health services in British India were still confined to the narrow limits of the European expatriate community and the army, and had not even begun to reach out towards the larger population. How could Rajnarayan be expected in 1873 to make a judgement on the miraculous advances of modern medicine in the twentieth century?

If this be the objection, then let us look at a few more examples. Addressing the All-India Sanitary Conference in 1912, Motilal Ghosh, founder of the famous nationalist daily, the *Amrita Bazar Patrika*, said that sixty years ago — that is to say, more or less at the time Rajnarayan referred to as 'these days' — the Bengal countryside of his childhood was almost entirely free from disease. The only illnesses were common fevers which could be cured in a few days by an appropriate diet. Typhoid was rare and cholera had not been heard of. Smallpox occurred from time to time, but indigenous inoculators using their traditional techniques were able to cure their patients without much difficulty. There was no shortage of clean drinking water. Food was abundant and villages 'teemed with healthy, happy and robust people, who spent their days in manly sports'.[3] I can produce more recent examples. Reminiscing in 1982 on her childhood in Barisal, Manikuntala Sen, the communist leader, writes: 'The thought brings tears to my eyes. Oh Allah, why did you give us this technological civilization? Weren't we content then with our rice and *ḍāl*, fish and milk? Now I hear there is no hilsa fish in all of Barisal!' Even more recently, Kalyani Datta in her *Thoḍ baḍi khāḍā* published in 1992 tells so many stories from her childhood about food and eating habits, that the people Rajnarayan Basu talks of as having lived in the late eighteenth century seem to have been very much around in the inner precincts of Calcutta houses in the 1930s. After having a full meal, she says, people would often eat thirty or forty mangoes as dessert.[4]

Examples can be easily multiplied. In fact, if I had suitably dressed up Rajnarayan's words and passed them off as the comments of one of our contemporary writers, none of you would have suspected anything, because we ourselves talk all the time about how people of an earlier generation were so much stronger and healthier than ourselves.

The question is: why have we held on to this factually baseless idea for the last hundred years? Or could it be the case that we have been trying all along to say something about the historical experience of our modernity which does not appear in the statistical facts of demography? Well, let us turn to the reasons that Rajnarayan gives for the decline in health from 'those days' to 'these days'.

The first reason, Rajnarayan says, is change in the environment.

---

[3] Cited in David Arnold, *Colonizing the Body: State Medicine and Epidemic Disease in Nineteenth-Century India* (Berkeley: University of California Press, 1993), pp. 282–3.

[4] Manikuntala Sen, Sediner Kathā (Calcutta: Nobapatra, 1982), p. 10. Kalyani Datta, *Thoḍ baḍi khāḍā* (Calcutta: Thema, 1992), esp. pp. 26–48.

Before, people would travel from Calcutta to Tribeni, Santipur and other villages for a change. Now those places have become unhealthy because of the miasma known as malaria . . . For various reasons it appears that there is a massive environmental change taking place in India today. That such change will be reflected in the physical strength of the people is hardly surprising. (Basu, pp. 38–9)

The second reason is food: lack of nutritious food, consumption of adulterated and harmful food, and excess of drinking. 'We have seen and heard in our childhood of numerous examples of how much people could eat in those days. They cannot do so now.'

The third reason is labour: excess of labour, untimely labour and the lack of physical exercise.

There is no doubt that with the advent of English civilization in our country, the need to labour has increased tremendously. We cannot labour in the same way as the English; yet the English want us to do so. English labour is not suited to this country . . . The routine now enforced by our rulers of working from ten to four is in no way suitable for the conditions of this country. (Basu, p. 39)

The fourth reason is the change in the way of life. In the past, people had few wants, which is why they were able to live happily. Today there is no end to our worries and anxieties. 'Now the European civilization has entered our country, and with it European wants, European needs and European luxuries. Yet the European way of fulfilling those wants and desires, namely, industry and trade, is not being adopted.' Rajnarayan here makes a comparison between two old men, one a 'vernacular old man', the other an 'anglicized old man'.

The anglicized old man has aged early. The vernacular old man wakes up when it is still dark. Waking up, he lies in bed and sings religious songs: how this delights his heart! Getting up from bed, he has a bath: how healthy a habit! Finishing his bath, he goes to the garden to pick flowers: how beneficial the fragrance of flowers for the body! Having gathered flowers, he sits down to pray: this delights the mind and strengthens both body and spirit . . . The anglicized old man, on the other hand, has dinner and brandy at night and sleeps late; he has never seen a sunrise and has never breathed the fresh morning air. Rising late in the morning, he has difficulty in performing even the simple task of opening his eyelids. His body feels wretched, he has a hangover, things look like getting even worse! In this way, subjected to English food and drink and other English manners, the anglicized old man's body becomes the home of many diseases. (Basu, pp. 49–50)

Rajnarayan himself admits that this comparison is exaggerated. But there is one persistent complaint in all of the reasons he cites for the decline in health from the earlier to the present age: not all of the particular means we have adopted for becoming modern are suitable for us. Yet, by imitating uncritically the forms of English modernity, we are bringing upon us environmental degradation, food shortages, illnesses caused by excessive labour and an uncoordinated and undisciplined way of life. Rajnarayan gives many instances of uncritical imitation of English manners, as for instance the following story about the lack of nutritious food.

Two Bengali gentlemen were once dining at Wilson's Hotel. One of them was especially addicted to beef. He asked the waiter, 'Do you have veal?' The waiter replied, 'I'm afraid not, sir.' The gentleman asked again, 'Do you have beef steak?' The waiter replied, 'Not that either, sir.' The gentleman asked again, 'Do you have ox tongue?' The waiter replied, 'Not that either, sir.' The gentleman asked again, 'Do you have calf's foot jelly?' The waiter replied, 'Not that either, sir.' The gentleman said, 'Don't you have anything from a cow?' Hearing this, the second gentleman, who was not so partial to beef, said with some irritation, 'Well, if you have nothing else from a cow, why not get him some dung?' (Basu, p. 44)

The point which this story is supposed to illustrate is that 'beef is much too heat-producing and unhealthy for the people of this country'. On the other hand, the food that is much more suitable and healthy, namely, milk, has become scarce: English officials, Muslims and a few beef-eating Bengalis 'have eaten the cows, which is why milk is so dear'.

Many of Rajnarayan's examples and explanations will seem laughable to us now. But there is nothing laughable about his main project, which is to prove that there cannot be just one modernity irrespective of geography, time, environment or social conditions. The forms of modernity will have to vary between different countries depending upon specific circumstances and social practices. We could in fact stretch Rajnarayan's comments a bit further to assert that true modernity consists in determining the particular forms of modernity that are suitable in particular circumstances; that is, applying the methods of reason to identify or invent the specific technologies of modernity that are appropriate for our purposes. Or, to put this another way, if there is any universal or universally acceptable definition of modernity, it is this: that by teaching us to employ the methods of reason, universal modernity enables us to identify the forms of our own particular modernity.

Western Modernity Representing Itself

How is one to employ one's powers of reason and judgement to decide what to do? Let us listen to the reply given to this question by Western modernity itself. In 1784, Immanuel Kant wrote a short essay on *Aufklärung*, which we know in English as the Enlightenment, i.e. *ālokprāpti*.[5] According to Kant, to be enlightened is to become mature, to reach adulthood, to stop being dependent on the authority of others, to become free and assume responsibility for one's own actions. When man is not enlightened, he does not employ his own powers of reasoning but rather accepts the guardianship of others and does as he is told. He does not feel the need to acquire knowledge about the world, because everything is written in the holy books. He does not attempt to make his own judgements about right and wrong; he follows the advice of his pastor. He even leaves it to his doctor to decide what he should or should not eat. Most men in all periods of history have been, in this sense, immature. And those who have acted as guardians of society have wanted it that way; it was in their interest that most people should prefer to remain dependent on them rather than become self-reliant. It is in the present age that, for the first time, the need for self-reliance has been generally acknowledged. It is also now that for the first time it is agreed that the primary condition for putting an end to our self-imposed dependence is freedom, especially civil freedoms. This does not mean that everyone in the present age is enlightened, or that we are now living in an enlightened age. We should rather say that our age is the age of enlightenment.

The French philosopher Michel Foucault has an interesting

---

5 Immanuel Kant, *On History*, Lewis White Beck, ed. (Indianapolis: Bobbs–Merrill, 1963), pp. 1–10.

discussion on this essay by Kant.[6] What is it that is new in the way in which Kant describes the Enlightenment? The novelty lies, Foucault says, in the fact that for the first time we have a philosopher making the attempt to relate his philosophical inquiry to his own age, and concluding that it is because the times are propitious that his inquiries have become possible. In other words, this is the first time that a philosopher makes the character of his own age a subject of philosophical investigation, the first time that someone tries from within his own age to identify the social conditions favourable for the pursuit of knowledge.

What are the features that Kant points out as characteristic of the present age? Foucault says that this is where the new thinking is so distinctive. In marking out the present, Kant is not referring to some revolutionary event which ends the earlier age and inaugurates the age of enlightenment. Nor is he reading in the characteristics of the present age the signs of some future revolutionary event in the making. Nor indeed is he looking at the present as a transition from the past to some future age that has not yet arrived. All of these strategies of describing the present in historical terms have been in use in European thought a long time before Kant — from at least the Greek age — and their use has not ceased since the age of Kant. What is remarkable about Kant's criteria of the present is that they are all negative. Enlightenment means an exit, an escape: escape from tutelage, coming out of dependence. Here, Kant is not talking about the origins of the Enlightenment, or about its sources, or its historical evolution. Nor indeed is he talking about the historical goal of the Enlightenment. He is concerned only with the present in itself, with those exclusive properties that define the present as different from the past. Kant is looking for the definition of enlightenment, or more broadly, of modernity, in the difference posed by the present.

Let us underline this statement and set it aside for the moment; I will return to it later. Let us now turn to another interesting aspect of Foucault's essay. Suppose we agree on the fact that autonomy and self-reliance have become generally accepted norms. Let us also grant that freedom of thought and speech is

[6] Michel Foucault, 'What is Enlightenment?', in Paul Rabinow, ed., *The Foucault Reader* (New York: Pantheon, 1984), pp. 32–50.

acknowledged as the necessary condition for self-reliance. But freedom of thought does not mean that people are free to do just as they please at every moment and in every act of daily life. To admit that would be to deny the need for social regulation, and to call for total anarchy. Obviously, the philosophers of the Enlightenment could not have meant this. While demanding individual autonomy and freedom of thought, they also had to specify those areas of personal and social living where freedom of thought would operate, and those other areas where, irrespective of individual opinions, the directives or regulations of the recognized authority would have to prevail. In his essay 'What is Enlightenment?' Kant did specify these areas.

The way he proceeds to do this is by separating two spheres of the exercise of reason. One of these Kant calls 'public', where matters of general concern are discussed and where reason is not mobilized for the pursuit of an individual interest or for the support of a particular group. The other is the sphere of the 'private' use of reason, which relates to the pursuit of individual or particular interests. In the former sphere, freedom of thought and speech is essential; in the second, it is not desirable at all. Illustrating the argument, Kant says that when there is a 'public' debate on the government's revenue policy, those who are knowledgeable in that subject must be given the freedom to express their opinions. But as a 'private' individual, I cannot claim that since I disagree with the government's fiscal policy I must have the freedom not to pay taxes. If there is a 'public' discussion on military organization or war strategy, even a soldier could participate; but on the battlefield his duty is not to express his free opinions but to follow orders. In a 'public' debate on religion, I may, even as a member of a religious denomination, criticize the practices and beliefs of my order; but in my 'private' capacity as a pastor, my duty is to preach the authorized doctrines of my sect and to observe its authorized practices. There cannot be any freedom of speech in the 'private' domain.

This particular use by Kant of the notions of 'public' and 'private' did not gain much currency in later discussions. On the contrary, the usual consensus in liberal social philosophy is that it is in the 'private' or personal sphere that there should be unrestricted freedom of conscience, opinion and behaviour, whereas the sphere of 'public' or social interaction should be subject to recognized norms and regulations that must be respected by all. But no matter how unusual Kant's use of the public/private distinction, it is not difficult for us to understand his argument. When my activities concern a domain in which I as an individual am only a part of a larger social organization or system, a mere cog in the social wheel, there my duty is to abide by regulations and to follow the directives of the recognized authority. But there is another domain of the exercise of reason which is not restricted by these particular or individual interests, a domain that is free and universal. That is the proper place for free thought, for the cultivation of science and art — the proper place, in one word, for 'enlightenment'.

It is worth pointing out that in this universal domain of the pursuit of knowledge — the domain which Kant calls 'public' — it is the individual who is the subject. The condition for true enlightenment is freedom of thought. When the individual in search of knowledge seeks to rise above his particular social location and participate in the universal domain of discourse, his right to freedom of thought and opinion must be unhindered. He must also have the full authority to form his own beliefs and opinions, just as he must bear the full responsibility for expressing them. There is no doubt that Kant is here claiming the right of free speech only for those who have the requisite qualifications for engaging in the exercise of reason and the pursuit of knowledge, and those who can use that freedom in a responsible manner. In discussing Kant's essay, Foucault does not raise this point; although he might well have done so, given the relevance of this theme in Foucault's own work. It is the theme of the rise of experts and the ubiquitous authority of specialists, a phenomenon which appears alongside the general social acceptance of the principle of unrestricted entry into education and learning. We say, on the one hand, that it is wrong to exclude any individual or group from access to education or the practice of knowledge, on grounds of religion or any other social prejudice. On the other hand, we also insist that the opinion of such and such a person is more acceptable because he is an expert in the field. In other words, just as we have meant by enlightenment an unrestricted and universal field for the exercise of reason, so have we built up an intricately differentiated structure of authorities which specifies who has the right to say what on which subjects. As markers of this authority, we have distributed examinations, degrees, titles, insignia of all sorts. Just think how many different kinds of experts we have to allow to guide us through our daily lives — from birth, indeed from before birth, to death and even afterwards. In many areas, in fact, it is illegal to act without expert advice. If I do not myself have a medical degree or licence, I cannot walk into a pharmacy and say, 'I hope you know that there is unrestricted access to knowledge, because I have read all the medical books and I think I need these drugs.' In countries with universal schooling, it is mandatory that children go to officially recognized schools; I could not insist that I would educate my children at home. There are also fairly precise identifications of who is an expert in which subject. At this particular meeting today, for instance, I am talking on history, social philosophy and related subjects, and you have come here to listen to me, either out of interest or out of plain courtesy. If I had announced that I would be speaking on radiation in the ionosphere or the DNA molecule, I would most definitely have had to speak to an empty room, and some of my well-wishers would probably have run to consult experts on mental disorders.

Needless to say, the writings of Michel Foucault have in recent years taught us to look at the relation between the practices of knowledge and the technologies of power from a very new angle. Kant's answer two hundred years ago to the question, 'What is Enlightenment?' might seem at first sight to be an early statement of the most commonplace self-representation of modern social philosophy. And yet, now we can see embedded in that statement the not-very-well-acknowledged ideas of differential access to discourse, the specialized authority of experts, and the use of the instruments of knowledge for the exercise of power. The irresistible enthusiasm that one notices in the writings of Western philosophers of the Enlightenment, about a modernity that would bring in the era of universal reason and emancipation, does not seem to us (witness to the many barbarities of world history in the last two hundred years — and I say this with due apologies to the great Immanuel Kant) as mature in the least. Today our doubts about the claims of modernity are out in the open.

A Modernity that is National

But I have not yet given you an adequate answer to the question with which I began this discussion. Why is it the case that, for more than a hundred years, the foremost proponents of our modernity have been so vocal about the signs of social decline rather than of progress? Surely, when Rajnarayan Basu spoke about the decline in health, education, sociability or virtue, he did not do so out of some post-modern sense of irony. There must be something in the very process of our becoming modern that continues to lead us, even in our acceptance of modernity, to a certain scepticism about its values and consequences.

My argument is that because of the way in which the history of our modernity has been intertwined with the history of colonialism, we have never quite been able to believe that there exists a universal domain of free discourse, unfettered by differences of race or nationality. Somehow, from the very beginning, we had made a shrewd guess that given the close complicity between modern knowledge and modern regimes of power, we would for ever remain consumers of universal modernity; never would we be taken seriously as its producers. It is for this reason that we have tried, for over a hundred years, to take our eyes away from this chimera of universal modernity and clear up a space where we might become the creators of our own modernity.

Let us take an example from history. One of the earliest learned societies in India devoted to the pursuit of modern knowledge was the Society for the Acquisition of General Knowledge, founded in Calcutta in 1838 by some former students of Hindu College. Several of them had been members of 'Young Bengal', that celebrated circle of radicals that had formed in the 1820s around the free-thinking rationalist Henry Derozio. In 1843, at a meeting of the Society held at Hindu College, a paper was being read on 'The Present State of the East India Company's Criminal Judicature and Police'. D.L. Richardson, a well-known teacher of English literature at Hindu College, got up angrily and, according to the Proceedings, complained that

to stand up in a hall which the Government had erected and in the heart of a city which was the focus of enlightenment, and there to denounce, as oppressors and robbers, the men who governed the country, did in his opinion, amount to treason . . . The College would never have been in existence, but for the solicitude the Government felt in the mental improvement of the natives of India. He could not permit it, therefore, to be converted into a den of treason, and must close the doors against all such meetings.

At this, Tarachand Chakrabarti, himself a former student of Hindu College, who was chairing the meeting, rebuked Richardson:

I consider your conduct as an insult to the society . . . if you do not retract what you have said and make due apology, we shall represent the matter to the Committee of the Hindoo College, and if necessary to the Government itself. We have obtained the use of this public hall, by leave applied for and received from the Committee, and not through your personal favour. You are only a visitor on this occasion, and possess no right to interrupt a member of this society in the utterance of his opinions.[7]

This episode is usually recounted in the standard histories as an example of early nationalist feelings among the new intelligentsia of Bengal. Not that there is no truth in this observation, but it does not lie in the obvious drama of an educated Indian confronting his British teacher. Rather, what is significant is the separation between the domain of government and that of 'this society', and the insistence that as long as the required procedures had been followed, the rights of the members of the society to express their opinions, no matter how critical of government, could not be violated. We could say that at this founding moment of modernity, we did genuinely want to believe that in the new public domain of free discourse there were no bars of colour or of the political status of one's nationality; that if one could produce proof of one's competence in the subjects under discussion, one had an unrestricted right to voice one's opinions.

It did not take long for the disillusionment to set in. By the second half of the nineteenth century, we see the emergence of 'national' societies for the pursuit of modern knowledge. The learned societies of the earlier era had both European and

---

[7] A report on this meeting that appeared in the *Bengal Hurkaru*, 13 February 1843, is reprinted in Goutam Chattopadhyay, ed., *Awakening in Bengal in Early Nineteenth Century (Select Documents)*, vol. 1 (Calcutta: Progressive Publishers, 1965), pp. 389–99.

Indian members. The new institutions were exclusively for Indian members, and devoted to the cultivation and spread of the modern sciences and arts among Indians — if possible, in the Indian languages. They were, in other words, institutions for the 'nationalization' of modern knowledge, located in a space somewhat set apart from the field of universal discourse, a space where discourse would be modern, and yet 'national'.

This is a project that is still being pursued today. Its success varies from field to field. But unless we can state why the project was at all considered feasible and what conditions governed its feasibility, we will not be able to answer the question I had asked at the beginning of this talk about the peculiarities of our modernity. We could take as an example our experience with practising any one of the branches of modern knowledge. Since I began this talk with a discussion on the body and its health, let me tell you the story of our acquaintance with the modern science of medicine.

In 1851, a Bengali section was opened at the Calcutta Medical College in order to train Indian students in Western medicine without requiring them first to go through a course of secondary education in English. The Licentiate and Apothecary courses in Bengali were a great success. Beginning with a mere twenty-two students in its first year, this section overtook the English section in 1864, and in 1873 it had 772 students compared to 445 in the English section. Largely because of the demand from students, nearly seven hundred medical books were published in Bengali between 1867 and 1900.[8]

But while the courses remained popular, complaints began to be heard from around the 1870s about the quality of training given to the students in the vernacular sections. It was alleged that their lack of facility in English made them unsuitable for positions of assistants to European doctors in public hospitals. This was the time when a hospital system had begun to be put in place in Bengal, and professional controls were being enforced in the form of supervision by the General Medical Council of London. From the turn of the century, with the institutionalization of the professional practices of medicine in the form of

---

[8] Computed from list supplied by Binaybhusan Ray, *Uṇiś śataker bāṅglāy bijñān sādhanā* (Calcutta: Subarnarekha, 1987), pp. 252–77.

hospitals, medical councils and patented drugs, the Bengali section in the medical school died a quick death. From 1916 all medical education in our country has been exclusively in English. But the story does not end there. Curiously, this was also the time when organized efforts were on, propelled by nationalist concerns, to give to the indigenous Ayurvedic and *Unani* systems of medicine a new disciplinary form. The All India Ayurveda Mahasammelan, which is still the apex body of ayurvedic practitioners, was set up in 1907. The movement which this organization represented sought to systematize the knowledge of ayurvedic clinical methods, mainly by producing standard editions of classical and recent texts; to institutionalize the methods of training by formalizing, in place of the traditional family-based apprenticeship, a college system consisting of lectures, textbooks, syllabuses, examinations and degrees; and to standardize the medicines and even promote the commercial production of standard drugs by pharmaceutical manufacturers. There have been debates within the movement about the extent and form of adoption of Western medicine within the curricula of ayurvedic training, but even the purists now admit that the course should have 'the benefit of equipment or the methods used by other systems of medicine . . . since, consistent with its fundamental principles, no system of medicine can ever be morally debarred from drawing upon any other branch of science . . . unless one denies the universal nature of scientific truths.'[9]

The very idea of the universality of science is being used here to carve out a separate space for ayurvedic medicine, defined according to the principles of a 'pure' tradition, and yet reorganized as a modern scientific and professional discipline. The claim here is not that the field of knowledge is marked out into separate domains by the fact of cultural difference; it is not being suggested that ayurveda is the appropriate system of medicine for 'Indian diseases'. It is rather a claim for an alternative science directed at the same objects of knowledge.

We have of course seen many attempts of this sort in the fields

[9] *Report of the Shuddha Ayurvedic Education Committee* (Delhi, 1963), cited in Paul R. Brass, 'Politics of Ayurvedic Education: A Case Study of Revivalism and Modernization in India', in Susanne Hoeber Rudolph and Lloyd I. Rudolph, eds, *Education and Politics in India* (Cambridge, Mass.: Harvard University Press, 1972), pp. 342–71.

of literature and the arts to construct a modernity that is different. Indeed, we might say that this is precisely the cultural project of nationalism: to produce a distinctly national modernity. Obviously, there is no general rule that determines which should be the elements of modernity and which the emblems of difference. There have been many experiments in many fields; they continue even today. My argument was that these efforts have not been restricted only to the supposedly cultural domains of religion, literature or the arts. The attempt to find a different modernity has been carried out even in the presumably universal field of science. We should remember that a scientist of the standing of Prafulla Chandra Ray, a Fellow of the Royal Society, thought it worth his while to write *A History of Hindu Chemistry*, while Jagadis Chandra Bose, also an FRS, believed that the researches he carried out in the latter part of his career were derived from insights he had obtained from Indian philosophy. In particular, he believed that he had found a field of scientific research that was uniquely suited to an Indian scientist. These researches of Jagadis Bose did not get much recognition in the scientific community. But it seems me to that if we grasp what it was that led him to think of a project such as this, we will get an idea of the principal driving force of our modernity.

Present History in the Age of Globalization

Whenever I think of enlightenment, I am reminded of the unforgettable first lines of Kamalkumar Majumdar's novel *Antarjali yātrā*:[10]

Light appears gradually. The sky is a frosty violet, like the colour of pomegranate. In a few moments from now, redness will come to prevail and we, the plebeians of this earth, will once more be blessed by the warmth of flowers. Gradually, the light appears. (p. 1)

Modernity is the first social philosophy which conjures up, in the minds of the most ordinary people, dreams of independence and self-rule. The regime of power in modern societies prefers to work not through the commands of a supreme sovereign, but through the disciplinary practices that each individual imposes on his or her own behaviour on the basis of the dictates of reason.

[10] Kamalkumar Majumdar, *Antarjali yātrā* (Calcutta: Kathasilpa, 1962).

And yet, no matter how adroitly the fabric of reason might cloak the reality of power, the desire for autonomy continues to range itself against power; power is resisted. Let us remind ourselves that there was a time when modernity was put forward as the strongest argument in favour of the continued colonial subjection of India: foreign rule was necessary, we were told, because Indians must first become enlightened. And then it was the same logic of modernity which one day led us to the discovery that imperialism was illegitimate; independence was our desired goal. The burden of reason, dreams of freedom; the desire for power, resistance to power: all of these are elements of modernity. There is no promised land of modernity outside the network of power. Hence one cannot be for or against modernity; one can only devise strategies for coping with it. These strategies are sometimes beneficial, often destructive; sometimes they are tolerant, perhaps all too often they are fierce and violent. We have, as I said before, long had to abandon the simple faith that because something was modern and rational, it must necessarily be for the good.

At the end of Kamalkumar's novel, a fearsome flood, like the unstoppable hand of destiny, sweeps away a decadent Hindu society. With it, it also takes that which was alive, beautiful, affectionate, kind. The untouchable plebeian cannot save her, because he is not entitled to touch that which is sacred and pure.

A single eye, like the eye mirrored on hemlock, kept looking at her, the bride seeking her first taste of love. The eye is wooden, because it is painted on the side of a boat; but it is painted in vermilion, and it has on it drops of water from the waves now breaking gently against the boat. The wooden eye is capable of shedding tears. Somewhere, therefore, there remains a sense of attachment. (p. 216)

This sense of attachment is the driving force of our modernity. We would be unjust to ourselves if we think of it as backward-looking, as a sign of resistance to change. On the contrary, it is our attachment to the past which gives birth to the feeling that the present needs to be changed, that it is our task to change it. We must remember that in the world arena of modernity, we are outcastes, untouchables. Modernity for us is like a super-market of foreign goods, displayed on the shelves: pay up and take away what you like. No one there believes that we could be producers of modernity. The bitter truth about our present is our subjection, our inability to be subjects in our own right. And yet, it is because we want to be modern that our desire to be independent and creative is transposed on to our past. It is superfluous to call this an imagined past, because pasts are always imagined. At the opposite end from 'these days' marked by incompleteness and lack of fulfilment, we construct a picture of 'those days' when there was beauty, prosperity and a healthy sociability, and which was, above all, our own creation. 'Those days' for us is not a historical past; we construct it only to mark the difference posed by the present. All that needs to be noticed is that whereas Kant, speaking at the founding moment of Western modernity, looks at the present as the site of one's escape from the past, for us it is precisely the present from which we feel we must escape. This makes the very modality of our coping with modernity radically different from the historically evolved modes of Western modernity.

Ours is the modernity of the once-colonized. The same historical process that has taught us the value of modernity has also made us the victims of modernity. Our attitude to modernity, therefore, cannot but be deeply ambiguous. This is reflected in the way we have described our experiences with modernity in the last century and a half, from Rajnarayan Basu to our contemporaries today. But this ambiguity does not stem from any uncertainty about whether to be for or against modernity. Rather, the uncertainty is because we know that to fashion the forms of our own modernity, we need to have the courage at times to reject the modernities established by others. In the age of nationalism, there were many such efforts which reflected both courage and inventiveness. Not all were, of course, equally successful. Today, in the age of globalization, perhaps the time has come once more to mobilize that courage. Perhaps we need to think now about 'those days' and 'these days' of our modernity.

The Bilingual Predicament

This is where I ended my lecture that warm September evening in Calcutta. Four months later, when I began to think of trying out the same ideas on an English-reading public, it immediately struck me that a mere translation would not do. The shift was not just one of language; I would in fact need to indicate a shift in the very terrain of discourse.

Let me therefore point out first what it is that remains the same. It was possible for me, as you would have noticed, to talk about Kant and Foucault in terms that would be entirely familiar to practitioners of the social sciences in modern academies the world over. This was possible precisely because of the success of the struggle carried out by bilingual intellectuals in the last hundred years to 'nationalize' modern knowledge by creating and constantly invigorating a field of modern social-scientific discourse in the Indian languages. On the other hand, even as I spoke of Kant and Foucault from texts that were familiar — were at least in principle accessible — to my audience, I was marking them out as situated at some distance from 'us'. These texts, we knew, were produced in a domain that was accessible to us; their results were available for us to use in ways that were authorized in the land of their emergence, so long as we chose to remain within the precincts of the modern academy. But there was no way in which we could count ourselves as belonging to the community of producers of that discourse. The distance was marked in the very language I was using.

On the other hand, lodged in the interstices of my Bengali prose were many figures and allusions that referred to texts and to practices whose meanings could only be available to those who were, like me and most of my Calcutta audience, daily practitioners of contemporary literary Bengali. Even as I tried, in translating for you the text of my lecture, to gloss those terms that were particularly significant for the texture of my argument, I was acutely aware of how much meaning I was losing. For instance, when I translate the binary opposition that recurs throughout my text as 'those days'/'these days', I know I have failed to convey the possibility of the meaning of *se kāl* varying with the age of the speaker: for someone affecting the wisdom of old age it could mean 'those good old days', whereas in the impatient voice of a youthful speaker the adjective *sekele* would refer to that which is outdated and no longer suitable for the present. Given the convenient fact that my own age is somewhere in between those two extremes, and with some skilful positioning of my voice between that of the hoary interpreter of tradition and the zealous prophet of modernity, I had tried, in my attempt to problematize the idea

of the present, to gain maximum mileage from the deep am-
biguities that have accumulated around the very dimension of
time in the contemporary Indian languages. I know that in my
translation I have lost that mileage.

Perhaps the most obvious, and in some ways the most crucial
loss, is my inability to translate several of those terms that are
in use in contemporary Bengali which carry a rich load of
conceptual meaning derived from various systems of philosophical and religious discourse in India, but around which have also
accreted a range of meanings borrowed from related concepts
in Western philosophy and social sciences. When I said 'plebeians of the earth' in my quotation from Kamal Majumdar's
novel, I was not displeased at the implied invocation of some
of the rhetoric of modern European socialism. But of course
the meaning *prākṛtajan* in the original was heavily loaded with
the language of a caste-divided society. *Prākṛta* therefore would
mean not just the populace, but specifically the lowly, the un-
refined, the vulgar. But not only that; *prākṛta* also carries with
it the sense of that which is primordial, natural, close to the
earth. The rhetorical gesture of counting oneself as one of the
prākṛtajan, therefore, was a move to identify with the lowly and
downtrodden, as well as to invoke a human collectivity that is
primary and hence in some ways closer to reality.

I have also spoken here about 'attachment to the past'. In
Kamal Majumdar's novel, the word is *māyā*. Some of you will
know of the enormous philosophical and religious baggage that
this word carries, and I have to say that there was much conceit
in my use, within a modernist social science discourse, of this
word as a description of our relation to the past. *Māyā* not only
means attachment, but in some metaphysical systems an attachment that is illusory; to valorize *māyā*, in opposition to that
metaphysics, is therefore also to humanize. But in this sense, of
course, *māyā* would mean not just attachment, but also affection,
compassion, tenderness. When I said that the driving force of
our modernity was our *māyā* for the past, I knew that I would
get my Bengali audience to sit up and take notice. I am certain
that I have failed to convey the rather startling effect of that
formulation when I say it in English.

Much has been said in recent years about the hybridity of
post-colonial intellectuals. It can hardly be denied that this recent

self-awareness has been immensely productive. No one who was not acutely aware of the sheer pain of an existential location that was always between cultures and never within any one of them, could produce the power that Salman Rushdie does when he writes of the ropes around his neck: 'I have them to this day, pulling me this way and that, East and West, the nooses tightening, commanding, *choose choose* . . . Ropes, I do not choose between you. Lassoes, lariats, I choose neither of you, and both. Do you hear? I refuse to choose.'[11]

But perhaps there is another figure that is far more ubiquitous in the history of non-Western modernities: that of the bilingual intellectual who is sometimes on one discursive terrain, sometimes on another, but never in between. He or she does not necessarily feel commanded to choose. When he is in the Western academy, he abides by the institutional rules of that academy. But he brings to it a set of intellectual concerns that have emerged somewhere else. Those concerns put him or her in an uneasy and intensely contestatory position in relation to the prevailing disciplinary norms of those institutions. There is no comfortable normalized position for the bilingual intellectual in the Western academy.

On the other hand, when the same person is a participant in an intellectual arena shaped by a modern non-European language, he or she is conscious of being an active agent in the forming of the disciplines in that arena, far more so than would be the case with him or her in the Western academy. But this role in the non-Western intellectual field is, paradoxically, premised on one's membership in the Western academy. Whichever way one looks at it, therefore, the relation between the intellectual and the academy in the two cases is not symmetrical.

One could, of course, say that the bilingual intellectual, operating as a full member in two different academic arenas, has a uniquely advantageous position of being interpretative and critical in both. This undoubtedly is what legitimizes his or her role. In that case, it must follow that what the bilingual intellectual does is actively reproduce the unequal relationship between the two academic arenas. On the other hand, if struggling with the act of translation, whether in this arena or that, is the very stuff

[11] Salman Rushdie, *East, West* (London: Jonathan Cape, 1994), p. 211.

of what the bilingual intellectual does, then even in the knowledge that there must always remain an untranslated residue, a loss of meaning, one would still be entitled to the belief that translation is an act of transformation — changing not only that which is being translated but also that to which the translation is a contribution. And if, as would be the case with many bilinguals, the act of translation works in both directions, then one might be entitled to the further supposition that in spite of the asymmetry between the two intellectual arenas of modernity I have talked about — the Western claiming to be the universal and the national aspiring to be different — one is contributing to the critical transformation of both. But how exactly that might happen, I am unable to tell you. That, as I said at the beginning, is a problem to which I do not have an answer. I can only invite you to ponder upon my predicament.

Index